AN INTRODUCTION TO
SWAMINARAYAN HINDUISM

An Introduction to Swaminarayan Hinduism is a comprehensive study of a modern form of Hinduism that is growing in the place of its birth in the Indian state of Gujarat and among Indian immigrants in East Africa, Britain, and the United States. It is the most prominent form of transnational Hinduism because it creates networks that define and preserve ethnic and religious identity in the modern context of rapid mobility and communication. Founded by Sahajanand Swami or Swaminarayan (1781–1830), a religious reformer in a time of great social and political change in Gujarat, Swaminarayan Hinduism expounds a path of devotion to Swaminarayan as the final, perfect manifestation of god.

Raymond Brady Williams provides a detailed introduction to the history, theology, discipline, and ritual of this important form of Hinduism. Based on and extending, with considerable updating and revision, his *A New Face of Hinduism: The Swaminarayan Religion* (Cambridge, 1984), the book places Swaminarayan in the context of transnational Hinduism and analyzes its current status in India and abroad.

RAYMOND BRADY WILLIAMS is Professor of Religion and Director of the Wabash Center for Teaching and Learning in Theology and Religion at Wabash College, Indiana. He is the author of several books, including *A New Face of Hinduism* (1984) and *Religions of Immigrants from India and Pakistan* (1988). A member of the Society of Biblical Literature and the Association of Disciples for Theological Discussion, he also serves on the board of directors of the American Academy of Religion and is founding editor of the journal *Teaching Theology and Religion*.

AN INTRODUCTION TO
SWAMINARAYAN HINDUISM

RAYMOND BRADY WILLIAMS

Wabash College, Indiana

CAMBRIDGE
UNIVERSITY PRESS

PUBLISHED BY THE PRESS SYNDICATE OF THE UNIVERSITY OF CAMBRIDGE
The Pitt Building, Trumpington Street, Cambridge, United Kingdom

CAMBRIDGE UNIVERSITY PRESS
The Edinburgh Building, Cambridge CB2 2RU, UK   www.cup.cam.ac.uk
40 West 20th Street, New York, NY 10011–4211, USA   www.cup.org
10 Stamford Road, Oakleigh, Melbourne 3166, Australia
Ruiz de Alarcón 13, 28014 Madrid, Spain

First published 2001

Printed in the United Kingdom at the University Press, Cambridge

Typeface Monotype Baskerville 11/12.5 pt   *System* QuarkXPress™   [SE]

A catalogue record for this book is available from the British Library

Library of Congress Cataloguing in Publication data

Williams, Raymond Brady.
An introduction to Swaminarayan Hinduism / Raymond Brady Williams.
p.   cm.
Includes bibliographical references and index.
ISBN 0 521 65279–0 (hardback) – ISBN 0 521 65422–x (paperback)
1. Swami-Narayanis.   2. Sahajānanda, Swami, 1781–1830.
BL1289.24 W54   2001
294.5′56–dc21   00-026754

ISBN 0 521 65279 0 hardback
ISBN 0 521 65422 x paperback

Contents

Plates

Plates 1, 2, 5, 6, 7, 8, 9, 10, 11, 12, 14, 16 and 18 reproduced from the
author's collection

Plate 3 reproduced by kind permission of Acharya Tejendraprasad Pande

Plate 4 reproduced by kind permission of the BAPS Swaminarayan
Temple, Amdavad

Plate 13 reproduced by kind permission of Vishal Video Tek

Plate 17 reproduced by kind permission of the Swaminarayan Temple,
Neasden, London

Figures

Tables

Preface

The Shri Swaminarayan Mandir located in Neasden in north London, which is illustrated on the cover of this book, is an impressive statement in stone that Swaminarayan Hinduism has been firmly planted by Indian immigrants in Britain and in other Western countries. The impressive architecture and intricate details that mirror traditional temples in Gujarat reveal an intimate connection with the roots of Swaminarayan Hinduism, which sink deeply into the fertile and variegated soil of Gujarati culture and Hinduism. A Gujarati poet stated, "Wherever a Gujarati resides, there forever is Gujarat." Others have added, "Wherever a Gujarati resides, soon a Swaminarayan temple appears." At the beginning of the twenty-first century Swaminarayan Hindus are experiencing steady expansion in India and abroad as part of a successful transnational religion.

On a first visit to Swaminarayan temples in Gujarat in 1976, I stayed in one of eight very modest guest rooms in a small temple in Ahmedabad (now Amdavad). Now that temple has a modern eight-story guesthouse with airconditioned rooms and a fully equipped medical clinic on the first floor. The guesthouse sits in a huge temple compound of multi-storied buildings that serve as the administrative hub for hundreds of temples and centers around the world. I also visited another temple in Ahmedabad where the *sadhus*' rooms in a nineteenth-century building still had dirt floors. Now the sadhus reside in a new modern residence hall. My first visit to the only Swaminarayan temple in New York in 1976 was to the basement of a private house on Bowne Street in Flushing, New York, where images had been set up in a small room. Now a large temple on that property in Flushing oversees 22 Swaminarayan temples and 148 centers in the United States. I first met Swaminarayan Hindus in London in a small abandoned chapel in Islington that had been converted into a temple seating approximately one hundred people. In 1996 Swaminarayan Hindus dedicated the new Swaminarayan temple in

Neasden which attracts both worshipers and tourists, hosting more than 600,000 visitors each year. Now images from these new temples are available for *darshan* on the Internet, which illustrates the rapidity of change and the power of new technologies.

Whether in modest surroundings or splendid new facilities – in India or abroad in East Africa, Britain, or the United States – Swaminarayan Hindus have been unfailingly kind and helpful to me as a researcher trying to learn about their religion. Indeed, many among the house-holders and sadhus have become friends. Often during my research I heard an old Gujarati saying, "Three people are to be treated as gods: your parent, your guru, and the guest in your house." I have enjoyed the hospitality enjoined by the saying and have been enriched by many friendships.

Acharya Tejendraprasad Pande and his son Koshalendraprasad Pande of the Ahmedabad diocese and Sadhu Narayanswarupdas, pop-ularly known as Pramukh Swami, who is the spiritual and administra-tive leader of the Bochasanwasi Akshar Purushottam Sanstha, were gracious in their welcome. Without their permission and assistance in arranging interviews, attendance at festivals, and visits to temples and residences of sadhus, research would not have been possible. In the course of research I interviewed scores of Swaminarayan sadhus and hundreds of householders. I have attended hundreds of Swaminarayan meetings and festivals. It is not possible to name the sadhus and house-holders who have contributed information and understanding to this work. I offer thanks to all of them by singling out for special thanks Atmaswarupdas Swami, who was one of the first Swaminarayan sadhus I met and who is now *mahant* of the Swaminarayan temple in Neasden, and the family of Dinker G. Ashier of London, who were among the first householders I met and who have remained good friends. I express to many more my gratitude for their hospitality to a non-Hindu who was a stranger in their midst.

My first book on Swaminarayan Hinduism was published by Cambridge University Press in 1984 as *A New Face of Hinduism: The Swaminarayan Religion*. Readers of this book will understand the enor-mous changes that have taken place in the interim that create the need for a revision of that work. The earlier book left Swaminarayan Hindus just having moved out of an abandoned chapel in north London in Islington and out of a basement in Flushing, New York and embarking on major building projects in India. This revision brings the story up to date and portrays Swaminarayan Hindus as the most important recent religious export of India and as a significant part of the new trans-national movement of religions. It will be fascinating to see what the shape and extent of Swaminarayan Hinduism will be when and if a new revision is called for in the future.

I continued to conduct research and to write about Swaminarayan Hinduism over the past two decades since the publication of the first book. (See the list of references for a list of publications during that period.) More specific research for writing this revision was conducted in India, Britain, and the United States in the winter and spring of 1999. I am grateful to Wabash College for its generous support of this research project.

Many Indian words have become assimilated into English; others remain quite foreign. The result is that any decision about the use of italics and diacritical marks in the text seems arbitrary. The practice in this work is to italicize the first appearance of words from Indian lan-guages about which some question may arise. Each such word then appears in the glossary with diacritical marks and a brief definition or description. Some variations in spelling in publications of the group result from the use of both Gujarati and Sanskrit forms of words. I have used the forms most common in the group.

I have dedicated previous books to several groups: family, academic department, and church. As one gets older, some things become more simple and clear. Hence, this book is dedicated simply to Lois.

Introduction

The final quarter of the twentieth century was a very good time for Swaminarayan Hinduism. Rapid social change provided the occasion and energy that propelled Swaminarayan Hinduism from a position of strength among Hindu groups into even more prominence in the State of Gujarat where it originated and on the expanded international stage where Gujarati immigrants live and have increasingly important roles. It began as a small Gujarati reform movement within Hinduism early in the nineteenth century and maintained considerable strength as an important modern manifestation of Hinduism into the twentieth century. Throughout the second half of the twentieth century it demonstrated significant resilience and adaptability which enhanced its importance and created its potential now at the beginning of the twenty-first century. It is one of the more recent and important of the religious exports of India.

Gujarat participated in the modernization of India's agricultural, industrial, and commercial base after Independence, creating both human and material capital that supports many new social institutions, including religious ones. The goal of universal public education following Independence and the increase in the numbers of graduates from secondary schools and universities produced numbers of highly educated young people beyond what the expanding industry could absorb. Gujarat also shared in the enormous population explosion that maintains India as the second most populous country on earth. Hence, many young people moved from Gujarat to major Indian urban centers and to other countries that opened doors to emigrants from India seeking their fortunes. Increased rapid mobility and almost instantaneous communication made possible by new technologies at the end of the twentieth century shaped them into new transnational communities that maintain complex infrastructures and communications between Gujarat, other locations in India, East Africa, Britain, Europe, and North America.

Swaminarayan Hinduism has become a transnational form of Hinduism while keeping its integrity and strength in the land of its birth. Adaptation and change have been hallmarks of Swaminarayan since its origin as a reform movement within Hinduism in Gujarat at a time of enormous social and political changes that accompanied the introduction of British rule throughout Gujarat in the nineteenth century. At the beginning of the twentieth century Gujaratis and Swaminarayan Hindus were prominent in the emigration to East Africa, where they established a strong and prosperous community. At mid-century the impetus for change came in India with Independence and in the West with emigration to Britain from both India and East Africa. Large numbers of Gujaratis and Swaminarayan Hindus have entered the United States and Canada since 1965 as part of the "new ethnics" and they have established temples and centers. Leaders do not seek to attract Western followers, but rather attempt to serve the Asian Indian community. The religion is, therefore, significant in the formation and preservation of ethnic identity and in the cultural negotiation of the Gujarati immigrants with the settled society. It promises to be that form of authentic Indian religion from which many non-Indians may get their first acquaintance with Hinduism.

One reason for its adaptability may be that it was born at the margin between the medieval and the modern in Gujarat. Sahajanand Swami, the founder, who attained the status of the manifestation of the divine as Swaminarayan, has been called the last of the medieval saints and the first of the modern sadhus of neo-Hinduism. Indeed, the Swaminarayan sect has become the most successful of the neo-Hindu reform groups. Hinduism is very old, and its Swaminarayan form preserves many of the ancient texts, beliefs, and practices. Sahajanand is called a reformer, and followers assert that he preserved the best of the beliefs and practices from the past and forged a new form of Hinduism well suited to the modern period. It is part of the Hindu devotional movement so popular in North and Central India, but here the devotion is directed to Swaminarayan, who is worshiped as the perfect manifestation of the eternal reality of god. Such devotion to Swaminarayan is the source of the commitment which is made by both ascetics and householders to follow the rather strict obligations prescribed in the sacred texts and to support the institutions founded by Swaminarayan. Devotion is the heart of Swaminarayan Hinduism.

Hinduism has many forms, but this work is about one group, the history, beliefs, religious specialists, and way of life that constitute the

Swaminarayan form of Hinduism. The Indian word is *sampradaya*, which is difficult to translate. It is not equivalent to a philosophical school, a monastic order, a denomination, a church, or a sect; it is definitely not a cult in the modern American sense. A sampradaya is a tradition which has been handed down from a founder through successive religious teachers and which shapes the followers into a distinct fellowship with institutional forms. Those who take initiation in this fellowship are called *satsangis*, companions of the truth, because they seek the truth in the company of others who share the same language, religious specialists, sacred scriptures, history, and rituals. To a large extent the individual's exposure to the elements that make up what is called Hinduism comes through participation in a particular sampradaya. Those aspects of belief and practice common to most persons who call themselves Hindus constitute what could be designated "Hinduism in general," but most individuals are first of all "Hindus in particular." Particularity is the essential feature of religious and group affiliation. Certainly it is the case with the satsangis of the Swaminarayan sampradaya.

The aim of this work is to present a comprehensive account of the history, doctrines, organization, discipline, and rituals of Swaminarayan Hinduism and to place all the subgroups and their practices in appropriate contexts. The first edition on Swaminarayan Hinduism was published in 1984 by Cambridge University Press with the title *A New Face of Hinduism: The Swaminarayan Religion*. This revised edition brings the story of the sampradaya up to date through the enormous changes that took place in India and abroad during the last part of the twentieth century. Thus, each chapter is an attempt to describe an aspect of Swaminarayan Hinduism as it exists at the beginning of the twenty-first century. The history of the foundation and the theology which developed from Sahajanand Swami's work are fundamental (chapters 1 and 3). The religious specialists and the rituals and rules prescribed by Sahajanand for both ascetics and householders (chapters 4 and 5) are essential to the religion as it is practiced. The methods of the transmission of the tradition, especially in contemporary mega-festivals (chapter 6), and the transplanting of the religion to the different soil of East Africa, Britain, and the United States and the development of transnational mission and infrastructure (chapter 7) are significant for the future prospects of the religion. What might be called in other contexts "the more delicate parts" – the disputes, quarrels, and divisions – and the contemporary status of the various groups are also included (chapter 2), even though some may wish that they were kept from public view. Much of the history and theology remains the same, but the contexts in which they are displayed have changed enormously in the past twenty years. The best approach to Hinduism is through acquaintance with a particular sampradaya in its contemporary settings because study of a sampradaya best fits the contours of the religious experience of many Hindus who worship in temples and discipline their lives according to the prescriptions and virtues of specific traditions. The study of this modern, ethnically based, and transnational form of Hinduism provides one such approach to the study of Hinduism in general. William Blake's statement, "But General Forms have their vitality in Particulars" is particularly apt with respect to religions. Hinduism in general certainly has a vital component in the Swaminarayan sampradaya.

CHAPTER ONE

The beginnings of Swaminarayan Hinduism

Several Swaminarayan temples prominently display pictures depicting the meeting of the founder, Sahajanand Swami, with Sir John Malcolm, Governor of Bombay. In the stylized paintings Sahajanand Swami, in elaborate dress and with a light shining around his head, is seated on a formal chair surrounded by his prominent ascetic disciples. Governor Malcolm stands before him in black official dress in an attitude of respect along with a few British and Indian officials. The two leaders met in Rajkot at the residence of the acting political agent for Kathiawar on 26 February 1830. The meeting has a prominent place in the iconography and literature of the group because it occurred during Sahajanand Swami's final illness and was one of his last public acts. He died later in that year. It was also near the end of Sir John Malcolm's long and distinguished career in India. He resigned from his position on 1 December 1830 and returned to England. No doubt he would have been astounded to learn that pictures of him now appear in Swaminarayan temples in London as well as India to mark the event, but he would have understood that their existence signifies more than the accidental meeting. They remain as silent witnesses to the fact that the popularity of the religious teachings and reforms of Sahajanand Swami and the growth of British political power in Gujarat developed at about the same time in the first half of the nineteenth century and to the fact that the two men shared a common interest in social order and harmony.

The British had by 1830 established political supremacy in Gujarat, which included South and North Gujarat proper, Kathiawar, also called Saurashtra, and Kutch. Sahajanand's religious movement had spread throughout this area as well. South Gujarat is the strip of land north of Bombay (now called Mumbai) on the Arabian Sea with Surat, Broach, and Baroda (now called Vadodara) as the main centers. North Gujarat is the land on the main land mass north of the Gulf of Cambay where Ahmedabad (now called Amdavad) is the major city. Kathiawar or

5

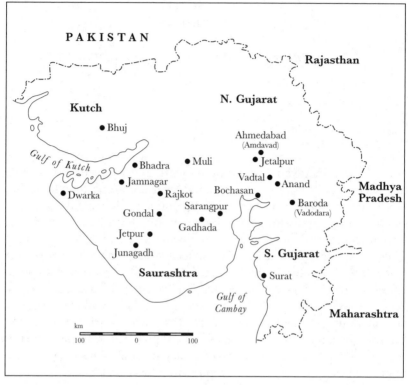

Figure 1 Map of Gujarat

Saurashtra is the large peninsula reaching out into the Arabian Sea between the Gulf of Cambay and the Gulf of Kutch. Rajkot, Junagadh, and Jamnagar are the important towns. Kutch, the most sparsely populated of the areas, is between the Gulf of Kutch and the desert areas to the north; Bhuj is the largest center. Kutch is fairly isolated from the rest of Gujarat by the large salt marsh covered at times by the tide, and until recently communication has been difficult (see figure 1). These are disparate areas with a great variety of peoples and social and religious customs. In the early nineteenth century Gujarat was divided politically among three or four competing political rulers striving for mastery over as much territory and as many chieftains in various parts of the territory as possible (Desai 1978: 3).

The legacy of the failure of the Maratha rulers was a territory of Gujarat divided into nearly three hundred states and principalities. There was no suzerain with the name or power to hold the princes and rulers in check or to provide for public order and security. The Maratha hegemony had not pacified the province. The Maratha rulers had been content to send an army to collect tribute from the local chiefs, Rajputs, Muslims, or Kathi. The intrigues between the rulers and the British did not ameliorate the situation until the establishment of British control about 1820. During the first two decades of the century, the Rajput and Kathi chiefs of Kathiawar and Kutch conducted many raids and wars resulting in a general breakdown of law and order in the territory. In short, Gujarat was a politically disunited area, lacking peace and security because of constant friction among various categories of chieftains and rulers. The Gujarati people were constantly subjected to the strains of war, plunder, changes in political rule, and hardships arising out of instability and the increasingly burdensome claims of a parade of victors.

According to the report of Sir John Malcolm, there was civil warfare in Kutch in 1812 and literally no government existed. Crops and cattle were destroyed, and land lay idle because of wars and brigandage. In the space of a few months 136 villages in Kathiawar were plundered by raiders from Kutch, 40,000 head of cattle were carried off, and property in the amount of 800,000 rupees was damaged or destroyed (Malcolm n.d.: 155–8). The times were made even more difficult by the natural calamities which occurred in parts of Gujarat in the first quarter of the century. There were three major famines. The worst was in 1810. In the previous year there was heavy rain and in winter the locusts settled in Rajasthan and Gujarat. Then in 1810 the rains failed and a dry famine came to Rajasthan, Kutch, Kathiawar, and North Gujarat. A lack of rain in 1813 resulted in a terrible famine in Kathiawar; this was followed in 1814 by an epidemic in which many people died. On 16 June 1819 Kathiawar experienced a severe earthquake. The third famine came in 1825. In these times of disaster and scarcity armed bands roamed the countryside killing and looting, and the weak were cowed by violence. Bishop Heber reported as he traveled through Gujarat in 1825 that no area was more disturbed, so the exercise of authority was more expensive in Gujarat than elsewhere. The officials maintained large armed forces to quell rebellions. Nevertheless, in no place was there more bloodshed or were the roads more insecure (R. Heber 1846 ii: 105). One writer summarized the situation in stark terms:

Never had there been such intense and general suffering in India; the native states were disorganized, and society on the verge of dissolution; the people crushed by despots and ruined by exactions; the country overrun by bandits and its resources wasted by enemies; armed forces existed only to plunder, torture and mutiny; government had ceased to exist; there remained only oppression and misery. (Dodwell 1963: 376–7)

Swaminarayan Hindus interpret these times and Sahajanand Swami's career in light of the traditional Vaishnava teaching that such periods of decay and despair call forth a great religious teacher, a manifestation of god, to bring peace and order. A reading of the pious literature distributed by members may lead one to believe that the account of social disruption is overdone in order to set the stage for the appearance of a religious leader. Contemporary reports of British officials confirm, however, that the situation was at least as bleak as portrayed in the literature. In this instance the Swaminarayan reformers and the British shared a common interest in reporting widespread disruption as a background for providential religious reform and colonial expansion into Gujarat.

The advent of the British East India Company added a new claimant to power and territory throughout Gujarat. Skillfully siding with one contestant or the other, the company gradually established a foothold in Gujarat and ultimately brought a large portion of the territory under its control. The British had been in a trading enclave at Surat since 1612. Significant political influence followed in 1759 when the company shared a certain amount of political authority with the Nawab of Surat. A great advance in British power came in 1782 when the Gaekwar detached himself from the Maratha confederacy, accepted British protection, and established an independent court at Baroda. In the first quarter of the nineteenth century British influence, military and political, gradually spread like a slow wave through greater Gujarat. The major accession came in June of 1818, when the forces of the Peshwa of Poona were defeated, and Sir John Malcolm negotiated an agreement whereby the rights of the Gaekwar of Baroda were confirmed and the territory of Kathiawar was ceded to the British.

To a degree the British were forced to establish control in Kathiawar because of their close association with the prince in Baroda. They extended their control into Kutch in order to protect Kathiawar and the coast from raiders and pirates and from the threat of invasion from the north. Sir John Malcolm described this process, in part, it must be noticed, to support a generally accepted view of the time that British rule in India was providential: "We did not obtain our influence and power in Guzerat and over the court of Baroda, as we had in other cases, by a war or treaty with a sovereign in the enjoyment of authority; we came in as mediators between parties in a country torn by factions, and in which all rule was disorganized" (Malcolm 1833: 6). Only after about 1820 was there established what could be called the "Pax Britannica" in

Gujarat. In 1822 the Nawab of Junagadh relinquished to the British all responsibility for collection of taxes, and all Kathiawar was under British control. Although absolute control was not immediately established over the whole territory, the British were clearly the only power in a position to bring order in the area.

They did not, however, annex the territories of all the chieftains and rulers in the country. They retained a large number of "native states." Thus, Gujarat was divided during British rule into two parts, one directly administered by the British and incorporated into the Bombay Presidency, and the other administered by princes of various grades operating under the supervision of residents and political agents appointed by the British government. During the British rule the significant political divisions were: (1) the British districts of Ahmedabad, Broach, Kaira, Panchmahal, and Surat; (2) the State of Baroda; and (3) a number of small princely states. By 1891 3,098,197 persons were under direct British rule in Gujarat and 5,542,349 persons were governed through the princely states (Desai 1978: 96). During the first part of the century this political organization was being forged out of the chaos of the earlier period. Some suggest that the first part of this century marks the transition in Gujarat from the social and political structure of medieval India to that of the modern period. At the time of Indian independence Gujarat became a part of Bombay State, but, upon the reorganization of that state on 1 May 1960, the linguistic and cultural difference was recognized with the establishment of the State of Gujarat as it presently exists.

The "Pax Britannica" brought significant cultural changes to the area and does mark the transition from medieval to modern. It was a time of great social change. However, neither the political nor the social changes occurred in a uniform pattern throughout Gujarat. The new pattern of political administration meant that in one part of Gujarat fragmented, multiple administration was abolished to be replaced by a uniform, unified administration which was in turn a part of a complex but uniform centralized administration. The other part lagged behind in establishing political integration. Nevertheless, there was a growing sense of the unity throughout the Gujarati-language area. Travel and communication were facilitated. The British rulers introduced legal structure, methods of production and exchange, and principles of educational organization founded on what Desai called the "legal-rational principle" (1978:96). The politics, economy, and education were secularized and separated from the overall religious and traditional matrix. These were superimposed upon the traditional social system of Gujarat over a relatively short period of time.

Governor Malcolm came to Rajkot in 1830 after a spectacular career in India that had affected Gujarat greatly. Born in England in 1769 as one of seventeen children in a poor family, he was commissioned at the age of thirteen by the directors of the East India Company. He served the company both as a military officer and as a diplomat. It was he who took the surrender of the Peshwa of Poona in 1818 and negotiated the settlement which finally placed Gujarat under British control. In that year he assumed military and political administration of Central India, in territories adjacent to Gujarat, where he attempted to establish order and root out the practices of brigandage and immolation of widows which he found particularly objectionable. His desire was to become Governor-General of India, but he did not achieve that high position. He did attain the rank of Major-General in the military, and his diplomatic skills were recognized by his appointment as Governor of Bombay from 1 November 1827 to 1 December 1830. He held this position when he met Sahajanand Swami. His biographer wrote of his career, "He left the country of his adoption having attained, if not its highest place, the highest ever attained by one who set out from the same starting point" (Kaye 1856 II: 541).

He was acutely aware of the social and cultural changes that were coming in India because of British rule, and he was especially concerned that changes forced too rapidly and without the willing cooperation of Indian leaders would lead to distrust, rebellion, and expulsion. Both his writings and his policies indicate that he had a great respect and sympathy for Indians. Even as he endeavored to eradicate from the territories under his control the evils of robbery, murder, immolation of widows, and infanticide, he wrote,

The chief obstruction we shall meet in the pursuit of the improvement and reform of the natives of India will be caused by our own passions and prejudices . . . This theme should be approached with humility, not pride, by all who venture to it . . . We should be humbled to think in how many points, in how many duties of life, great classes of this sober, honest, kind and inoffensive people excel us. (Malcolm 1824 II: 154)

In recognition of his statesmanship his statue by Chantrey stands in Statesmen's Aisle of Westminster Abbey. The inscription reads in part: "Disinterested, liberal and hospitable, warm in his affections and frank in his manners, the admirer and patron of merit, no less zealous, during the whole of his arduous and eventful career, for the welfare of the natives of the East than for the service of his own country . . ."

Two principles which guided him in his efforts at reform were consonant with his desire to meet with Sahajanand Swami. The first was his desire to bring about limited social reform through persuasion, by using the influence of responsible and respected Indian leaders rather than by the use of force to support the acts of legislation. He indicated that he would rather court the people than compel them by force to abandon their objectionable habits. He wrote: "To wean them from those habits by a conciliatory but firm course of proceeding may have to be a process both difficult and slow . . . but a statesman will hesitate to effect, by forcible means, objects which are safely and permanently secured by the slower process of moral persuasion and political management" (Malcolm 1824: 26–7 and App. A: 84). Thus, even though he said that the abolition of the practice of the immolation of widows (*sati*) through gradual means and with the aid of influential Indians had occupied his attention from the day of his arrival at Bombay, he did not immediately apply in Bombay the Sati Act of 1829 from Bengal. He circulated the Act, but indicated that he did not wish to introduce it as legislation; rather, he said, the officials under his authority "should scrupulously act upon the instructions already sent which it is hoped may have the desirable operation of rendering the most respectable natives instruments in effecting the abolition of suttees" (Judicial Department 20/213, 1830 quoted in Desai 1978: 322 note). When he arrived in Kutch after his meeting with Sahajanand Swami, he gathered the leaders of the Jarijah caste of Rajputs and tried to persuade them to give up the practice of killing infant daughters (Kaye 1856 II: 541). Governor Malcolm believed that true reform would come by persuasion and through the leadership of enlightened Indians, and he believed that such reform would be effective and lasting where the force of arms failed.

A second characteristic of his conduct of affairs, one which caused him some difficulty with the more evangelical members of the company, was his reluctance to interfere with the religious practices of the Hindus. He believed that official government policy should not disturb or create offense to Hindu sensibilities. Thus, even when he came to feel that legal action must be taken against "this horrid rite" of sati, he wrote, "This measure must be quoted to our subjects as an exception to that rigid rule we prescribed to ourselves, and meant scrupulously to maintain, as a general rule, of not interfering on any point with their religious usages" (Malcolm 1833: App. A: 84–5). It is certain that Malcolm was very pleased to meet a religious reformer who taught that sati and other such practices were not a legitimate part of orthodox Hinduism.

When Governor Malcolm left Bombay in 1829 for Gujarat, he was anxious to investigate for himself the troubled politics of Baroda, Kathiawar, and Kutch and the progress made in the stabilization and ordering of society in the preceding decade of British influence. His investigation continued the work of a Secret Committee which had to recommend whether the British should withdraw from Kutch and parts of Kathiawar because of continued disturbances and lawlessness in the area or should increase their presence and influence there. His mission is an indication of the unsettled character of the social and political situation in Gujarat even at that late date. Malcolm recommended that the British remain because it was essential to protect the area from invasion by pirates and plunderers. He referred to the object of humanity in removing infanticide as well as the object of political policy to create a secure and peaceful territory in the north as a buffer zone (Malcolm n.d.: 200). Better than most of his contemporaries he recognized, however, that healing from the ravages caused by earlier political instability and the battle for social and moral reform would be effected and won by Indian leaders among whom Sahajanand Swami was, by 1830, one of the most influential in Gujarat. These are the factors which caused Governor Malcolm to invite Sahajanand Swami to travel from Gadhada to Rajkot and, when he arrived, to show him great respect.

Sahajanand Swami came to the meeting in Rajkot as he neared the end of his ministry in his adopted land of Gujarat and after he had gained a large following. His followers point with pride to the salutary effect his preaching and teachings had in leading the residents of the territory to morally upright and peaceful lives in the midst of the chaotic situation. Alongside of the "Pax Britannica" they place the "Pax Swaminarayana" and suggest that it both complemented and was more effective than the former in the positive transformation of Gujarati society in the first quarter of the nineteenth century. His influence in Gujarat is somewhat surprising because he could be viewed, with Sir John Malcolm, as an outsider; he was from the Hindi-speaking area of the Upper Provinces and came to Gujarat as a young man.

The story of Sahajanand's life is told in great detail in the literature of the movement, but it is impossible to construct from the materials a biography in the modern sense. As Parekh suggests, "In a life like that of Swaminarayan it is very difficult to decide what is strictly historical and what is superimposed by the faith of his followers" (Parekh 1980: xi).

These materials provide the basis for a hagiography. Most of the stories are legendary and are transmitted in the satsang to demonstrate the divine character of Sahajanand, even as a child, and the miraculous character of his deeds. While it is not possible on the basis of materials currently available to give a modern historical account, it is necessary to give a brief sketch of his life story as it provides the basis for much of the literature, iconography, and ritual of the fellowship. In harmony with common Hindu practice, he is called by different names to indicate different status and stages in life. His childhood name was Ghanashyam. As a youth he was a wandering ascetic pilgrim and was called Neelkanth. When he was initiated as an ascetic in the tradition of Ramananda, he was given the name Sahajanand Swami, and when he became leader of the group of ascetics and was accepted as the manifestation of god, he was revered as Swaminarayan. These four stages provide an outline for the life of the saint.

He was born outside Gujarat in Chhapia, a village near Ayodhya, in the Hindi-speaking area of present-day Uttar Pradesh, on the day of the festival of the birth of Rama, Ramanavami. His birth fell on the ninth day of the bright fortnight of the lunar month of Chaitra in the year 1837 according to the lunar Samvat calendar, and it corresponds to 3 April AD 1781 of the solar calendar.[1] The birth is celebrated with a festival on that date every year, and the bicentenary of his birth was celebrated in April 1981. His parents were Hariprasad Pande and Premavati of the Brahmin caste of Sarvariya. His father was a Samaveda Brahmin of the Kauthumi branch of the Savarna *gotra*. His elder brother was Rampratap, and a younger brother, Ichcharama, was also born to the family. These family details are important because the family of the brothers provide religious specialists for the sect, the *acharya*, and wives of the acharyas come from the same caste in Uttar Pradesh.

His childhood name is Ghanashyam, which is one of the childhood names of Krishna. This is thought to be especially appropriate because

---

[1] Several of the early English accounts of his life give the date of his birth as AD 1780, an error resulting from the difficulty of transposing the date from the lunar calendar to the solar calendar. Generally one can arrive at the corresponding date in the Christian era by subtracting fifty-six from the Samvat number, but, because the beginnings of the solar and lunar years do not coincide, between the beginning of the lunar year in mid October and the first of the solar year in January, one subtracts fifty-seven. The beginning of the year in the lunar calendar is not the same in all parts of India, so there is an added complication. The result is that variations of one year are common in early accounts, and these incorrect dates for the birth and other events in Sahajanand's career have been repeated in more recent studies. The most careful parallel dating of Sahajanand's teaching career has been done in H. T. Dave's translation of the *Vachanamritam* (1977), but the material does not date major events of his career or the early period of his life.

the legendary stories of the childhood of Ghanashyam resemble the stories in the *puranas* about the childhood of Krishna. Indeed, some of the stories of Krishna may have been transformed to apply to Ghanashyam. Devotees do not accept this judgment. They maintain that these stories were told by Suvasini Devi, Rampratap's wife, who came to Gujarat with the family twenty-eight years after Ghanashyam left home. Therefore, the stories are accepted as accurate accounts of his childhood. His parents are believed to have been manifestations on earth of heavenly beings. They are given the names Dharmadeva and Bhaktimata, and images of the parents and the holy family are found in the temples. Stories of the childhood are told to support the claim that he was a divine child. Some of the stories are mythological, as when he was threatened by the demon Kalidatta, or when he was protected by the invocation of the monkey god Hanuman, through the mantra *Hanuman chalisa*. In another group of stories he manifests the attributes, powers, and character of divinity. One records the incident when an image of god in a temple took living form and placed a garland of flowers on the child. Another recounts the story of when a prince challenged Ghanashyam, and he showed the sure sign of divinity; the sixteen signs or sacred marks appeared on his feet.

Similarities between some of the stories and those from the Christian gospels are evident in some of the story traditions in Gujarat. A story about his childhood often told in the satsang concerns his encounter with the teachers of philosophy in the holy city of Varanasi. He was taken to Varanasi by his father, and there he defeated in debate the philosophers of two important schools, the representatives of the *Advaita* non-dualism of Shankara and the representatives of the *Dvaita* dualism of Madhva. He was victorious in propounding the philosophy of Ramanuja, the modified non-dualism of *Vishistadvaita*. As a young boy, according to the stories, he confounded the demons, false teachers, evil princes, and the unbelievers with his great powers.

His parents died when he was eleven years old, and this brought about a major change in his life. Though he would have been cared for by his older brother, he renounced the world in the time-honored practice of ascetic wandering students (*brahmachari*). He traveled for seven years and received his religious and philosophical training in what M. C. Parekh calls, "the school of spiritual vagrancy" (1980: 5). Such spiritual vagrancy was not an uncommon practice, and some other nineteenth-century leaders also left home at early ages for travel and study according to this ancient pattern. These include Rammohan Roy, the founder of the Brahmo Samaj, and Dayananda Sarasvati, the founder of the Arya Samaj.

During this time of itinerant wandering, he took the name Neelkanth. As has been the practice of Indian holy men, ancient and modern, he began his pilgrimage with a period in the Himalayas, where he met and talked with a number of religious teachers. There he studied the science of yoga for a year with a teacher called Gopalyogi. He visited the pilgrimage centers of Haridwar, Badarinath, and Mathura, the latter the legendary birthplace of Krishna. His tour of other pilgrimage centers took him from the north to the south of India. Leaving the Himalayas, he went through Bengal to Jagannathpuri in the east and on to the famous pilgrimage temples in South India. He visited the sacred places associated with the career of Ramanuja including his birthplace at Sriperumbudur and the famous pilgrimage temple at Srirangam. His journey through Kanchipuram, Kumbakonam, Madurai, and Rameshwaram took him to the southern tip of India. He traveled up the western side of India, and after seven years of wandering entered Gujarat to visit the famous Krishna temple at Dwarka. From that time he remained in Gujarat, the land of his adoption.

The travelogue provides the framework in the literature for many stories, similar to those of his childhood, which portray him as the perfect student (brahmachari). He came into contact with false ascetics and evil princes, and was delivered from their temptations and power by the influence of his pure austerities. The pictures and icons of Neelkanth in the temples show him to be extremely emaciated. It is said that during this period he undertook such a severe penance that the blood in his body dried up so that the blood from his mother, the sign of his physical attachment to family, was completely removed. He is said also to have practiced perfect celibacy in avoiding all contact with women. Muktananda described him at the end of this period of wandering in a letter to Ramananda:

This yogi has yellow hair on his head, a big tutsi bead around his neck, a girdle round his waist, a deer skin, a rosary, a kerchief, a piece of cloth for filtering water and a small manuscript [a summary of scriptures]. He does not take any solid food and so all the veins in his body look green in color, nor does there seem to be any blood in his body, and if a woman's shadow approaches him, he vomits. (Parekh 1980: 16)

His strict celibacy is one source for the strict rules for ascetics of the sect and for the separation of males and females in satsang meetings. When he arrived in Kathiawar in Gujarat, he came into contact with a group of ascetics who were followers of Ramananda Swami, a Vaishnava teacher of the philosophy of Ramanuja. He met these ascetics at Loj, near Junagadh, in 1799 or 1800, and was persuaded to remain with them until Ramananda returned from a visit to Bhuj in Kutch. Muktananda Swami, later a close disciple of Sahajanand, was the leader of the group in the absence of Ramananda. Association with this group of ascetics was important in the development of the teaching and the community that developed into Swaminarayan Hinduism.

Ramananda Swami (b. AD 1739), not to be confused with the earlier North Indian religious leader of the same name, was born to a Brahmin family in Bihar. At the age of twelve he undertook a pilgrimage to the sacred shrines to learn from famous scholars. Eventually he came to Dwarka, the home of Krishna in Kathiawar. In this province he met an ascetic named Atmananda who initiated him in the Advaita school of philosophy following Shankara. Later he traveled to the south to Srirangam, where he became convinced of the truth of the modified non-dualism of Ramanuja which developed as an alternative to Shankara's philosophy. The story is told that one night after nearly six months at Srirangam, Ramananda concentrated on Ramanuja and went to sleep. Ramanuja appeared to him in a dream, initiated him, and gave him the marks of Vishnu which, it is said, remained on his body when he awoke. Thus, he entered the line of acharyas appointed by Ramanuja, and received his commission to return to the north, to Kathiawar, to spread the teachings of Ramanuja. The initiation as acharya is significant because through him the connection is established for the leaders of the Swaminarayan movement back to Ramanuja (*Vachanamritam*, Vadtal 18).

When he returned to Gujarat, Ramananda gathered a following of both ascetics and householders, though it is difficult to determine the size of the movement at this time. In *Satsangijivan* and the *Vachanamritam*, sacred texts of the Swaminarayan fellowship, Ramananda is associated with Uddhava, the cousin-friend of Krishna. In Hindu mythology Uddhava, who was also the chief disciple of Krishna, was ordained to spread his message in a future birth, and some satsangis believe that he reappeared as Ramananda to prepare the way for another manifestation of Krishna in the form of Sahajanand. Because of this, his followers are sometimes called Uddhavi Sampradaya.

After having been summoned back from Bhuj to meet the new ascetic, Ramananda accepted Neelkanth into his group and gave him initiation as a Vaishnava ascetic. With this initiation he received a new name, Sahajanand Swami, to signify his new status. He remained as one of the ascetics in the ashram of Ramananda for almost two years (AD 1800–2). Then, according to the story, Ramananda perceived the spiritual excellence and divinity of this young ascetic and, despite his youth and the maturity of other possible successors, such as Muktananda, he appointed Sahajanand as the acharya and successor in a public ceremony at Jetpur. Shortly thereafter Ramananda died. Thus, he appears in the story in the role of a John the Baptist who prepares the way for the greater teacher.

Sahajanand Swami became the acknowledged leader of the group only in face of considerable opposition. Some members separated from the group. Two women, named Valbai and Harbai, who were long-time associates of Ramananda and leaders and preachers of the group, refused to accept the authority of Sahajanand, who was young enough to be a grandson to them. He had decreed that strict separation of the sexes should be observed and that they should confine their preaching to women only. They protested vigorously and were excommunicated by Sahajanand. One male leader in Ahmedabad (now called Amdavad) took fifteen ascetics from the group along with one of the four temples associated with Ramananda (Parekh 1980: 29). Other temples seem also to have been alienated. Fortunately for his success, Muktananda Swami, the ascetic with the greatest claim on the succession, accepted the leadership of Sahajanand, and the followers who remained became the nucleus of the new religious movement based on the teaching and example of the new leader.

Very soon thereafter Sahajanand Swami was regarded not only as the undisputed leader of the satsang, but also as a manifestation of god. He is so described in the first work written by a disciple in the year AD 1804, the *Yama Danda*. He had been given the name Narayan Muni by Ramananda, but from this time the name takes on special meaning, and he is called Swaminarayan or Swami Narain. He gave his followers a new mantra to repeat in their rituals: Swaminarayan. In very short order the preacher became the message and the object of the cult ritual (see plate 1).

The change in status brought a change in his style of life. Previously he had exercised a very strict discipline in his renunciation of the world. He had abandoned all family ties and contact along with all worldly possessions. He followed strict rules of celibacy which kept him from touching, looking at, or talking with women. He had renounced the world. Indeed, it is reported that he did not wish to become the acharya

1 Image of Sahajanand Swami in temple

of the group following Ramananda because it would mean that he would have to be responsible for financial and administrative affairs and to have conversations with female devotees. As the divine leader of the fellowship he was forced to relax some of his personal austerities, at least in their external form, though he continued to demand renunciation by his ascetic followers. His followers showered him with extravagant gifts of food and clothing, gold and costly ornaments. He traveled with an entourage befitting a prince in a land where princes lived in great luxury. This paradox is no problem for his followers. As a divine figure he was totally without attachment to material affairs and their attraction, which allowed him to live entirely for the benefit of his devotees. Thus, when he received a gift, perhaps the fine shawl from Governor Malcolm, he accepted it, not because he had any desire for the material thing, but because it was appropriate for the person to give, and the donor received a blessing through the act of giving. There are many stories in which he received gifts or ate very fine food, not because he wanted them, but to satisfy the devotional needs of his followers. It is said that he had reached the spiritual state in which a nugget of gold and a lump of clay were the same to him. It is clear that this dramatic change in conduct required some explanation, and toward the end of his career he said on one occasion:

I speak to you from a realised state which is my own. Wherever I go, women flock for My darshan, people shower wealth and offer Me valuable objects . . . Rich clothes, precious ornaments, vehicles and beautiful places for living are placed at my disposal, but when I meditate inwardly and think about the greatness and glory of God, I discard them as absolutely insignificant and totally devoid of any attraction . . . attachment to mundane objects fades away by the influence of this divine knowledge. (*Vachanamritam*, Gadhada III, 39. All translations from the text are from H. T. Dave 1977)

Thus, he explained that he remained completely unattached to the luxuries that came to him as leader of a large religious community just as he had lived a life of complete renunciation earlier in his career.

The movement grew during his public ministry between AD 1802 and his death in 1830, but it is not possible to chart the course of its development except in general outline. During most of this time his main place of residence was at Gadhada, in the Bhavnagar State, in the house of a Kathi devotee, Dada Kachar. He was the feudal chief of twelve villages which comprised the Gadhada estate. The house is preserved as a part of the large temple in Gadhada. Stories of the devotion of Dada Kachar and his two sisters are prominent in the literature. They made their home a residence for Sahajanand and his ascetics and a center for the movement. From there he undertook preaching tours which led him throughout Kathiawar and into Kutch to the north and into Gujarat to the west and south. The attempt to estimate the number of followers of the movement, both then and now, is surrounded with great difficulty, but the earliest reference to the group in British sources, written in AD 1823, reports that "the number of his followers is very great, estimated by the most intelligent natives at about one hundred thousand (100,000) principally from Kateewar [*sic*] and the western districts of Guzerat" (n.a. 1823: 348–9). The reporter goes on to say, however, that Sahajanand Swami led 50,000 people to Ahmedabad for the dedication of the temple there (the dedication was in 1822), which suggests a larger number for the total of followers even at this early date. The government census of AD 1872, the last census which gives a breakdown of membership in religious groups, gives the membership of the Swaminarayan religion as 287,687 from a total population of 6,693,289 (*Gujarat State Gazetteer*. Reprinted from the 1972 *Gazetteer*). Census figures for this period are notoriously inaccurate partly because of the hesitancy many persons had in giving accurate personal information to government officials. It is now claimed by some leaders in the community that Sahajanand had gathered during his lifetime a total of 1,800,000 followers, though they indicate that this number is based on one reference to the number of households. This reveals a serious difficulty in all estimates; some refer to the number of heads of households while others include the family members, and all are subject to great error. There is greater agreement on the estimate that he initiated about two thousand ascetics during that period. After some initial hesitation, he allowed women to undertake the ascetic life. They lived in separate locations in the temples, called *havelis*, or in separate temples. They followed the strict rules of the male ascetics as appropriate to women.

All devotees took the five principal vows which Sahajanand required of followers: (1) not to steal; (2) not to commit adultery; (3) not to eat meat; (4) not to drink intoxicants; and (5) not to receive food from persons belonging to a caste lower than one's own. These continue to be the vows that are taken at the time of initiation into the satsang. Those who receive initiation as ascetics undertake more strenuous vows as prescribed by Sahajanand. The early account referred to above said that they

receive a name and are instructed to submit to any usage without resistance, or without allowing the slightest resentment to remain in their minds; they are to forswear all worldly goods and all the concerns of this world; they are not even to possess any article made of metal, except a needle to sew their clothes and a knife to mend their pen for writing holy works; they are not to see, nor to think of a woman; if they do see one so as to distinguish her as such, if the idea of a woman comes into their minds, or if they touch one, they must fast for that day. (n.a. 1823: 348)

One phenomenon of this period, noted by both outside observers and in the literature of the group, was that followers were induced into a trance state called *samadhi* by contact with Sahajanand Swami. In this state their thoughts are said to have been so merged with his that they lost normal consciousness and enjoyed a divine bliss. What made this unusual was that it did not result from long practice of the yogic path of ascent to higher consciousness – thought by many to be the only path to its attainment; it came immediately through contact with or meditation on Sahajanand Swami. There are hundreds of stories of persons in the trance state, especially from the early period of his ministry. A constant theme in the stories is that the men and women who had such visions saw Sahajanand Swami as the supreme being served by other divine figures, for example, Rama or Krishna (Parekh 1980: 40–2). Many found fault with this practice, and even Muktananda thought that the attainment of the trance state was not possible or appropriate without the traditional yogic discipline. The writer in the *Asiatic Journal* gave a Western account:

His [Sahajanand Swami's] votaries are sometimes indulged with what they call *sumadhee*, in which the spirit is said to leave the body, and to be transported to the blissful regions their imaginations are taught to expect after death; and during the period of absence, no wound or infliction produces the slightest effect, or pain, the trunk is represented to be perfectly senseless, and after its return, the favoured person gives lively descriptions of what he has seen, generally abundance of gold and jewels, with palaces, according to the fertility of his imagination. (n.a. 1823: 348)

The author concluded that the most intelligent people in the country believed that his preaching had produced great effect in improving the morals of the people, and, he said, "my own intercourse with natives leads me to form the same opinion." The reports of British observers of Sahajanand's impact in Gujarat were generally favorable.

Sahajanand was faced with great opposition, especially in the chaotic period of about fifteen years from the beginning of his ministry until the more stable period gradually ushered in by the "Pax Britannica." During that early period several incidents are reported of attempts made

on his life by both religious and secular powers. When he first went to
Ahmedabad to preach his message, he was expelled by the ruler, and he
was not permitted to return until the British gained control of the area.
His follows were also harassed, especially the ascetics, who were required
to avoid any retaliation or angry response. They were physically attacked
and abused. Because they observed caste rules in matters of eating and
drinking, it was easy to contaminate their food and drink with the touch
of a polluting person or with unclean food such as meat. Also, if they
were touched by a woman, they were required by their discipline to
undergo a complete fast. It is said that they were harassed because of the
anger of the religious and political leaders at the size of the following
attracted by Sahajanand.

One response to the harassment was to initiate 500 of the ascetics into
the highest state of asceticism, called *paramhansa*. In this state, which
signifies total renunciation, no rules or regulations that are prescribed in
the scriptures applied to them and they had no actions to perform. They
gave up all external marks and rituals, including the sacred thread of
caste, the sect mark on the forehead, the clothing and the tuft of hair
worn by ascetics, and even the outward ritual observances of worship.
Their new status raised them above the consideration of purity and
impurity, and, as David Pocock suggests, made them "socially invisible"
(1973: 130). They were told that they should not have any outward distinguishing marks that would cause them to be easy prey to their enemies.
Those ascetics who were initiated into this higher status were all given
names which end in "ananda." The group includes some of the prominent ascetics honored by the fellowship, for example, Muktananda,
Brahmananda, Gunatitananda, Premananda. Several of these are regarded as companions who accompanied Sahajanand from the heavenly
abode to suffer the difficulties at the time of the beginning of the movement. They are called *muktas*. Sahajanand initiated paramhansas as a
temporary accommodation to the persecutions, and he ceased to ordain
persons to this highest status after his position was more secure and the
British government was established in Gujarat. Then he returned to the
practice of ordaining ascetics who would conform to the orthodox standards of caste and ritual.[2]

Another source of protection was the support of followers of the military class, called Kathis, who gave some armed protection to him and his

---

[2] Some accounts suggest that Sahajanand initiated only 500 ascetics during his career. They
confuse the number of paramhansas with the total number of ascetics, which was 2,000.

followers. He traveled with a large entourage of armed bodyguards who had other than decorative functions. When he arrived in Ahmedabad with a large force to meet the new British administrator, there was some concern, shown to be unfounded, that he had come to take over the city. The times required such precautions.

Even under such circumstances Sahajanand inspired the growth of what the historian R. C. Majumdar calls "the greatest of the reforming sects of Gujarat" (1997: 716). He spread a message of social and religious reform and organized a new religious community in Gujarati society. A major element of reform was the strict discipline he required of the band of ascetics who became his disciples. The disorder in Gujarati society at the turn of the nineteenth century discussed above was reflected in the breakdown of ascetic discipline. Some men were banded together as ascetic warriors who hired themselves out to fight in the military conflicts even during the early years of British rule, especially in the princely states (Ghurye 1964: 112). They had a reputation for immorality as well as violence. In contrast to the others, Sahajanand demanded of his ascetic followers a strict discipline of renunciation. They could not resort to violence, even in self-defense. They had to avoid all contact with women and money.

The ascetics were organized for works of social welfare which would help to restore order and some security to the area. Even though they renounced the world and took vows of poverty and celibacy, they resided and worked in the towns and villages. In a departure from the recognized convention that ascetics were above doing manual labor, Sahajanand ordained that his ascetics would engage in manual work. He ordered them to dig wells and reservoirs for water and to repair old ones that were out of use. Followers still point with pride to the large reservoir at Vadtal which was dug by Sahajanand and his disciples, and they praise him for his reforming work. The ascetics assisted villages in the building and repair of roads. They worked as masons and carpenters in the construction of temples and residences, and it is said that Sahajanand also worked. Visitors to Vadtal are shown thirty-seven bricks built into the temple which were carried by him. This manual labor by the ascetics marked a clear departure from custom. Some recent converts to the fellowship say that whereas they had once thought that ascetics were worthless and a burden to society, they were converted because of the role of the ascetics in the Swaminarayan movement in labor and projects of social welfare and reform. They trace this activity to the example of Sahajanand and his early disciples.

In times of famine and plague the ascetics opened kitchens to feed the destitute. Sahajanand was able to marshal the resources of his followers from different parts of Gujarat to meet the relief needs of those areas of Gujarat hit by disaster. During the famine in Kathiawar in 1813–14, he sent his ascetics into the Kaira district in South Gujarat to beg for food-grains to be sent for relief of the people in Kathiawar. He seems to have made no distinction in caste and religion in these relief activities.

The ascetics were also trained as preachers and teachers to visit the villages to spread the teachings of Sahajanand. Their organized preaching tours were responsible for the rapid growth of the movement. Some were poets and singers; others were philosophers and writers. Together they are responsible for the sacred literature of the movement. They, along with Sahajanand himself, represent what Philip Singer called the "sadhuization" of the Hindu revival (1970). The modern ascetic, quite different from the old parasitic sadhu, leads in the revival of the religious values and in the ordering of social life that responds to the requirements of modernization. They were important in the process by which some Hindus redefined the essential character of their religious beliefs and practices in the face of the social and intellectual forces active during the period of British control.

Sahajanand emphasized the doctrine of non-violence or non-killing (*ahimsa*), an emphasis which he shared with the large Jain community in Gujarat. All his followers were required to become vegetarians and to avoid killing or harming living creatures. It is reported that many people from the lower castes were induced to give up meat-eating. The rules given in the *Shikshapatri* (H. T. Dave 1977: 236–59), a sacred scripture of injunctions for various classes of disciples recited daily by devout followers, prohibited the killing of even insects and bugs (11). Homicide and suicide were strictly forbidden (13, 14). He taught that violence has its origin in love for and attachment to the world, whereas non-violence has its origin in the attachment to the other world. Sahajanand attempted to change the character of the sacrificial rituals which, during his time, involved animal sacrifices, which many Hindus considered an essential part of Vedic religion. Sahajanand condemned animal sacrifices, taught that they were not a part of true Vedic religion, and performed public rituals of bloodless sacrifice in their place. In AD 1808 he staged a large sacrifice (*yajna*) without animal sacrifice in Ahmedabad. Soon after the sacrifice a relative of the Peshwa officer in Ahmedabad died; Sahajanand's opponents persuaded the officer that the death was caused by the unauthorized sacrifice. Sahajanand was expelled from the city. He went to Jetalpur, where he performed another large bloodless sacrifice. The large gatherings gave him the opportunity to proclaim his doctrine of non-violence, not only in ritual affairs, but also in personal morals. After some years he gave up the idea of celebrating these large sacrifices and replaced them with smaller and better-organized meetings of the members of the satsang which were held twice a year. These conventions are still held by members.

Some Western contemporaries of Sahajanand reported that he preached a monotheism and condemned the superstitious belief in false deities (R. Heber 1846 II: 106, 110 and Burgess 1872: 333). These reports resulted from his rejection of the superstitious placation of various evil spirits and inferior deities (*Shikshapatri*, 85). People were frightened of ghosts, demons, and evil spirits, and consequently they were under the power of various types of unscrupulous exorcists. He rejected the forms of magic and superstition that were a part of village and tribal religions. There are many stories of people literally throwing away their gods and goddesses on joining the sect (Parekh 1980: 97). His followers were taught to give primary allegiance to Narayana or Krishna; hence, the impression was given that he taught a doctrine of monotheism. However, followers were also instructed to give worship to five important deities of the Hindu pantheon, Vishnu, Shiva, Ganapati, Parvati, and Surya, the major deities worshiped by Smarta Brahmins.

Sahajanand was not a monotheist in the Western or Muslim sense, but he did reject many of the rituals associated with the spirits and divinities of the regional traditions in Gujarat. In this regard, as in the prohibition of meat-eating and liquor-consumption and the emphasis upon the Vedic and Sanskrit religious texts, his teaching can be identified as a movement toward Sanskritization of the religious practices in Gujarat, which M. N. Srinivas indicated was facilitated by British rule (1962: 42–62; see also Staal 1963: 261–75). In the complex relationship between the regional cults and the all-India Sanskrit tradition, the Swaminarayan along with other devotional groups emphasized the regional languages in pilgrimage festivals and religious dramas to convey to a vast and unlettered populace the ideals, rituals, and rules of Sanskritic Hinduism. Srinivas indicated that the Sanskritization of the Patidar caste owed much to the influence of the Vallabhacharya and Swaminarayan sects (1966: 15). The history of the Swaminarayan group shows that the process of Sanskritization is not limited to caste organizations, though upward social mobility may be marked there. Devotional groups and religious organizations, which to some extent transcend caste groupings, were agents of change in belief and conduct for those who became members, some of whom had come from non-Hindu segments of the population. Though itself a regional movement associated with a particular regional language, the satsang required members to give up those practices and traditions which would exclude them from participation in rituals and groups associated with the all-India Sanskrit tradition.

Sahajanand's ethical teachings prohibited various forms of misconduct which he believed were contributing to the debased character of both the religious and the social order. Charles Heimsath observes that many reforming groups were concerned with similar religious malpractices: sexual license under the guise of religious ceremonies, fraudulent religious mendicancy, gross superstition and faith in magic, self-torture to gain religious merit, and excessive ritualism (1964: 39 n. 34). Sahajanand's reforms were directed at the social conduct of lay followers as well. Personal dishonesty and theft were forbidden. As has been said, he was especially strict about sexual morality. Men and women were strictly separated in the temples and in the meetings of the satsang. Adultery and sexual license were condemned. He reacted strongly against the bawdy songs and lewd practices associated with the Holi festival and forbade his followers to participate in the Holi celebration. Likewise, marriage songs full of jokes and *double entendres* were replaced with songs composed to dignify the wedding ceremonies. Gambling and the use of alcohol and drugs were forbidden. In the regulations about intoxicating drugs, especially opium, he was taking a position antithetical to British policy. From AD 1811 to 1831 the East India Company had a legal monopoly on the opium trade in Gujarat as a part of its commerce with China, and the British had a vested interest in the production of and trade in opium (Gillion 1969: 50). Bishop Heber believed that the greatest blot on the record of the British in Gujarat was the opium monopoly (letter to C. N. Williams in March 1825 quoted in A. Heber 1830 ii: 290). Sahajanand's puritanical teachings included the use of opium in the list of personal vices that were strictly forbidden.

These puritanical teachings of Sahajanand were aimed at what he believed to be the immoral and improper practices of some religious groups of his day, but some commentators have incorrectly identified these religious leaders as the Vallabhacharya Maharajas. Monier-Williams referred to the Vallabhacharyas as "the Epicureans of India" (1882b: 308–9) and to the "Augean stable of Vallabhacaryan licentiousness." The *Gujarat State Gazetteer* for 1872 stated: "The epicurean principles of the Vallabhachari sect sometimes assumed very unseemly forms and the reaction against them led to the reform of the Vaishnava church early in the nineteenth century by Sahajanand Swami" (*Gujarat State Gazetteer* for 1872, Surat District: 249). The point has been repeated by Majumdar: "The epicurean principles of the Vallabha sect led to the reform of the Vaisnava church early in the nineteenth century by Sahajanand Swami" (1964: 221). Constant repetition by one scholar after another has made this a standard explanation of the source of the decadence that Sahajanand attacked.

The accusation that the Vallabhacharya Maharajas were sensualists whose appetites were served by their devotees who gave over to them body, soul, and property, including their wives and daughters, came from the Maharaja libel case heard in the High Court in Bombay in 1862. In the midst of a controversy about religious authority, an editor printed an accusation that a Vallabhacharya Maharaja was guilty of many abuses of authority including sexual indulgence with wives of devotees. The Maharaja filed a libel suit against the editor. After a long case, complicated by the charge of a conspiracy to keep followers from testifying against the Maharaja, the Chief Justice, Mr. Arnold, gave the verdict that the charge of libel was unfounded (Desai 1978: 117). N. A. Toothi concludes that the case was "overstated, exaggerated, and in some instances even fabricated" (1935: 97–8). Whatever the merits of the case, the charge against the Vallabhacharyas received wide publicity, and produced a reaction against them both among Indians and among Western observers. Note that this furor occurred several decades after Sahajanand's ministry, and there is no evidence in his writings or in the writings of his contemporaries that the Vallabhacharyas were believed to be such sensualists. It seems that later writers incorrectly read the reactions to the Vallabhacharyas back into the time of Sahajanand Swami.

There were, indeed, many followers of Vallabhacharya in Gujarat in the time of Sahajanand Swami. Two of the seven principal seats or *gadis* of the sect, presided over by descendants of Vallabhacharya, were in Gujarat at Ahmedabad and Surat. However, the major adversaries of Sahajanand were not the disciples of Vallabhacharya. Nowhere in the literature is it mentioned that Sahajanand criticized the followers of Vallabhacharya or the Maharajas. On the contrary, he adopted the pattern of temple worship, fasts, and observances of festivals as prescribed by Vitthalanath, the son of Vallabhacharya, and ordered in the *Shikshapatri* that his followers should continue to follow these practices (81, 82). Françoise Mallison is correct in her conclusion that Western writers, under the influence of the libel case, misinterpreted the relation of Sahajanand with the Vallabhacharis, and their error was later taken up by Indian writers (1974: 449). It was not the case, as Monier-Williams held, that "it was this utter confusion of the Vaishnava faith (i.e., Vallabhacharya) that led to a modern puritan movement under a reformer Swami Narayan" (1877: 101–2). Rather, his chief adversaries were followers of the left-handed Shakti cult, known as Vama-Marga, which was popular in the province at the time. Its ritual included animal sacrifices, meat-eating, drinking of intoxicants, and sexual license. Sahajanand's puritanism was a reaction against the cult of the mother and other disreputable practices associated with village and tribal deities, and not against the Vallabhacharya sect.

Sahajanand Swami and Governor Malcolm both abhorred two practices known in the province, infanticide and immolation of widows. It was the custom among some Jariyah Rajputs and Kathis to kill a newborn female child by drowning her in milk. This was to avoid future spending on a large dowry. The custom was not common among the lower castes; it was limited to some chiefs of high rank and small fortune. Major A. Walker investigated infanticide in Kathiawar in 1807 and received an estimate that every year 20,000 girls were put to death in Kutch and Kathiawar. Though he believed the estimate to be exaggerated, he could find only five instances of Jadejas who preserved their daughters. One brave man had two daughters, but he dressed them as boys as though ashamed to acknowledge their sex. In 1841 the entire male Jariyah population of Kathiawar was 5,760 and that of females 1,370; in Kutch there were 2,625 boys to 335 girls (Panigrahi 1976: 41–2). Sahajanand taught that infanticide was forbidden because it comprised three sins: murder of a member of one's family, child murder, and the murder of a woman who deserved protection. He even promised to raise money to defray the marriage expenses of their daughters if the parents would give up the practice of infanticide. He traveled throughout the territory to preach against it. Finally infanticide was banned by a government Act in 1870 and the Jariyah Rajputs and the Patidars of Gujarat not only were threatened with punishment if found guilty, but were compelled to register the births and deaths of their children.

The problems connected with widows were of two types. One was the practice of the immolation of widows on the funeral pyre of their husbands. The other was the wretched and humiliating position of surviving widows in society, which made the early death at times the lesser of two evils. The practice of widow suicide was rare in Gujarat compared to some other provinces; most acts of widow suicide were in

Bengal and led to the Sati Regulation Act of 1829 in Bengal. Malcolm reports that in 1819 there were 650 widow immolations recorded in the company's territory and 421 were in Bengal. In 1820 the numbers were 597 and 390 (Malcolm 1824 II: 446). Nonetheless, Sahajanand campaigned in Gujarat against the practice of widow suicide. Moreover, he emphasized the excellence of a life of devotion to god lived by the widows. The act of voluntary immolation was depicted as belonging to those who did not possess a desire for salvation and who did not know what their true duties as widows were. He made provision for women desiring a life of devotion to shave their heads, put on distinctive clothing, and live an ascetic life. They did not receive formal initiation, nor did they follow the strict discipline of the male ascetics. They could look at and talk to men, though they were prohibited from touching them. These provisions for women were, at least in part, an attempt to make a place in society where widows and other unmarried women could make a contribution and receive honor and respect. While Governor Malcolm had given much evidence of his reluctance to interfere with the religious affairs of the Hindus, he and other British officials were willing to encourage and to give some support to the reforms initiated by Sahajanand Swami.

During the last ten years of his life Sahajanand Swami supervised the construction of six large temples, in Ahmedabad, Bhuj, Vadtal (see plate 2), Junagadh, Dholera and Gadhada.[3] In AD 1820 the Collector of Ahmedabad offered him land in Ahmedabad on which to build a temple, and the first temple was constructed there. Thus, the British were involved in the building of the first temple of the fellowship, a vivid symbol that the "Pax Britannica" and the "Pax Sahajananda" were parallel movements toward common goals. A report in AD 1823 indicates that on a "recent visit to Ahmedabad for the purpose of consecrating the temple to Nar-Narayana, Sahajanand was accompanied by 50,000 people" (n.a. 1823: 349). While the first years of his ministry prior to British rule were filled with opposition and persecution, the last ten were marked by great success, high honors, and the development of the movement into a large and influential reform movement. Soon after the meeting with Governor Malcolm, he returned to his residence in Gadhada and died later in AD 1830 at the age of forty-nine on the tenth day of the bright half of Jyeshtha in Samvat 1886.

---

[3] Followers in the territory associated with the Vadtal temple refer to six major temples, but followers in Ahmedabad add two others at Dholaka and Muli.

2 Vadtal temple

Sahajanand and his followers continued to influence the changes in Gujarat. His career spanned an important era of change as there was the transformation from the social and political organization of the rival princely territories to the unified administration of the British Raj. In the period between AD 1802 and 1830 the British gained control, either directly or by treaty with princely states, of the whole area. Other changes followed directly. The change from traditional and caste regulations supported by religious sanctions to a secular law based on the British court system brought about significant changes, not only in law, but in how religious ethics could be perceived. The improved communication facilitated by the "Pax Britannica" and encouraged by the advent of the vernacular printing presses, first in Bombay in 1812 and then in Ahmedabad in 1845, and the railroad which reached Ahmedabad in 1864, bound the Gujaratis more into a unified regional linguistic and ethnic group. The effects of Western education were not directly felt in Gujarat in Sahajanand's lifetime, but they came upon the second and third generation of his followers to bring significant changes in Gujarati language, literature, and culture. Sahajanand stood at the critical point in the change of the times.

His contribution to the change was great. He traveled throughout the area of Gujarat, Kathiawar, and Kutch, and the new community which he established helped to bind the territory together. The associations which his followers formed across territorial boundaries unified the state, though there were few followers south of Surat during his lifetime. The establishment of holy places and temples as pilgrimage sites started a movement of people and forms of association that have provided a significant element in Gujarati cultural identity. The literature of the movement coming from Sahajanand and the poets, hymn writers, and theologians who were his companions gave momentum to the standardization of the Gujarati language and slowly helped to form the various dialects into a distinct, unified language for the entire Gujarati population (Desai 1978: 307). It is not too much to claim that the existence of a separate Gujarat State in independent India today is in part a legacy of the movement which Sahajanand started.

He has been identified correctly as the last of the medieval Hindu saints and the first of the neo-Hindu reformers. He began his career in the midst of medieval India. His teachings hold fast to the ancient traditions. His world-view, manner of life, and the devotional path he set forth are in continuity with the famous medieval saints of Hinduism. The reforms he instituted, based, he believed, on the correct interpretation of the ancient tradition, make him the best early representative of neo-Hinduism. He developed a new religious organization based on voluntary membership with a clearly defined hierarchy of laymen, ascetics, and acharyas and a definite world of sacred people, places, and times which met the needs of the Gujaratis during the period of modernization and Independence. The new religious structure prospered in the new socio-political context. The "Pax Britannica" and the "Pax Swaminarayana" complemented each other.

The meeting between Sahajanand Swami and Sir John Malcolm is recorded in the iconography of the temples and remembered with interest and told with enthusiasm because it symbolizes the conjunction of the political changes and the religious reforms in Gujarat. Members of the satsang generally look upon British rule as providential in its time; the British imposed order and political stability in the area which permitted the growth of the new religious movement. Indeed, the British extended their protection to the person of Sahajanand Swami and provided other tokens of support. Followers maintain, however, that what the British could not accomplish in the ultimate transformation of individuals and society by the force of arms was accomplished by the preaching of Sahajanand. With this Governor Malcolm would have heartily agreed: that hope was one of the reasons he was prepared to meet him.

Mahatma Gandhi, a son of Gujarat, is quoted as having said: "The work which Sahajanand could do in Gujarat, the rulers by their might could not do and would not be able to do . . . The era of Sahajanand has not yet passed away" (Thakur n.d.: 209). Gujaratis have long recognized the conjunction of British rule and Sahajanand's ministry. There is an old Gujarati saying, "The topi [the British pith helmet] and the tilak [the characteristic mark worn on the forehead by satsangis] came together, and they will leave together." The British came and were agents of enormous change in Gujarat. Their legacy is everywhere evident, but they are gone. The tilak is very much in evidence in Gujarat and England, and the religious institution founded by Sahajanand continues to be a major force in the religious life of Gujarat and wherever there are Gujaratis.

CHAPTER TWO

Growth, administration, and schism

A traveler finds ample evidence of the success of Sahajanand and his disciples in spreading his message throughout Gujarat, Kathiawar, and Kutch. Large and prosperous temples are found in the city centers, several built during his lifetime. The temple compounds have residence halls for large numbers of sadhus who have taken ascetic vows and for pilgrims who flock to the temples for the festivals. Every day, thousands crowd into the shrine for *darshan* of the images of the gods. It seems that everywhere there is new construction of more residences in the older temples and new temples on the edge of the cities or in the villages. Most small villages have shrines dedicated to Swaminarayan, and annual gifts from the harvest and products of the villages are sent to the temples. Schools, colleges, medical clinics, and libraries as well as temples and residence halls are supported by the income. The sect is now a large religious institution with vast wealth, many followers, religious and charitable trusts, and all the problems of administration that result.

In the early days Sahajanand exercised direct control of both the spiritual and the administrative affairs of the satsang. He personally directed the conduct of the sadhus, received the tithes and gifts of the followers, and appointed the sadhus who were to be the *mahants* (chief ascetics) and *kotharis* (managers) in the temples. Yet even during his lifetime it became necessary to delegate some of the responsibility and authority. The ways in which Sahajanand decided to delegate the responsibility among the sadhus, householders, and the members of his own family have had profound effect on the growth and development of the movement. The history of the group provides illustration of the ways new religious groups and sects are formed, the modes of administration employed by leaders with different loci of power, and the types of administrative structure developed in some Hindu sects.

Tension which developed between the sadhus led to delegation of authority. It is not surprising that conflict and competition arose among the ascetics because they came into the satsang from different classes of society and from different parts of Gujarat. It is reported that some had been leaders of groups of ascetics in their own communities before they became followers of Sahajanand (Parekh 1980: 204). Though they all gave allegiance to Sahajanand, their relations gave rise to early problems, which proved to be a great disappointment to Sahajanand. His response was to appoint Muktananda, Brahmananda, Chaitanyananda, and Mahanubhavananda as *sadgurus* over four groups of ascetics. He placed them in positions of honor at his side in the assemblies, and he made the other ascetics give homage to them. As early as AD 1820 he promoted other ascetics to the position of senior ascetics (*Vachanamritam*, Gadhada 1, 78). The sadgurus helped him oversee the spiritual affairs and conduct of the sadhus.

Problems were created by the increase in numbers, wealth, temple institutions, and activities which those who had taken ascetic vows could not easily handle. Sahajanand then appointed householders, not ascetics, to some positions of administrative authority. Householders could handle money and financial affairs, move freely in society, come into contact with women, and thus administer the daily affairs of the sect. An important result of this decision, whether or not it was a part of his intent, was the separation of the spiritual leadership of the satsang under the control of the sadhus from the administrative leadership of the chosen householders. In the first instance Sahajanand chose a Brahmin disciple, Gopinath Bhatt, and made him a paid administrator of the temple at Ahmedabad (now called Amdavad). He was charged to take care of the ascetics and to provide for their needs. Subsequently, it was discovered that Gopinath Bhatt was mismanaging the affairs of the temple for his own benefit. He was dismissed.

APPOINTMENT OF ACHARYAS IN VADTAL AND AHMEDABAD

Then Sahajanand decided to establish a line of acharyas (preceptors) taken from among the members of his family (Williams 1982: 61–97). As members of his family they had a certain spiritual authority, and as householders they were free to oversee the affairs of the satsang. Sahajanand had lost contact with members of his family in the period of his wandering and teaching, so when he decided to appoint acharyas from his family, he sent representatives to search out his family in the United Provinces, the present-day Uttar Pradesh. As in the story of Joseph, members of his family were brought to be reunited with their illustrious relative who had gained position and power in another territory. He had an older brother, Ramapratap, and a younger brother, Ichcharama. In AD 1826 he formally adopted a son of each brother and installed them in the office of acharyas; Ayodhyaprasad, son of the elder, was made acharya of Ahmedabad, and Raghuvira, son of the younger, was made acharya of Vadtal. Sahajanand decreed that the office should be hereditary so that the acharyas would maintain a direct line of blood descent from his family. That claim to direct descent as members of the founder's family remains a significant aspect of the acharyas' claim to authority in the religion.

The initiation into the role of religious specialist as acharya placed them in a line of religious specialists whose authority is traced back to Ramanuja, the founder of the philosophical school of modified non-dualism (vishistadvaita). This sacred line of tradition (*guruparampara*) provides a source of spiritual authority in addition to the claim of blood descent. The Shrivaishnavas of South India trace their heritage to Ramanuja, who taught at Srirangam in the twelfth century and installed seventy-four acharyas, both householders and ascetics, to initiate followers into Vaishnavism and to spread his philosophy. The acharyas in that tradition maintain a hereditary relation as religious specialists for a group of families. The acharyas of the Swaminarayan movement claim descent in this spiritual line through Ramananda, who initiated Sahajanand. Sahajanand was initiated by Ramananda, and the nephews of Sahajanand were initiated into this line of specialists by him. They are not Shrivaishnavas, but they do propagate a philosophy similar to the modified non-dualism of Ramanuja and follow the devotional path within Vaishnavism.

The *Shikshapatri* contains a section of regulations and duties for the acharyas:

The acharyas, the sons of my elder and younger brothers, shall never preach to females other than those of their kindred. 123 They should never touch or talk to females not closely related to them, nor should they be cruel to any living being, nor accept money from others as deposits in their charge. 124 They should never stand as surety for others in their general dealings; they should subsist on alms to tide over the period of austerity but should never incur debts. 125 They should never sell food grains offered to them as alms by their followers. However, old cereals may be exchanged for new, and such an exchange does not amount to a sale. 126 They should perform a special ceremony on the fourth day of the bright half of the month of Bhadrapada, which is the birthday of Ganapati. On the fourteenth day of the dark half of Ashwina month they should perform a similar ceremony for the propitiation of Hanuman. 127 The acharyas, namely Ayodhyaprasada and Raghuvirji, appointed by me as the religious heads of my disciples, should initiate the male aspirants in our holy order and fellowship. 128 These acharyas should behave according to their appropriate duties (*dharma*). They should respect the saints and should study the scriptures with a spirit of reverence. 129 They should perform with due rites the worship and devotion of Laksmi Narayana and other idols installed by me in large temples. 130 Anyone who enters the temple with a desire to have food should be so served with food and treated hospitably, according to the means available. 131 A pathasala for teaching Sanskrit should be established, and a learned Brahmin preceptor should be appointed therein to impart the knowledge of truth, for verily the propagation of the scriptural lore is an act of great benediction. 132

These regulations for the acharyas are diverse and occasional, and no attempt was made in them to give all the duties of the office. It is clear, however, that the acharyas were left to be the chief administrators to oversee the affairs of the satsang.

Diocesan organization

The institution of a hereditary line of religious specialists is common in Hinduism, but what is strikingly novel in Sahajanand's institution of this office is that he designated an administrative division of the followers into two territorial dioceses. This administrative division is set forth in minute detail in a document written by Sahajanand, called *The Lekh*.

A dividing line was extended from Calcutta in the east to Dwarka in the west, running near Baroda (now called Vadodara) and Rajkot in Gujarat, and all of the temples, villages, and devotees in the territory north of that line are under the authority of the diocese of Ahmedabad, centered in the large temple in Ahmedabad dedicated to Nar-Narayana. Those south of the line are under the authority of the diocese of Vadtal, where there is the large temple dedicated to Lakshmi-Narayana. In the course of a lawsuit in the first decade of the twentieth century the boundaries as set forth in *The Lekh* were accepted by the Bombay High Court as the legal boundaries of the two dioceses, and they have not been an object of dispute since that time.

The assignment of the two acharyas was by lot, as described in *The Lekh*:

The temples having been apportioned, along with the country divided as above, lots were cast by means of two pieces of paper. The lot pertaining to the temple of Shri Nar-Narayana fell to Pande Ayodhya Prasad. So the whole of the income as above written that arises from the temples of Shri Nar-Narayana and also the territory are the income and territory of Pande Ayodhya Prasad. Also the lot pertaining to the temple of Shri Laxmi Narayana fell to Pande Raghuvir.

So the whole of the income as above written that arises from the temples of Shri Laxmi Narayana and also the territory are the income and territory of Pande Raghuvira. (3, 4)

Thus, the geographical extent of the authority of each of the acharyas was established. The similarity of this principle of organization to the dioceses of the Church of England has led some to suppose that Sahajanand was influenced in the establishment of these dioceses by contact with Christians, perhaps his discussions with Bishop Heber. Certainly the organization of the sect into territorial dioceses seems to be unique in Hinduism. But no proof of direct influence exists. Bishop Heber mentions that when they met, Sahajanand was on his way to attend a ceremony "on occasion of his brother's son coming of age to receive the Brahminical string [*sic*]," but he makes no mention of any discussion of the office the young man was to hold or the type of organization that was to be instituted (R. Heber 1846 ii: 109). In the twentieth century there were more disagreements over the duties, succession, and authority of the acharyas than about the extent of the dioceses.

Administration of temples and sadhus

The acharya was given the responsibility of managing the material wealth and temples of the diocese and of seeing to the welfare of the ascetics associated with the temples. The two dioceses receive a large amount of wealth in property, money, and produce. Three types of gifts are given to the temple. A small annual fee is received from every member of the fellowship as a kind of dues. Major income comes from the tithe that is prescribed for all devotees in the *Shikshapatri*: "My disciples should donate one-tenth of their income or the food grains that may be their agricultural income. Those who have insufficient means should donate one-twentieth of their income, either in money or in kind" (147). This is a progressive tithe and it is often stressed that the poor pay a lesser amount, and if a poor member is in great need, provision is made for some support from the fellowship. The third source of income is the special offering which the followers give when they visit the temple or when the acharya or his representatives visit the homes of devotees. These resources are often "placed at the feet of the acharya," and in the early days they were handled as the personal income of the acharya which he used to discharge his official and personal obligations. The separation of his personal and official obligations and the propriety of the use of the funds became a point of contention in the twentieth century, as we shall see.

The acharyas have the right to perform the ritual of installation of the images in the temples built in their dioceses and the ritual for the rededication of the images after the renovation of a temple. In this ceremony, called *pran pratistha*, the acharya places his hand over the image or picture and with the appropriate chant (mantra) enshrines the deity. After this act, the image is ready for worship and service. This important function of the acharya as the religious specialist is emphasized in the *Shikshapatri*: "My devotees should worship only those images of the lord that are given by the acharya or installed by him. Only obeisance should be offered to other images" (62). The acharya installs the images in the women's temples and shrines, but not in the presence of the women because he is prohibited from direct spiritual oversight over women. The acharya is expected to attend the major festivals in the temples, as on the day of the anniversary celebration of the installation of the images, and he is always given a place of honor.

The day-to-day affairs of the temples and of the ascetics who reside in them are conducted by a senior sadhu who is appointed by the acharya to be mahant to oversee the temple and the work of the lay employees of the temple. Prior to the appointment of the acharyas, Sahajanand chose some of the chief ascetics to be in charge of the larger temples; Gunatitanand Swami served as mahant of the Junagadh temple for forty years. Now the acharyas have the authority to appoint the mahants; the appointment is for a period of three years. An exception is made in the case of the mahant of the Bhuj temple, who is appointed for life. Each of the senior ascetics, from whom the mahants are chosen, has a group of ascetics who are his disciples and who move with him to the new temple assignment to help in the conduct of the affairs and rituals of the temple. Groups of ascetics go out from the larger temple to administer the smaller temples in their area; thus, there is a movement of mahants and ascetics from temple to temple. Some older ascetics have been the mahants for several temples during their career, always coming back to their home temple for the interim periods. The mahants have considerable prestige and exercise great control, so the acharya's authority to appoint the mahants is a major administrative power. It is also a source of considerable tension because, as in any organization, the desire for advancement and prestige leads to jealousy, competition, and even division.

Sahajanand bestowed on the acharyas the authority to perform the initiation of the men who enter the ascetic order of the fellowship. All followers take a simple initiation as devotees, but the higher initiation, complete with the appropriate Vedic rites, is reserved for those taking the vows of a sadhu. The aspirant, usually a youth – though the general age limit is from ten to fifty years – comes to the acharya after a period of discipline under the instruction of a senior ascetic to whom he has attached himself. When the sponsor thinks he is ready, the youth is brought to the acharya for initiation. He renounces the world, and takes a new name to mark his new status. He takes the five vows to renounce wealth, sexual pleasure, indulgence in food, family ties, and ego. After he receives the mantra, "I take refuge in Swaminarayan," he is given the sacred mark, the clothes of an ascetic, and the wooden bowl from which he will eat. From that time the satsang provides all the necessities for the sadhu, including food, housing, and clothing. The appropriate care of the ascetics as well as of the capital resources of the fellowship is a prime responsibility of the acharya's administration.

The acharya is expected to lead a pious, exemplary life according to the duties of the householders in the fellowship. In the words of the *Shikshapatri*: "The acharyas should behave according to their appropriate dharma [duties]. They should respect the saints and should study the scriptures with a spirit of reverence" (129). The acharya and his wife are expected to maintain strict observances which are appropriate to a Brahmin household and to be faithful devotees of Swaminarayan. They observe the food regulations for Brahmins, and will not accept food other than fruit and milk in disciples' houses except for those of high Brahmins. When they travel abroad, they are accompanied by ascetics from their household staff who purify the kitchens and prepare appropriate food. Some have wanted to make the conduct of the acharya the main criterion of his worthiness for the office, and some acharyas have been attacked by those who believed them to be unworthy of the office in spite of the blood descent from Sahajanand.

The acharya's family

The strictures on conduct are even more demanding of the wives of the acharyas because they have special functions to perform. Their purity is carefully protected. The acharyas, as descendants of Sahajanand's family, are members of the Sarvaria Brahmin caste still located in Uttar Pradesh. Wives for the acharyas are chosen from that caste; therefore, they come to Ahmedabad or Vadtal from the Hindi-speaking area of North India. Prior to marriage the young woman chosen usually is not a member of the Swaminarayan religion, though a Vaishnava, and does not read or speak Gujarati. She may know little of the history or theology of the fellowship. Nevertheless, marriage to the acharya, or soon-to-be acharya, gives her the position of a religious specialist. Verses from the *Shikshapatri* give some indication of the duties and restrictions: "The wives of the acharyas, Ayodhyaprasad and Raghuviraji, with the permission of their husbands, shall preach to females only and shall initiate them into the Krishna mantra (133). They shall never touch, talk to, or even show their faces to the males other than those who are closely related to them" (134).

The acharya's wife lives in strict separation from contact with men outside her household. Male disciples are not permitted to see her or her picture. She has separate rooms in the family residence and does not greet the visitors of the acharya. She does not go about openly in the city; she does not attend the cinemas, dramas, or other secular functions. When she and her maids leave the house, she is covered, and the car has dark glass and curtains. The wife of the Acharya of Ahmedabad goes to the temple every morning and visits the women's precinct to worship openly at the shrine there where men are not allowed entrance. When she goes to the main shrine of the temple to have darshan of the god, she is covered by an umbrella, and men are not allowed in the shrine area during her visit. Thus, her social existence is marked by complete separation from men and mixed company apart from her own relatives. In the latter part of the twentieth century this discipline became very difficult to maintain. In part this is because marriages take place at an age of greater maturity after both the young man and the young woman have completed university studies and have been engaged in active social life. It is then very difficult for both to maintain the strict regulations regarding social isolation. Some devotees have wondered aloud how long such an absolute separation can be maintained. It may be that in the future the acharyas' wives will maintain their ritual status on the official occasions of the fellowship but have somewhat more freedom in the conduct of their personal and unofficial affairs.

Since the acharya is not permitted to be the religious specialist for women, his wife becomes a religious specialist in her own right. She receives training after marriage from her mother-in-law for her role as a religious specialist for women followers. The strict separation of men and women in the meetings of the fellowship and the prohibitions of contact between the ascetics and persons of the opposite sex create the need for female leaders. There are separate temples, shrines, and meetings for women, and the acharya's wife occasionally gives lectures on religious subjects to the women. She performs the initiation rituals for women who take ascetic vows.

An important function of the wife of the acharya is to provide a male heir who can succeed his father as acharya. Under normal circumstances the eldest son becomes acharya if he is judged worthy. The red turban, worn at official functions, is one of the symbols of his authority, along with the golden staff and the umbrella. It is believed that the office should not be unoccupied, so as soon as the father's body is removed after death, the son is installed and receives the turban from another acharya. Preferably the acharya of the other diocese will perform the ritual, but that has not occurred in recent years. In his absence another Vaishnava acharya may perform the appropriate ritual. The younger sons of the acharya have no special office or power and are "just like any other person." This prevents the brothers of the new acharya from challenging his authority and causing a division in the fellowship.

The acharya's brother's son has on one occasion been adopted to succeed the acharya. The acharyas feel that in cases where there is no male heir, they have the right to nominate and adopt a person to succeed them. Without doubt, they would choose a descendant from the family of Sahajanand. It has happened that an acharya has died without an heir. Then it was necessary to go back to the family home in the United Provinces and trace the ancestors of all the candidates. The young man having the most direct line of descent from Sahajanand was installed as acharya. The blood line must be preserved. Though in the beginning the acharyas descended from Ayodhyaprasad and Raghuvira, the line from Raghuvira has ended, and both current acharyas trace their lineage from Ayodhyaprasad. It is legitimate for the father to abdicate and hand over the office to his son as Narendraprasad, the Acharya of Vadtal, did in 1983.

The acharyas' lineage

The acharyas of the Vadtal diocese have been: (1) Raghuvira; (2) Bhagavatprasad, who was the son of Raghuvira's elder brother; (3) Viharilal; (4) Lakshmiprasad, who was adopted into the Vadtal line from the Ahmedabad line; (5) Shripatiprasad; (6) Anandprasad; (7) Narendraprasad; and (8) Ajendraprasad. The acharyas of the Ahmedabad diocese have been: (1) Ayodhyaprasad; (2) Keshavprasad; (3) Purushottamprasad; (4) Vasudevprasad; (5) Devendraprasad; and (6) Tejendraprasad. See table 1. Pictures of the acharyas of the diocese

Table 1. *Acharyas of the two major dioceses*

Vadtal diocese		Ahmedabad diocese
Raghuvira (37 years) b. 21 March 1812 d. 9 Feb. 1863 10 Nov. 1826	initiation	Ayodhyaprasad (42 years) b. 25 May 1809 d. 18 Feb. 1868 10 Nov. 1826
Bhagavatprasad (17 years) b. 11 Oct. 1838 d. 12 Aug. 1879 9 Feb. 1863	initiation	Keshavprasad (22 years) b. 16 April 1835 d. 9 April 1890 18 Feb. 1868
Viharilal (20 years) b. 19 April 1852 d. 27 Sept. 1899 12 Aug. 1879	initiation	Purushottamprasad (12 years) b. 7 Feb. 1870 d. 25 Nov. 1901 9 April 1890
Lakshmiprasad (10 years) b. 15 Aug. 1892 24 April 1909 (retired) 27 Sept. 1899	initiation	Vasudevprasad (35 years) b. 17 July 1899 d. 29 Nov. 1937 25 Nov. 1901
Shripatiprasad (22 years) b. 18 Aug. 1875 d. 12 Feb. 1931 26 April 1909	initiation	Devendraprasad (32 years) b. 5 Oct. 1922 d. 12 Oct. 1969 30 Nov. 1937
Anandprasad (28 years) b. 22 July 1906 d. 8 July 1974 30 April 1959 (retired) 12 Feb. 1931	initiation	Tejendraprasad b. 11 April 1944 13 Oct. 1969
Narendraprasad (14 years) b. 25 Jan. 1930 d. 13 May 1984 25 May 1983 (retired) 30 April 1959	initiation	Kosalendraprasad b. 19 Oct. 1972
Ajendraprasad b. 16 Aug. 1949 25 May 1983	initiation	Vrajendraprasad b. 29 July 1997
Nrigendraprasad b. 13 March 1974		

are found in each of the temples of the diocese. Biographies of some of the acharyas have been prepared which contain the small amount of remaining history of the group in the period after the death of Swaminarayan.

The acharyas have had to deal with conflicts and divisions in the satsang caused by power struggles among the ascetics, householders, and acharyas. Sahajanand recognized the danger of conflict among these three, just as he recognized the jealousy and conflict that existed among the ascetics mentioned above. In *The Lekh* (p. 12), he decreed that if there was a dispute between the two acharyas, it should be adjudicated by four householders, two from each diocese. Disputes between the wives of the acharyas should be dealt with by married women. In no case should the ascetics, male or female, be a party to these disputes. Conflict is to be avoided. The prescriptions in the *Shikshapatri* urge respect: "My disciples should never enter into futile debate with the Acharya and should respect him and serve him with money, clothes, and the like according to their means (71). On hearing of the arrival of the Acharya, my disciples should proceed up to the outskirts of the town to receive him with respect. And on his departure they should accompany him to the outskirts and bid him farewell" (72). Nevertheless, in the twentieth century numerous controversies erupted which resulted in divisions in the fellowship and in court cases to define the power and authority of the acharyas.

One of the acharyas of the Vadtal line was deposed in AD 1906 because he was found guilty of misconduct. It is said that Lakshmiprasad did not observe the rules of the office of acharya because he came under the influence of bad companions. A meeting of sixty members of the fellowship, leaders of the ascetics and of the householders, voted unanimously to depose him. He seems to have been relieved to give up the position because he said that he did not feel fit for the office. He was given a sum of money and the income from a few villages, and he retired to the United Provinces. The office of acharya was given to another man from Swaminarayan's family. Later some followers called into question the integrity of the acharya line because Shripatiprasad was not chosen according to the prescriptions of the scriptures. After Lakshmiprasad left Vadtal he had a son who later claimed that he was the legal successor to the position. He filed a suit in court to obtain the office, but it was rejected.

There was also a dispute early in the century over the succession to the position of acharya of the Ahmedabad diocese. In AD 1901 Acharya

Purushottamprasad died, and his adopted son Vasudevprasad was immediately designated as the successor though he was only two and a half years old. The problem was complex because there was an adult claimant with considerable support who had been adopted by Purushottamprasad's senior wife. She and her supporters claimed that a will written shortly before the acharya died, in which he gave the office to a son born to his junior wife, was not valid. There was a division between those who supported the claims of the young child and those who supported the claims of the older man.

The rival claims came to the District Court at Ahmedabad for adjudication (Civil Suit No. 22 of 1902 in the Court of the District Judge at Ahmedabad; the decision was given on 23 June 1905). The two major points before the court were raised by the nature of the will left by Purushottamprasad. He treated the office as his personal possession and designated his successor without consulting the leaders of the religious community or making provision for any such consultation. Moreover, he treated the property and wealth of the sect as the personal property of the family to be disposed of as he stipulated. Those who sought to break the will disputed his right to appoint the acharya without consultation and his assumed ownership of the wealth and property. They argued that he had been guilty of misusing the income of the temples because he had treated it as his personal income.

The district judge, Mr. B. Knight, ruled on both these points. He indicated that the acharya did have the right to designate his successor, so the right of Vasudevprasad to be acharya was affirmed. He ruled against the acharya, however, with the decision that all the property of the sect is public religious property and that the use of the property and income is subject to review by the leaders of the community and, by implication, by the court. Reference was made to the fact that in *The Lekh* Swaminarayan said that money and property given as donations are given to the deities, to Nar-Narayana in Ahmedabad and to Lakshmi-Narayana in Vadtal. He ruled, however, that no evidence was before the court to support the complaint that the acharya had misused any property of the satsang. Some critics still call into question the religious, if not the legal, legitimacy of the acharya line because Vasudevprasad took office when he was only a baby, when he obviously could not perform the duties of an acharya.

The imposition of the power of the courts in the affairs of the sect has been very important in the subsequent development of the acharya's role in the administration of the spiritual and administrative affairs. Swaminarayan left three centers of power in the fellowship: (1) the acharyas, who had ascribed authority because of their hereditary blood ties to Swaminarayan; (2) the ascetics, who had acquired authority because of their manner of life and role in teaching and the ritual affairs of the temples; and (3) the householder disciples, whose authority was less centralized, but who increasingly exercised oversight in the affairs of the community as mandated by judicial and legislative action. In the twentieth century, government officials, both British and Indian, exercised increasing authority over this and other religious institutions. Numerous court cases have been filed which have seriously weakened the acharyas' administrative power. The development of the Public Trust System in the states of independent India has introduced a government official in the State of Gujarat who has oversight over the affairs of the Swaminarayan fellowship as well as over other trusts. The Charity Commissioner is *custodia legis* of all the trusts in the state. The property of all the trusts rest in him, and no property can be changed without his authority. His responsibility is to see that the affairs of the religious and charitable trusts in the state are run in an appropriate manner and that the property and wealth of the organizations are used in a way consonant with the purposes of the trust. The courts and the charity commissioners have been active in the definition of the role and authority of the acharyas of Vadtal and Ahmedabad.

Administration in the Vadtal diocese

The major instruments of the government's influence in the affairs have been the Bombay Public Trusts Act of 1950, along with its companion Acts after Gujarat became a separate state on 1 May 1960, and the scheme for administration of the Vadtal diocese set forth by the Bombay High Court in 1922 and amended at various times since. The Vadtal acharyas have been engaged in bitter public controversies with leading ascetics and householders in their diocese which have led to a curtailment of the acharya's power. As presently defined, the acharya has little administrative authority in the diocese, but considerable spiritual authority. He has the right to administer the initiation to ascetics. Usually he performs the official installation of images in the temples associated with his diocese, although images have in the past been installed by ascetics. His authority in the appointment of mahants and kotharis of the temples in the diocese is less clear. He still maintains the right to issue the appointment, but the selection is currently made by the Trustees.

The Board of Trustees is made up of representatives elected from and by the ascetics and the householders of the fellowship. Any member who has given a donation of fifteen rupees per year for the previous three years is entitled to vote in the election. The mahant of the Vadtal temple is a member *ex officio* of the committee. The acharya of Vadtal is in the position of Custodian Trustee, and the elected members are in the position of Managing Trustees. As Custodian Trustee the acharya does not take an active part in the deliberations of the committee. According to the Scheme: "The members of the Board as Managing Trustees shall manage and administer the trust properties and all affairs relating thereto in the name and under the order of the Acharya, who shall concur and perform all acts necessary to enable the members of the Board to exercise their powers of management."

Some of the larger temples in both the Vadtal and the Ahmedabad dioceses have their own resident ascetics and their own local temple committees. These temples – Junagadh and Gadhada in the Vadtal diocese are examples – manage most of their affairs. Junagadh has 228 sadhus and 150 *parshads*, men at the first stage of initiation, associated with the temple, and forty-eight groups go out from that temple to take posts in the temples in the area of Junagadh. The certificate of appointment for the mahants comes from the hand of the acharya in Vadtal, but the decisions have been taken from his hands.

Acharya Narendraprasad made a declaration in writing to the court that he did not want to have chief administrative authority and handed over the office to his son so he could retire with a pension of two thousand rupees a month from the trust in addition to the provisions for his house, household expenses, and automobile expenses. His son, Ajendraprasad, was initiated as acharya on 13 May 1984, one year before his father died. Ajendraprasad was educated at Sadar Patel University in Gujarat and had a career as a lawyer before his initiation. His wife is the daughter of a renowned Sanskrit scholar from Varanasi. Ajendraprasad's tenure and relations with the Managing Committee have been marked, nonetheless, with bitter disputes and rumors.

Administration in the Ahmedabad diocese

The Ahmedabad acharya has retained greater support from the ascetics and householders in his diocese, and hence there has been less diminution of his authority. Formerly in the Ahmedabad diocese the acharya acted as the sole owner of the property and wealth and treated it as his private property. Then the Ahmedabad diocese fell under the scheme of the Bombay High Court. As the scheme was applied in Ahmedabad, the acharya was the sole trustee and the committee was advisory. The acharya was not under legal obligation to follow the advice of the committee. Still, the property was designated as a public trust, and the acharya received the specified income from the trust and was prohibited from using as private income any of the gifts received by him, his wife, or his son.

In AD 1962 a suit was filed by the Charity Commissioner to change the administration of the Ahmedabad diocese. In contrast to the court cases filed against the Vadtal acharya by ascetics and householders of the diocese, this case was filed by an outsider and was opposed by the leaders of the diocese. The case is still under review in the courts, which will take some years. The Ahmedabad acharya retains rights as primary trustee and works with a board of trustees made up of five householders, three sadhus, and the mahant of the Ahmedabad temple, who is appointed by the acharya.

The administration of the Ahmedabad diocese is made rather complex because two areas of the diocese, Bhuj in Kutch and Muli in Kathiawar, are administered under schemes separate from that under which the rest of the diocese operates. Separate trusts were established because in the early days Muli and Bhuj were in different princely states. Each has a separate board of trustees to advise the acharya and to help administer the affairs in their area. Nevertheless, some differences exist in the procedures. For example, members of the board of trustees in Muli are not elected by vote of the members; individuals are nominated for the positions and then the selection is by lot in a drawing of names by a young child. The Bhuj temple was in the past more independent and self-sufficient because of the difficulties of travel and communication between Kutch and Ahmedabad. Until military conflict with Pakistan led to the rapid improvement of roads and other forms of communication, it took several days of difficult travel to reach Bhuj from Ahmedabad. Therefore, the mahant of the Bhuj temple exercised considerable independent power. Contrary to ordinary practice, the mahant of Bhuj is selected by the ascetics at Bhuj, and the acharya appoints him to his position for life. In the early days the mahant of Bhuj performed the initiation ceremony for young ascetics, but during the tenure of Devendraprasad the right to perform the initiation was returned to the acharya. Now the acharya visits Bhuj regularly, and senior ascetics travel to Ahmedabad to discuss temple affairs.

3 Acharya lineage of Ahmedabad diocese: Tejendraprasad Pande, his son
Koshalendraprasad, grandson Vrajendraprasad and attendants

The current Acharya of Ahmedabad is Tejendraprasad Pande, who
received the office from his father in AD 1969 (see plate 3). His training
for the position involved several years' apprenticeship during which he
learned the sacred texts and details of the various rituals he is expected
to perform. A unique aspect of his education is that he attended schools
with Western curricula and studied in English at St Xavier's High School
and St Xavier's College in Ahmedabad. He is active in presiding over
the meetings of the committees and in administering the religious and
charitable work of the Ahmedabad diocese. He travels throughout the
year to visit the temples and homes of the members of his diocese. He
reserves to himself the rights to perform the initiation ceremony for
ascetics and to install the images for worship in the temples of his
diocese. He exercises some minimal control over the affairs of the ascetics who reside in the temples in his diocese by appointing the mahants
of the temples.

He has traveled extensively outside of India to visit disciples among
overseas Gujaratis. In 1957, when he was thirteen years old, he undertook a tour for his father to Nairobi. In 1971 he went to East Africa and
Britain, and he returned to Britain in 1976. In 1978 Tejendraprasad

established the International Swaminarayan Satsang Organization, which subsequently has been incorporated in several countries including the United Kingdom, the United States, Australia, and New Zealand. He is the Founding Trustee and approves other trustees who oversee national activities. He and his son, Koshalendraprasad, travel abroad every year to visit satsangis and dedicate new temples.

In preparation for the twenty-fifth anniversary of Tejendraprasad's initiation as Acharya of Ahmedabad, Koshalendraprasad vowed to visit every temple in the diocese and in the process he established a network of over 300 centers for a youth organization that he administers. The organization now includes centers and summer conferences in the United Kingdom and the United States. This work is a significant preparation for his future work as acharya.

Even though the diocese organization as described in *The Lekh* made provision for administration of temples in other parts of India, it made no provision for the temples which have now been built in East Africa, Britain, the United States and other countries. No way exists for deciding under which diocese a temple in the United States belongs when that temple is built by devotees who have come from various parts of Gujarat. Because the devotees overseas have grown in numbers and in material prosperity, they have become an important constituency for the leaders of the movement. The International Swaminarayan Satsang Organization represents one response to the growth and prosperity of satsangis outside of India. The leader who has a claim on their support will gain significant additional resources for his administration.

Providing leadership for temples abroad has been difficult because it was not customary for Swaminarayan sadhus to live abroad until the end of the 1990s. Reluctance to travel or live abroad has been based on considerations of ritual purity. Moreover, in the organization of the diocese there has not been a natural right or call for individual ascetics to leave the temples of their residence in India to travel abroad. Sadhus traveled with the Ahmedabad acharya on his trips abroad, and some independent sadhus visited their followers. Growth in the numbers of satsangis, temples, and programs made it necessary for the acharya to establish sadhus in the temples of the International Swaminarayan Satsang Organization. Other Swaminarayan groups have also appointed sadhus to temples outside India even though immigration regulations in the various countries make it difficult, if not impossible, for the sadhus to become permanent residents.

Ascetics as administrators

The diminution in recent times of the legal administrative powers of the acharya, especially in the Vadtal diocese, has resulted in the increasing independence of the leading sadhus of the fellowship. The achieved moral authority of the leading sadhus has been preferred by some laymen to the ascribed hereditary authority of the acharyas. Some senior ascetics attract numbers of loyal disciples among both the ascetics and the householders. A young man who wishes to become a sadhu attaches himself to a senior ascetic for instruction and serves him. If the senior sadhu has achieved some prominence, he has a separate apartment in the temple in which he and his ascetic disciples reside. If he is appointed to be the mahant of one of the temples for a three-year term, he takes his group of sadhus with him to that temple to help him in the administration. Moreover, the prominent sadhus have householders who come to them for instruction and advice. Some sadhus receive support from these followers. These senior sadhus thus have considerable power and support.

Many established sadhus reside in their own apartments of several rooms with their own kitchens in the temple complex in Ahmedabad or Vadtal. Each has several ascetic disciples who reside with him and has several thousand loyal followers throughout the diocese who look to him as their primary religious teacher (guru). The ascetics who live in his complex take instruction from him in an apprenticeship that was in previous generations the primary type of religious instruction. They tour the villages to visit the homes of loyal followers. Every day some fifty or sixty people come to his rooms to listen to him teach or recite scripture or to ask his advice about some quandary or problem. These prominent sadhus are often appointed as mahants of temples of the diocese, where they establish their cadre of sadhus to help them conduct the affairs of the temple. These leading sadhus recognize the authority of the acharya and have the picture of the appropriate acharya prominently displayed in their apartments, but they have considerable authority and prestige in their own right.

An administrative problem for the acharyas of Ahmedabad and Vadtal is that after they perform his initiation, the acharyas can exercise very little direct authority over the individual sadhu. Except for the power to appoint the mahant of the temple, who can exercise some authority, the acharya does not have the power to designate the tasks which the ascetics will perform, nor does he have the power to discipline

Table 2. *Major administrative divisions*

Vadtal diocese and trust	Ahmedabad diocese and trust
Junagadh temple	Bhuj temple and trust
Swaminarayan gurukuls	Muli temple and trust

Swaminarayan Gadi (Maninagar)
Akshar Purushottam Sanstha (Bochasan)
Yogi Divine Society (Vidyanagar and Sokhda)

them. The sadhus have a legal claim on the institution for their requirements of food and housing. Even if the acharya attempts to discipline the ascetic by expulsion, he must be careful to do it in a legally acceptable manner. Moreover, if the sadhu has gained many followers and some financial resources, such an attempt at discipline will tend to cause a schism in the fellowship. The sadhu can leave the temple and take his disciples and resources with him. Thus, the practical power of the acharya to exercise authority over the institution is severely limited. His only recourse is through direct contact with the members. Acharyas prior to the current ones, especially in the Vadtal diocese, have not been very successful in maintaining a constructive relationship with the leading householders which would enable them to counter the growing influence of the ascetics.

THE SWAMINARAYAN *GURUKULS*

The administrative division into the two dioceses has been augmented by further schism and division as leading sadhus have separated themselves to form new religious movements or independent religious or educational trusts. Our aim now is to examine the more important of these, shown in table 2, to illustrate their diversity. Many separate educational trusts have been established by independent sadhus as *gurukuls*, some to establish hostels at universities and others to establish schools.

Dharmajivandas Swami left the Vadtal temple in AD 1947 to establish institutions which provide hostels and education for high-school and college students in three major centers: Rajkot, with 900 students living in the hostel with 40 sadhus; Junagadh, with 300 students and 5 sadhus; and Ahmedabad, with 85 students and 7 sadhus. Dharmajivandas developed an educational trust separate from the Vadtal administration, but all of the sadhus received their initiation from the Acharya of Vadtal. In

1979 he and fifteen of his sadhus undertook a six-month tour of East Africa, Britain, and the United States to visit former students and other devotees who might support the educational trust.

Dharmajivandas precipitated a territorial dispute by establishing a hostel in Ahmedabad near Gujarat University clearly outside the territory of the Vadtal diocese. The students and sadhus constructed a temple building with the desire to install the images of the gods for worship in the temple, but the selection of the person willing and able to perform the appropriate installation ceremony was a major problem. The Acharya of Ahmedabad understandably was not willing to perform the ceremony for a separate institution of the other diocese in the shadow of his own headquarters. The Acharya of Vadtal did not have the authority to enter the other diocese to perform the ceremony. After Dharmajivandas' death the images were installed by sadhus, which signaled a separation from the dioceses. Subsequently, the gurukul has separated into the major centers.

Hariprakash was initiated by the Vadtal acharya in 1941, but left the Vadtal temple in 1975 to establish the Swaminarayan gurukul and high school in Gandhinagar, the new capital city established for the Gujarat State in 1970. In twenty-five years the gurukul grew to 8,000 students in its schools in Gandhinagar, with a total of 40,000 students from kindergarten through high school in fifteen schools. Fifteen sadhus are associated with him in this educational enterprise.

The Acharya of Ahmedabad recognizes as many as fifteen gurukuls in his diocese, and a couple are started each year. Those that are recognized give regular financial reports to the diocese and their endowments revert to the diocese if the gurukul is closed. Even though he maintains some relationship with these educational institutions, their existence complicates the administrative structure and the fund raising for the diocese as a whole.

SWAMINARAYAN GADI

A small separate sect has been founded by a sadhu who left the Ahmedabad temple in the 1940s. Muktajivandas was born in 1907 and as a youth took initiation in Ahmedabad and eventually became a prominent sadhu in the Ahmedabad diocese. He left the temple in a dispute with the father of the present acharya and established his own sect. He went to Maninagar, just outside Ahmedabad, and began to build up his own institutions, which came to be called the Swaminarayan Gadi. In an explicit rejection of the claims of the householder acharyas to be the legitimate successors of Swaminarayan, followers in this sect claim that Swaminarayan appointed an ascetic, Gopalanand Swami, to be his successor. The spiritual leadership is thought to be in the hands of the ascetic who is the successor to Gopalanand. According to the tradition handed down in this group: "Lord Swaminarayan handed over the responsibility of the religious sect and the key of eternal salvation to Sadguru Shree Gopalananda Swami. That key of eternal salvation lies with the lineage of the Acharyas of the Shree Swaminarayan Gadi. Therefore, one can only achieve the motive [*sic*] of salvation at the resort of Shree Swaminarayan Gadi" (Divyavigrahdas n.d.: 3–4). Muktajivandas is thought to be the fourth acharya to take his place on the Swaminarayan Gadi. Opponents point out that the first three were not known as acharyas. The traditions concerning Gopalanand Swami and the other sadhus who are accepted as ascetic acharyas in this line are preserved in the group. One of the four, Abjibapa (AD 1844–1928), was a householder and social reformer, and followers believe that he was an incarnation of Swaminarayan. Abjibapa was associated with Kutch, and some Kutchis are followers. They have built a temple in Bhuj and also overseas in Nairobi and in North London, where many Kutchis reside.

Muktajivandas was the first in the line to claim divine authority for himself. He constructed temples, residences, and other institutions. Most importantly, he personally conducted the initiation of sadhus and the installation of the images in temples of his group which signaled the separation from the Ahmedabad diocese. Although the group is relatively small, the devotees seem to be very loyal and lavish in their support. In 1957 they celebrated a golden jubilee of his birth by giving him a gift of his weight in gold; ten years later they celebrated his platinum jubilee with a gift of platinum; and when he was seventy he was weighed against five types of jewels. A large part of these gifts were from wealthy devotees in East Africa. Muktajivandas used the gifts to build a school, a library, and other social institutions. On 7 October 1972 he revealed that he was the personification of the Swaminarayan Gadi, and thereafter he received the honors appropriate to a god. His images were placed in the temples of the sect, one depicting him being weighed with gold and another depicting him being taken in procession on an elephant. He died in Bolton in 1979 while on tour to visit his disciples in Britain.

His successor is an ascetic of the sect, Purushottam Priyadasji, and under his leadership the silver jubilee of the establishment of the

Swaminarayan Gadi was celebrated in 1997. From its headquarters at Maninagar near Ahmedabad he leads an organization with 100 sadhus (60 at Maninagar and 40 in other temples), 20 women ascetics (5 in Maninagar and 15 at other locations), and some 100,000 followers, including 1,500 in Britain, 1,000 in the United States, and 1,000 in East Africa. The last quarter of the twentieth century was a time of significant growth.

AKSHAR PURUSHOTTAM SANSTHA

The most important event in the modern history of the Swaminarayan movement is the founding of the Bochasanwasi Akshar Purushottam Sanstha. This event involves the major doctrinal split as well as the major institutional division within the movement. The independent trusts and religious institutions separate from Vadtal and Ahmedabad mentioned above are relatively small in both numbers and resources. The Akshar Purushottam Sanstha, on the other hand, is a very large and growing religious community with its own group of sadhus, a separate administrative organization, many large temples in Gujarat and abroad, and claims to over a million followers. Thus, the two major divisions of the Swaminarayan movement are the "old school," as I refer to it, which encompasses the institutions associated with the traditional acharyas of Ahmedabad and Vadtal, and the "new school" of the Akshar Purushottam Sanstha. Both sections of the movement are growing, and the Akshar Purushottam Sanstha is one of the fastest-growing religious groups in Gujarat and perhaps in all of India.

The split came when Swami Yagnapurushdas (AD 1865–1951), commonly called Shastri Maharaj, left the Vadtal temple in 1906 and was expelled from the fellowship by a hastily called meeting of the sadhus. He left to establish his own group with a few ascetics and a small number of householders who supported him. This was during the acharyaship of Lakshmiprasad, who was soon to be deposed for his failure to live up to the moral requirements of his office. It may well be that the immorality of the acharya, caused as some suggest by the bad influence of the mahant of the Vadtal temple, created a condition which caused Yagnapurushdas to leave the temple. It is clear that he found fault with the lax behavior of some of the ascetics of the Vadtal temple. They were accused of accumulating wealth, of not observing the rules concerning ritual observances, and of failure to observe the restrictions concerning contact and conversation with women. Shastri Maharaj reinstituted for

Table 3. *Line of succession*

Gunatitanand Swami	1785–1867	(Brahmin)
Pragji Bhakta	1829–1897	(Sat Shudra, tailor)
Yagnapurushdas (Shastri Maharaj)	1865–1951	(Vaishya)
Jnanjivandas (Yogiji Maharaj)	1891–1971	(Vaishya)
Narayanswarupdas (Pramukh Swami)	1921	(Vaishya)

the sadhus who became his disciples a strict observance of the rules regarding money, women, and ritual observances. Yet the primary cause of his departure from the Vadtal temple was a doctrinal issue.

Yagnapurushdas had come to believe and teach that Swaminarayan had appointed one of his close followers, Gunatitanand Swami, to be his spiritual successor. He taught that Swaminarayan promised that he would always be manifest in the world with his devotees in the person of his chief devotee, who is, in fact, *akshar* as the manifestation of an eternal principle and the abode of god. Gunatitanand Swami (AD 1785–1867) was a Brahmin ascetic, an early disciple of Ramananda Swami, and one who remained loyal to Sahajanand Swami when he became the preceptor of the group. During the time of Sahajanand he was a prominent ascetic of the group, a teacher, an author of a commentary on the *Vachanamritam*, and the mahant for almost forty years of the large temple at Junagadh. Yagnapurushdas revered him as the true spiritual successor of Swaminarayan. The sadhus of the Vadtal temple came to fear that he would attempt to place images of Gunatitanand Swami in the temple, and they would not accept this innovation. Therefore, he left the temple.

Members of the Akshar Purushottam Sanstha do not believe that it was an innovation. They believe that Gunatitanand Swami was appointed by Swaminarayan, and that the early acharyas looked to Gunatitanand Swami for advice and help in the administration of the fellowship. Gunatitanand Swami established a line of spiritual authorities who are believed to have the right to administer the affairs. They indicate that Swaminarayan gave authority to devout ascetics to initiate ascetics and install images in temples. The theory is that Swaminarayan is always manifest in the perfect disciples who have continued in a line of succession from Gunatitanand. Images of those in the line of succession are placed in the temples. Though the doctrine has on the whole resulted in the strengthening of the authority of the sadhus of the group, the second man in the line of succession was a householder, not a sadhu. See table 3.

The line of succession in the Akshar Purushottam Sanstha

Pragji Bhakta (AD 1829–97) is described as the faithful disciple and successor of Gunatitanand Swami. His inclusion is remarkable because he was a Sat-Shudra and a householder. (A distinction is made between two categories of Shudras; the lower are called Shudras and untouchability is practiced with Shudras and not Sat-Shudras.) He was born in Mahuva on the Gujarat coast into a family of a tailor caste. He became a loyal follower of Gunatitanand Swami at Junagadh. He is supposed to have wished to renounce the world and become an ascetic, but he was told to remain a householder. He thus demonstrated the teaching of the group that a person can attain the realization of god in any status, even as a householder in a relatively low caste, because realization depends upon devotion and nonattachment. Though Pragji Bhakta faced opposition from the authorities at Vadtal, he continued to teach and preach as a householder. He did not, however, organize a separate religious community. That task was left to Yagnapurushdas.

Swami Yagnapurushdas left Vadtal in 1906 and immediately began to build up the new institution. The first of several large temples was built in Bochasan, and the images of Swaminarayan and Gunatitanand Swami were placed in the central shrine for worship. The seventy-fifth anniversary of the installation of the images was celebrated at Bochasan on 18 May 1982 with 15,000 followers in attendance. Five large temples were built during his lifetime; currently there are fifteen main temples of the Akshar Purushottam Sanstha which contain full sculptured images of the major deities: Ahmedabad, Atladara near Vadodara (previously called Baroda), Bhadra, Bochasan, Gadhada, Gondal, London, Mahelav, Mehsana, Mumbai (previously called Bombay), Rajkot, Sankari, Sarangpur, Surat and Surendranagar. There are hundreds of smaller temples and shrines in Gujarat and abroad which contain other sculpted images or pictures. Swami Yagnapurushdas performed the installation ceremonies of the images and pictures in the temples built during his life, and his successors have continued the practice of performing the installation ceremonies (pran pratistha). This effectively signals the separation of this group from the dioceses of Ahmedabad and Vadtal.

Yagnapurushdas had only six ascetic disciples and a handful of householders who were his loyal followers when he left Vadtal. Later he had some success in attracting candidates for initiation as sadhus and householders who admired the strictness of his observance of the ascetic rules and believed his teaching about the manifestation of the abode of god as Gunatitanand Swami. Although neither he nor his successors have claimed the title or office of acharya, they have performed the major rituals of installation of images in the temples and the initiation of the sadhus. There is no exact record of the number of men who were initiated by Swami Yagnapurushdas, but it is estimated that the number of sadhus grew to about fifty by the time of his death in AD 1951. Their primary activities were to preach in the villages and to help in the construction of the temples. They had to visit the villages to beg alms for their food. They faced opposition from the leaders of the Vadtal diocese, which restricted their activities somewhat. Elderly sadhus now comment on the striking contrast between the early days when there was a lack of financial support, few followers, and significant opposition and the size and prosperity of the Akshar Purushottam Sanstha today.

Swami Yagnapurushdas seems to have had some success in attracting followers both from families and villages associated with Vadtal and from groups that had not previously been associated with the Swaminarayan fellowship. It is reported in the stories of his life that he, like Swaminarayan, performed miracles to attract people to his teaching and caused people to enter the trance state. Again, there is no accurate record of the number of devotees attracted to the new sect during this period. The fact that there was some success even at the expense of the Vadtal diocese is shown by the opposition that was aroused. The dispute reached its legal conclusion in a suit filed against Swami Yagnapurushdas and the Akshar Purushottam Sanstha by the Acharya of Vadtal. The rulings of the judge and the appeal judge provide insights into the points of division between the two groups (Appeal no. 165 of 1940 in the Court of the District Judge, Kaira, at Nadiad from Decree in Reg. Civil Suit No. 519 of 1936 of the Court of the Sub-judge Mr. P. B. Patel of Borsad).

The original suit arose out of an incident in 1935 when some sadhus of the Akshar Purushottam Sanstha visited the small village of Ishnav. With the approval of some of the villagers, but against the wishes of the trustee of a small temple in the village, the sadhus entered the temple and spent the night there. Though it seems clear that there was some division of loyalty in the village, the temple had always been under the administration of the Acharya of Vadtal. He filed a suit asking the court to prohibit the sadhus of the Akshar Purushottam Sanstha from claiming to be sadhus of the Swaminarayan movement or from entering temples or properties belonging to the Vadtal diocese. The local court ruled in his favor, but Swami Yagnapurushdas appealed the ruling to a higher court. In the higher court the issues between the two groups had a fuller hearing.

The District Judge, Mr. J. D. Kapadiya, who delivered his judgment on 29 November 1943, recognized the importance of the issues between the two groups. He investigated the administrative and theological principles which separated the two because of the far-reaching significance of the case. He wrote:

> Then there is a more important question. The suit trust [*sic*] is a religious trust. The Ishnav Harimandir is after all a small property but on this question of doctrinal differences hang far more important issues. If it is decided that the defendants are entitled, as they follow the Swaminarayan creed according to the scriptures as laid down by the founder, to the benefit of this particular temple under the Vadtal Gadi, this is merely a test case. If the defendants win on this point, they will get rights far more extensive than those covered by the right to stay and preach in the Harimandir at Ishnav. Both the parties have realized this and that is why they have tenaciously fought in the trial court here. (par. 51, p. 18)

He made judgments on a number of issues. He overruled the local judge's statement that Swami Yagnapurushdas had been properly expelled from the Vadtal temple. He wrote: "The laws of natural justice have clearly been broken in these proceedings [of 1906] and I have no hesitation in holding that as far as the law courts are concerned they would not recognize the excommunication of defendant No. 1 [Yagnapurushdas] and would not deprive him of his rights to property on the grounds of that excommunication" (par. 38, p. 11). It was clear to the judge, however, that his followers formed a separate group which did not give allegiance to Vadtal or claim the properties of the diocese. He entered into the record an affidavit from Swami Yagnapurushdas: "I say that since about twenty-four years ago I and some other Sadhus who were formerly of the Swaminarayan sect attached to the said Vadtal Gadi, owing to certain differences, seceded from the said Vadtal Gadi, and we have erected new temples in different places in Gujarat and we are managing the same and neither I nor my associates who have so seceded have any connection whatever either with the holders of the Vadatal [*sic*] or Ahmedabad Gadi" (par. 24, p. 9). On the basis of this affidavit the judge ruled that the ascetics of the Akshar Purushottam Sanstha did not have the right to stay or preach in the temple in Ishnav, and he restrained Swami Yagnapurushdas from sending his sadhus to stay and preach in that temple.

The lawyer of the Akshar Purushottam group impressed upon the judge that a decision of the court that the new group did not follow the Swaminarayan creed would affect them adversely. The judge agreed that it was not for him to decide whether their doctrines were within the scriptures. The court of law was not concerned with that point. Nevertheless, the evidence given on matters of faith and practice and the reflections of the judge do give some indication of the points at issue.

At the time there seems to have been a difference in the interpretation of Sahajanand's teaching concerning his divinity. The lawyer for the Akshar Purushottam Sanstha gave an analysis of the scriptures to show a development in his teaching. He argued that the founder first started as a devotee of Krishna and bowed to Krishna as the supreme deity. Then he made his followers understand that he was himself a manifestation of Krishna. Finally, he taught that he was superior to Krishna. The leaders of the Vadtal group held that Krishna was the supreme deity. The judge reviewed the Hindu doctrine of avatars and the Swaminarayan scriptures and came to agree with the position of the Vadtal spokesmen. He continued, however, to place the controversy in a different perspective.

> Though this is only my opinion, it appears to me that this new sect is a more ascetical sect than the original one. The founders seem to have been horrified or repulsed at the idea of the sensual and other pleasures enjoyed by Shri Krishna. They seem to be horrified at the idea of the supreme god indulging in such pleasure. They think only of an ascetical religion devoted to prayers and self-mortification. This explains why they have put Sahajanand Swami, an ascetic, over Shri Krishna, who admittedly enjoyed the pleasures of human beings. That is why the new sect has set aside Golok as the supreme heaven because there Krishna is supposed to be enjoying himself with his Gopis. This is I think one of the fundamental differences between the two sects and the schism cannot be bridged. (par. 97, p. 36)

Leaders of the Akshar Purushottam Sanstha emphatically reject the judge's opinion and indicate that the entire life of Krishna is accepted as totally divine by all groups of the Swaminarayan religion. Thus the judge's statement about Krishna is held to be blasphemous.

Also at issue was the position of Gunatitanand Swami and his successors. The Vadtal group argued that Gopalanand Swami was the chief ascetic disciple of Sahajanand and that the acharyas have the sole authority to initiate sadhus and to install images in the temples. The lawyer for the Akshar Purushottam Sanstha presented evidence which showed that Gunatitanand Swami had been appointed to be the leader of the movement after the death of Sahajanand. Moreover, he argued that the chief ascetics had been given the authority to perform the primary rituals of the group, including the initiation of sadhus, and that this authority had not been revoked when the acharyas were appointed. He questioned the legitimacy of the Vadtal acharya line because there had been acharyas who did not live up to the requirements. He quoted the statement from the *Satsangijivan*: "In case you have sons you must set up for the Acharyaship one meritorious son. It is not the rule that you must set up the eldest son, but should place on the Gadi the meritorious of the sons. That son is fit for the Acharyaship and none other who possesses virtue, inspires life in the religion and who is able to protect the religion of his followers and who has faith in the religion established by his sampradaya" (par. 133, p. 50). The emphasis is upon the spiritual lineage rather than the hereditary lineage, and the claim is that the one who observes the rules should be the acharya. Though the judge was not convinced, the presentation did set forward the primary theological claims of the new group. The judge did not attempt to adjudicate the theological claims, but his ruling did indicate that the two major sections of the movement were legally and in fact separate institutions.

The separation became even more clear with the reorganization of the Akshar Purushottam Sanstha in a new constitution approved in December of AD 1946 and certified in 1947. Prior to the reorganization, the properties of the sect had been registered in the government registers in the name of Swami Yagnapurushdas or in the names of the mahants and kotharis of the major temples. The point of the reorganization was to assure that the properties were all a trust of the Bochasanwasi Shri Akshar Purushottam Sanstha, as the legal name was established, and that no individual had rights to any of the property. An administrative committee with twenty-six members was formed with Swami Yagnapurushdas as president to hold title to all the property and to oversee the work of the temples and the sadhus. Provision was made in the by-laws of the committee for the appointment of an acharya for the group from the family of Swaminarayan who would clearly be subordinate to the president, but this provision was never implemented. In AD 1950 Swami Yagnapurushdas appointed a young ascetic named Swami Narayanswarupdas (AD 1921–) to work under Swami Jnanjivandas as the administrative president of the group and to be his spiritual successor.

The period after the death of Swami Yagnapurushdas in AD 1951 was one of shared authority and responsibility. Swami Narayanswarupdas, given the title Pramukh Swami because Pramukh means "president," continued as president for twenty years with principal responsibility for administration. Swami Jnanjivandas (AD 1891–1971), also called Yogiji Maharaj, became the spiritual leader of the group as third in line following Gunatitanand Swami. Both were active, and the arrangement seems to have worked well. Swami Jnanjivandas was particularly effective in attracting the strong devotion of his followers and greatly expanding the numbers of followers. He also attracted and initiated a large number of well-educated young university graduates as sadhus. Because Swami Narayanswarupdas was an effective organizer and administrator, the period was marked by very rapid growth of the sect through the institution of new programs, expansion into new areas, and the construction of new temples and buildings. As one disciple remembered, "Yogiji Maharaj was the one who willed, but Pramukh Swami was the one who executed and carried it out." In addition to their joint activities in India, Pramukh Swami accompanied Yogiji Maharaj on tours of East Africa and Britain in 1960 and 1970. When Swami Jnanjivandas died shortly after the tour in January of 1971, Swami Narayanswarupdas became his successor, and the two functions of temporal administration and spiritual oversight were reunited in him. He is the current president and leader of the Akshar Purushottam Sanstha.

He was born in December 1921 in the village of Chansad in Baroda district. (For details of his life see Pandya 1974.) Swami Narayanswarupdas received his education and training for his office within the sect. His father, Motibhai Prabhudas Patel, was a non-Brahmin householder and follower of Swami Yagnapurushdas. The boy received initiation into the fellowship from Swami Yagnapurushdas. After he finished his primary education to the fourth standard in the village school, he joined the group of ascetics and entered the probationary stage at Ahmedabad, during which he wore the white turban and robes. He was given a new name, Shanti Bhagat, which signified that his attachment to family and his previous life was broken. After two years, in AD 1940, he received full initiation as a sadhu from the hands of Swami Yagnapurushdas.

His preceptor sent him to Sanskrit school in the town of Bhadaran and later to Khambhat to study the *Vedas*. He earned the title "Shastri," signifying competence in sacred scripture and philosophy, a title which several of the learned ascetics received. He was involved in the practical affairs of the sect as kothari of the temple at Sarangpur and as supervisor of the construction of the large gate of that temple. In 1947 he was chosen to be the private secretary to Swami Yagnapurushdas, and he was then in a position to observe all the rituals and to become well acquainted with all of the affairs of the ascetics and of the institution. He was twenty-eight when he was appointed to the newly formed position of president of the group in 1950.

Organization of the Akshar Purushottam Sanstha

Pramukh Swami has developed an extensive administrative structure to manage the expanding activities of the Sanstha from its headquarters at the Ahmedabad temple. He is the president of five tax-exempt charitable trusts: Bochasanwasi Shree Akshar Purushottam Swaminarayan Sanstha for general activities, Swaminarayan Aksharpith for publications, Gnanyagna Vidyapith for educational institutions, Bochasanwasi Shree Akshar Purushottam Gaushala Trust for animal husbandry, and Bochasanwasi Shree Akshar Purushottam Public Charitable Trust for medical clinics and hospitals. Various schools, hospitals, hostels, and many disaster relief programs in response to droughts, earthquakes, and floods are supported by these trusts. One of the distinctive organizational characteristics of this group is its large and well-organized volunteer corps. The Ahmedabad center, for example, maintains a volunteer force of 3,000 men and women who receive specialized training. They assemble at the call of Pramukh Swami to assist with the activities of the sanstha and to engage in emergency relief work under the direction of the sadhus.

Because of rapid growth in membership and programs in the last quarter of the twentieth century, an extensive organization is required that reaches down to the smallest village and covers all the programs of the women, men, children, and youth. In 1953 Yogiji Maharaj started twelve centers for regular meetings by sending postcards to followers. The number of centers in India grew to 180 by the time of his death in 1971. By the end of the century there were over 1,900 centers in India (1,800 in Gujarat and 100 outside) and more than 100 abroad where regular weekly sabhas are held. Sadhus are the acknowledged leaders of all satsang activities and they reside in the main temples and travel throughout their districts to instruct and inspire satsangis. Each zone and region also has a committee of volunteers who oversee activities and report to the sadhus and to Pramukh Swami through his boards of national trustees. At each level there are coordinators of the various activities such as the children's program, the youth organization, the women's work, the program of examinations, and publications. The lay members of these local committees receive regular instructions through publications sent out from Ahmedabad and they work with the sadhus to plan the programs in their towns and villages. Regular weekly program reports and financial reports are sent to the trustees for review and audit. The result is an effective modern administrative organization and a powerful central decision-making body, with almost absolute authority in the hands of one man, Swami Narayanswarupdas, because of the divine position he holds according to the theology of the sanstha.

An advantage which the new group has over the old is that it is not constrained by any territorial limitation of the diocese division. The new group has spread all over Gujarat wherever it has been able to attract followers without territorial limitation of the diocese organization. It has attracted followers from both the Vadtal and Ahmedabad dioceses. The Akshar Purushottam Sanstha has not had much success in reaching into Kutch because the people there have remained loyal to the Bhuj temple and to the Acharya of Ahmedabad. Only one temple is in Kutch, and the few followers there have returned from East Africa and Britain. In Gujarat proper and in Saurashtra there are examples of villages which have changed allegiance from one group to the other. No legal transactions have taken place to change the designation, but the shrine contains pictures of Gunatitanand Swami and Swaminarayan together which mark the shrine as belonging to the new school. The annual donations of rice, wheat, and millet at harvest time are given to the Akshar Purushottam Sanstha. Outside of Gujarat the group is free to establish temples and centers at any place having a concentration of Gujaratis, and they have been very successful in attracting followers from Gujaratis who have migrated to the cities of India and abroad.

Administrative committees have been established in each of the countries where there is a temple. These committees are registered or incorporated according to the laws of the countries where they are located, but in each case Swami Narayanswarupdas is the president of the committee. There are now committees in Kenya, Tanzania, Uganda, Australia, New Zealand, South Africa, Singapore/Malaysia, Britain, the United States, and Canada. The chairman and members of each committee are appointed by Swami Narayanswarupdas. The work of the Akshar Purushottam Sanstha in all the countries is coordinated through the central committee in India. The effective administrative structure combined with a centralized and respected authority to make decisions is one of the major factors leading to the growth and success of the Akshar Purushottam Sanstha during the last thirty years.

Another factor leading to growth is the work of the sadhus, who have taken the vows of renunciation to devote themselves to religious work. There were in 1980 approximately 250 ascetics working in and out of the temples. A few still remain who were initiated by Swami Yagnapurushdas, but most were attracted to the ascetic life through their contact with Swami Jnanjivandas. It was his custom to take young men and university students with him on his preaching tours. During his time many highly trained university graduates became sadhus, including many from East Africa. In 1973 on the occasion of the birthday of Swami Narayanswarupdas a group of fifty-six young men took initiation as sadhus as a sort of birthday present. During the bicentenary celebrations of the birth of Swaminarayan 207 young men presented themselves for initiation. Swami Narayanswarupdas performed the initiation ceremony, which almost doubled the number of ascetics associated with the Akshar Purushottam Sanstha. By 2000 the number had grown to between 650 and 700 sadhus. They will do many jobs as assigned by Pramukh Swami: cooking and cleaning in the temples, caring for the images, preaching in villages, working on publications, studying philosophy and theology, art, and music. The growth in the number of sadhus and expansion of the sanstha are linked, and at the end of the twentieth century Pramukh Swami found it necessary to restrict the expansion until more sadhus were trained to assist with the growth (see plate 4).

Pramukh Swami appoints the mahants and kotharis of the temples. In some cases the two duties are combined. There is a difference in the appointment from the practice in the Vadtal and Ahmedabad dioceses. The appointment is not for a specific period of three years; rather, the mahant serves at the pleasure of Swami Narayanswarupdas. The senior sadhus do not have coteries of ascetic disciples, though the managers of prominent temples are shown great loyalty and respect by both sadhus and householders. Sadhus are moved from temple to temple and from job to job by Swami Narayanswarupdas without the cumbersome intrusion of intermediate authorities. The ability to deploy ascetics geographically throughout Gujarat and abroad and to assign them to the range of activities required for the life of the satsang has been a significant factor in making this one of the fastest-growing religious movements in India.

YOGI DIVINE SOCIETY

The history of the Akshar Purushottam Sanstha has not been without controversy and division. In AD 1966 Dadubhai Patel and his brother, Bapabhai, left to form a separate group called the Yogi Divine Society.

4 Initiation of sadhus by Pramukh Swami

Dadubhai Patel was one of the outstanding lay preachers and devotees of the Akshar Purushottam Sanstha. Controversy arose over a trip which he took to East Africa. He carried a letter from Swami Jnanjivandas requesting satsangis to assist him on a preaching tour. He showed this letter to Mr. C. T. Patel of Mombasa. A dispute arose because Dadubhai interpreted his mandate to include recruiting young women to become ascetics and to raise funds for a temple and residence for female ascetics that he planned to build on property at Vidyanagar which he was prepared to donate for that purpose. Because he was popular in East Africa, he was able to raise a large sum of money for the building of the temple. He also announced that Swami Jnanjivandas had agreed to initiate young women as ascetics. Several young girls agreed to be initiated and prepared to travel to India. The trustees decided that Swami Jnanjivandas had not authorized the raising of funds and certainly not the initiation of girls. They maintained that Swami Jnanjivandas commanded him to stop preaching to women. Though there are a few older widows affiliated with the new school who live the ascetic life, leaders maintain that Swami Jnanjivandas explicitly forbade the initiation of women as ascetics. After an investigation the trustees decided to expel both brothers.

Dadubhai Patel was a well-known leader with a significant following. Thirty-nine ascetics who were associated with the Bombay temple left the temple to show their displeasure and said that they would not return unless the brothers were readmitted. Some of this group returned, but others followed Dadubhai when he started a separate movement. He started a mission at Vidyanagar and established some of the young women from East Africa as women ascetics. He has constructed some temples in which there are pictures of Swami Jnanjivandas along with the pictures of Swaminarayan. He claimed that Swami Jnanjivandas approved all his activities and wished him to stay in the Akshar Purushottam group but that it was Swami Narayanswarupdas who was against him and persuaded the committee to vote against him. Members of the Akshar Purushottam who witnessed the events point out, however, that official notice was given by Swami Jnanjivandas and the trustees in the organization's Gujarati monthly, *Swaminarayan Prakash* (July, 1966) for those who left to return and that Swami Jnanjivandas signed the order of expulsion when Dadubhai and his followers did not obey. Still, Swami Jnanjivandas has a major place in the preaching and iconography of the Yogi Divine Society, but the group rejects the authority of his successor. Thirty-six men took initiation as ascetics with this group at the bicentenary celebration of Swaminarayan's birth at Sokhda near Baroda in April 1981, which increased the number of ascetics to about one hundred. Twenty-three women became *Samkhya Yoginis* at the same time. After Dadubhai's death in 1986, a sadhu named Hariprasad became leader of the Divine Yogi Society, which includes approximately 175 sadhus and 225 female ascetics who dress in white saris and follow disciplines similar to those of sadhus.

Two separate but cooperating organizations have been established that follow a different discipline. The Anoopa Mission has its headquarters at Mogri near Anand and is led by Jashbhai Saheb, who was a youth leader under Swami Jnanjivandas. The Mission initiates men who are celibate, but who neither shave their heads, don saffron robes, nor adopt new names. They dress in a uniform of blue shirts and cream pants and engage in secular occupations to support their institutions. They have even established their own electronics firm. A separate organization for female ascetics was established as the Gunatit Jyot. These ascetics are also engaged in secular activities but live a disciplined life in the ashram. There are followers of this movement in East Africa, Britain, and the United States.

GURU MAHARAJ OF NORTH GUJARAT

The adaptability and fluidity within Swaminarayan Hinduism are demonstrated by the Guru Maharaj, a still smaller group which developed a line of religious teachers who were successors of Pragji Bhakta, the householder disciple of Gunatitanand Swami. This group followed a religious leader (guru) who is a householder; it is said that he lives a very strict, simple, and pious life. He attracted a localized group with between four and five thousand followers, with a couple of temples, but there are no sadhus associated with them. Over the years they grew much closer to the Akshar Purushottam Sanstha, and for several years all of their festival days were celebrated in Akshar Purushottam temples. Their donations of grains have been given to the Akshar Purushottam temple in Ahmedabad. They accepted the hierarchy of the Akshar Purushottam Sanstha but also showed respect to their own line of teachers. Gradually they have merged with the Akshar Purushottam Sanstha, and some of their young men have become sadhus.

The formation of these various groups within the Swaminarayan movement indicates some of the pressures – theological, administrative, and personal – which lead to schism and separation. Though there are many groups and trusts, the two largest and most important divisions of the fellowship are the old school, which follows the acharyas of Vadtal and Ahmedabad and supports the temples and sadhus under their charge in the two dioceses, and the new school of the Akshar Purushottam Sanstha, which gives allegiance to Narayanswarupdas Swami as the current abode of god in succession from Gunatitanand Swami and supports the temples, ascetics, and institutions under his administration. The chief administrative leaders of the old school are two Brahmin householders; the undisputed leader of the new school is a non-Brahmin ascetic. They have different sadhus, temples, trusts, and institutions as well as different theological positions.

Great difficulty exists in the attempt to estimate the number of followers of these groups. One estimate of the total number of followers of the Swaminarayan religion is about 5 million, about one-sixth of the population of the state of Gujarat – 3.5 million associated with Vadtal and Ahmedabad and 1.5 million associated with the Bochasanwasi Akshar Purushottam Sanstha. A basic problem in all estimates is that the same follower may be counted by more than one group. Each group has a core of followers who express allegiance to that form of the religion. In fact, many followers practice what may be called a double allegiance. They participate in the temples of more than one group, show respect to sadhus from each group, and give their donations to various trusts. Some movement occurs among groups as both individuals and villages change their allegiance. Moreover, many Gujaratis who may not technically be considered members are nonetheless sympathetic to the Swaminarayan movement and participate in rituals and festivals. Many Gujaratis consider themselves to be Vaishnava as followers of Krishna and support Swaminarayan activities. Such joint participation and sympathetic support of the various groups is very evident among overseas Indians for whom only in the last two decades have the institutions become more distinct. The dioceses of Ahmedabad and Vadtal are more wealthy, have more followers, both sadhus and householders, and support more large temples than the other groups. The Akshar Purushottam Sanstha grew at a very rapid rate in the last quarter of the twentieth century. Competition for allegiance and support of Gujaratis exists among the groups – competition which has resulted in court cases in the past. But now there seems to be less direct competition. The movement as a whole has grown rapidly over the past three decades and can now make the claim to be the most important of the indigenous Gujarati religious movements. Discussions with religious leaders, community leaders, and newspaper editors leads to a conclusion that the world-wide membership approaches 5 million. It is a specifically Gujarati form of modern Hinduism.

CHAPTER THREE

The structure of Swaminarayan theology

Reginald Heber, the well-known poet, hymn writer, and Lord Bishop of Calcutta, was on tour through his diocese from Calcutta to Bombay (now called Mumbai) when he met Sahajanand Swami at the small town of Nariad north of Baroda (now called Vadodara) on 26 March 1825 (R. Heber 1846 II: 106–15).[1] Sahajanand was in Kaira district on tour to visit some 5,000 disciples in neighboring villages and to attend a large gathering in the next few days to celebrate the sacred thread ceremony of his brother's son. Two hundred horsemen and a large body of armed disciples accompanied him. Bishop Heber himself had an armed guard of one hundred men. He commented on the irony, "in some degree painful and humiliating," of the idea of two religious teachers meeting at the head of little armies and "filling the city, which was the scene of their interview, with the rattling of quivers, the clash of shields, and the tramp of warhorses." Such protection was made necessary by the unstable social situation described in chapter 1, but it provided a strange backdrop for the discussion of theology which engaged the two men.

Bishop Heber had heard a report about the Swaminarayan religion a few days earlier in Baroda from a prince of Kathiawar who had attempted to put down this new Hindu sect by force of arms. The British stopped him. He complained of the sect that "there were too many of them," and that, "they had no religion at all, but hatred of their superiors and of all lawful authority" (R. Heber 1846 II: 101). In spite of this introduction and his own negative evaluation of the Hinduism of his previous experience, Bishop Heber approached the meeting with a high regard for this Hindu reformer. He had been told by Mr. Williamson, a British official near Ahmedabad (now called Amdavad), that Sahajanand followed a strict moral code and had a profound influence for good in the lives of his

---

[1] Nariad, a town north of Baroda with a population of about 15,000 when they met, is present-day Nadiad.

followers, many of whom came from the least restrained portion of the population. The villages and districts where Swaminarayan was popular were among the best and most orderly in the provinces. Heber was also told that Sahajanand preached faith in one god. The appearance of what he took to be an ethical monotheism attracted his interest. He mused: "I could not but hope he might be an appointed instrument to prepare the way for the Gospel." Thus, Heber's goal in the meeting was to introduce Sahajanand to Christianity, to provide him with a copy of the Bible, and to persuade him to accompany him to Bombay, where he could contact the Church Missionary Society.

For his part, Sahajanand requested the meeting hoping to enlist Heber's support and good influence with the British government officials for some projects underway in the area. After the meeting he requested Heber's assistance in getting an endowment for the temple to Lakshmi Narayana at Vadtal and for a residence hall and hospital (R. Heber 1846 II: 115). Thus, each participant wished to make a good impression upon the other, and the discussion progressed in cordial good will. Sahajanand could not accept the invitation to travel with Heber because of his commitments to his thousands of followers. Heber refused to give any support for the construction of a temple or to idolatry, as he viewed it, but he agreed to convey the request for support for the hospital and residence hall to Mr. Elphinstone, the Governor of Bombay.

The discussion and the major point of disagreement were about the doctrine of god and Sahajanand's presentation of a Hindu doctrine of the manifestation of god in the particular form it took in the Swaminarayan religion. Sahajanand began the exchange with a statement of belief, translated by Heber into Christian idiom "in one God, the Maker of all things in Heaven and on earth, who filled all space, upheld and governed all things, and more particularly, dwelt in the hearts of those who diligently sought him." Heber was sufficiently conversant with Hindu doctrine to ask if he referred to *Brahman*. Sahajanand replied, "Many names there may be, and have been, given to him who is and is the same, but whom we as well as other hindoos call brihm [*sic*]" (R. Heber 1846 II: 110). Heber accepted this as a type of monotheism.

It was not the monotheism of the Christian West, however, and Heber was repelled by Sahajanand's explanation that Krishna was a form of god which he worshiped and by the intimation that Sahajanand considered himself to be a manifestation of God. Sahajanand explained his belief "that there had been many avatars of God in different lands, one to Christians, another to the Hindoos in time past, adding something like a hint, that another avatar of Krishna, or the Sun, had taken place in him." The theological discussion ground to a halt when he gave Heber a picture of the form of god he worshiped, which Heber described as "a large picture in glaring colours, of a naked man with rays proceeding from his face like the sun, and two women fanning him; the man white, the women black." Even though Sahajanand explained that "it was not God himself, but the picture or form in which God dwelt in his heart," Heber confessed that at this point his fluency in Hindi failed him.

What was a hint to Heber has developed into a complex teaching concerning the manifestations of god in the Swaminarayan religion. Followers of the religious tradition which he founded worship Sahajanand as Swaminarayan, a manifestation of god, though differences exist among them regarding the nature of the manifestation. This regional form of Hinduism provides an illustration of the unity and diversity within the generally accepted Hindu doctrine of manifestation of god. It also shows that in spite of the general Hindu tolerance, the individual Hindu operates within a theological scheme in which the doctrine of the manifestation of god as experienced within a particular sect or regional form is accepted as the most adequate. The manifestation of god is real to the devotee in its particular form or set of forms. Moreover, the doctrine of the manifestation is related to other spheres which cohere to form a conceptual unity which provides a base for thought and action. The important point to observe is that the interrelation of these spheres makes each more significant for the follower than it would be in isolation. Thus, we can see how the manifestations of god are variously conceived in one regional Vaishnava tradition.

Four interrelated spheres form a structure for the apprehension of the manifestation of god in the religion: the theanthropic sphere, which is the identification of the physical form with one or more of the divine beings; the cosmological sphere, which provides the conceptualization of the heavenly states or abodes of the gods; the devotional sphere, which charts the stages of development of the individual toward release, and the iconographic sphere of the images in the temple. See table 4. Reference is made to all four of these in the brief conversation between Bishop Heber and Sahajanand Swami. In the Akshar Purushottam Sanstha the spheres are thought to intersect in the person of the president and guru, Narayanswarupdas Swami.

THEANTHROPIC SPHERE

"Theanthropic" refers to an important teaching of Swaminarayan Hinduism, that the most exalted of the manifestations of god are in

Table 4. *Swaminarayan theology*

Theanthropic	Cosmological	Devotional	Iconographic
Swaminarayan as Purushottam	Akshardham	Released souls	Images of Swaminarayan
Akshar	Personal akshar	Narayanswarupdas	Living icon
Swaminarayan as Krishna			
	Goloka		Images of Krishna
Krishna			
Other deities		Worship of other deities	Images of other deities in human form
	Vaikuntha and other abodes		
Deities in human form		Concern with material	Images in non-human form
Deities in non-human form			Hanuman
			Ganapati
Forms of deities	States or abodes	Stages to release	Images

human form. Sahajanand taught that god is in human form in his eternal abode. His teaching is based on the traditional Vaishnava teaching regarding the manifestations of god (*avatara*), but in this case the Hindu deities are arranged in a hierarchic pattern with those in fully human form in the superior position. He shared with other nineteenth-century reformers and intellectuals a preference for the representations of deities in human form.

According to the traditional teaching, whenever there is a great need, god manifests of his own free will on earth in the created order to assist men. Whereas other creatures take birth as compelled by karmic law, god acts of his own will. The manifestation of god occurs freely when needed, and there may be more than one in an age. Ramanuja gave the classic statement of the reason god takes the form of an avatar:

I am born from age to age in the forms of gods, men, etc., for protecting them by giving them opportunities of seeing, talking about, and doing similar things in regard to my body and my activities: (I am born) also for the destruction of those who are the opposite of these: and for the firm establishment, when in decline, of the Vedic dharma, which is of the nature of worship of myself, by showing my form which is adorable. (Ramanuja 1969: 117)

Sahajanand also taught that no limit exists in principle on the number of manifestations. Just as Krishna assumed as many forms as the number of maidens (*gopis*) with whom he danced, so god can manifest himself simultaneously in his divine form in each and every universe whenever he desires (*Vachanamritam*, Gadhada 11, 42). He agreed with traditional Vaishnava teaching that, as Parrinder indicates, these manifestations of god are not isolated events (Parrinder 1970: 122f.). Avatars do not just drop into the human scene unrelated to what has gone before. Each is in the succession of earlier forms and is succeeded by the next avatar, who comes whenever there is a decline in righteousness. Ten major avatars of Vishnu or Narayana have appeared, some in human and others in animal form, and these ten were given priority by Ramanuja because they came with three general purposes: to protect the devotees, to destroy evil-doers, and to establish the rule of sacred law (Chakaravarti 1974: 323f.). They are the superior manifestations (*purnavatara*) of the supreme god Narayana. Fourteen partial avatars (*amsavatara*) also appear in Vaishnava iconography and literature. Other avatars have come as well, and the list grows very long (for traditional stories about manifestations of Vishnu and Krishna see Dimmitt and van Buitenen 1978: 59, 146).

Thus, Sahajanand supported the general Vaishnava tradition when he affirmed that there have been many avatars, and he demonstrated traditional Hindu tolerance when he included Christ among the avatars. Sahajanand told his followers to revere all the manifestations of god, but to give primary worship only to images in human form. Of these, Rama and Krishna are preeminent, and Sahajanand followed the example of most of the Vaishnava sects of Gujarat in the worship of Krishna in a variety of forms as depicted in the *Bhagavata Purana* and the *Bhagavad Gita* (Toothi 1935: 72).

Jarring notes entered the conversation between Bishop Heber and Sahajanand when Sahajanand identified the god who was to receive primary worship as Krishna and when he offered as a gift to Heber the large picture of god with two female attendants. Heber admitted that he did not receive a clear understanding of Sahajanand's teaching regarding these points. Heber can be excused because the correct interpretation of Sahajanand's teaching about avatars and about the relation of Krishna and himself has remained a matter of discussion and some disagreement among his followers to the present. At least three different interpretations exist.

Krishna as manifestation of god

A few followers hold the position that Sahajanand taught that Krishna was the highest manifestation of *Parabrahman* or *Purushottam* and that he was the only appropriate object of devotion and meditations.[2] Hence, the Swaminarayan religion is sometimes identified, somewhat inexactly, as a Krishnavite sect of Gujarat (Mallison 1974: 437–71). There is, one must admit, considerable support for this identification in the literature, temples, and rituals of the satsang. In general, Vaishnavas in Gujarat are worshipers of Krishna. Bishop Heber understood him to say that Krishna was the avatar of Parabrahman for the Hindus. Sahajanand had a distinct preference for the manifestations in the human forms and thought that spiritual advancement comes from meditating on the human but divine form of Narayana who manifests himself on earth. Thus, he praised both Rama and Krishna as forms of god and said that devotees should meditate on that form of god who has assumed human form and has become visible before them (*Vachanamritam*, Loya 11). One verse of the *Shikshapatri*, written in the year after the meeting with Bishop Heber, contains the injunction: "That Being, known by various names – such as the glorious Krishna, Parabrahman, Bhagavan, Purushottam – the cause of all manifestations, is to be adored by us as our one chosen deity" (108; trans. Monier-Williams 1882a: 762).

Sahajanand explained that Krishna appears in many forms. When he is together with Radha, he is regarded as supreme lord under the name of Radha-Krishna; with Rukmini he is known as Lakshmi-Narayana; when joined with Arjuna he is known by the name of Nar-Narayana; when associated with other divine figures, he is called by other names. Sahajanand told his disciples, "Out of the various incarnations emanating from Narayana . . . Krishna is dearest to me. And I feel that this incarnation is the greatest of all the incarnations and the most powerful. It is distinguished as the source out of whom the other avatars emerge" (*Vachanamritam*, Loya 14). In this preferential order of avatars, Krishna is supreme because he reveals the divine nature to the highest degree. All of the different names Radha-Krishna, Lakshmi-Narayana, Nar-Narayana, Krishna-Balarama refer to different forms of the one

---

[2] The two terms are used for the same reality. Currently the term "purushottam" is generally used by members to refer to this reality. Some use "brahman" to refer to akshar, as aksharbrahman. I generally use "supreme person" to translate purushottam, following the practice of John Carman (1974:159f.). The terms "god" and "deity" are also used, but these are used in reference to the ishvara and to the forms of the avatars as well. Some Swaminarayan scholars use the term "demigod" to translate ishvara.

deity, and it is felt by believers that from the point of ontology and identity no one should make a distinction between these forms and names.
Many texts indicate that Krishna is the god to whom worship is to be
offered, and they teach that although he appeared under different names
and with different attendants, all are related to Krishna as the highest
god.

Sahajanand continued the use of the Krishna mantra, "Shree
Krishna, thou art my refuge," at the time of initiation, and the mantra
is still used in the rituals of Ahmedabad and Vadtal. The rituals and ceremonies highlight the events from the career of Krishna, especially as
portrayed in the tenth chapter of the *Bhagavata Purana*. The teaching that
Krishna is the supreme manifestation of god closely parallels the position of the Vallabhacharya sect, which directs primary worship to
Krishna (Marfatia 1967: 33–42). Hence, there is some justification for the
identification of the sect as Krishnavite and in the statement that
Sahajanand taught that Krishna is the primary avatar of god to be worshiped by his followers. But the situation is more complex than this.

Swaminarayan as manifestation of Krishna

A more widely held position is that Sahajanand was a manifestation of
Krishna. Bishop Heber understood him to be saying that Krishna was
the form of god which the group worshiped, "adding something like a
hint, that another avatar of Krishna, or the Sun, had taken place in
Himself" (R. Heber 1846 ii: 110). Krishna is thought to have taken many
different forms in the various worlds and at different times for the benefit
of men in this world. Some followers believe that there is no essential
difference between Sahajanand, called Swaminarayan in his exalted
role, and Krishna. He manifested himself in one form in Krishna at a
particular time and in another form in Swaminarayan, the latest of the
manifestations.

During Sahajanand's lifetime there was a growing acceptance of his
divinity as Swaminarayan. In spite of significant opposition even within
the group, opposition based in part on his claims to divinity, many
accepted his leadership and his divinity. Muktananda Swami was the
most senior disciple of Ramananda Swami and was twenty-two years
older than Sahajanand Swami. When Sahajanand became leader,
Muktananda accepted him without argument, but continued to give
precedence in reverence to Ramananda. At last, it is said, he had a
vision in which Ramananda set forth the correct relationship between

them: "I am merely the drum beater [one who goes through the town to attract attention and make the announcements], whereas he is the real performer [the one whose act has been advertised]." As a result, Muktananda spontaneously composed a chant which he sang as he performed the waving of the ceremonial light (*arti*) before Swaminarayan.

Hail to Sahajanand Swami who is an eminent preceptor and who is
  omniscient. Sahajanand is gracious and compassionate. He has many
  names and great divine prowess.
I offer my humble respects at your lotus feet with folded hands, bowing at
  your feet; you have dissolved all my miseries.
You, Lord Narayana, who were born in a Brahmin family, have redeemed
  innumerable fallen and demonic souls [*jiva*].
You perform divine sport anew every day, and you are eternal. The sixty-eight
  holy pilgrimage places rest at your feet, and to serve you results in greater
  merit than to visit Kashi [Vanarasi] millions of times.
Those who have darshan of the manifest Lord will be freed from the clutches
  of time moving to death and rebirth, and they will be redeemed along with
  their whole families.
Now you are very gracious and the source of grace. You have shown us an
  easy path to emancipation.

This chant is used at the regular times of daily worship (arti) in all the temples associated with the fellowship, and on special festival days the full chant is sung.

As early as AD 1804 Sahajanand was described as a manifestation of god in a work called *Yama Danda*, a work of great historical value because it is the first work written in the sect. Nishkulananda Swami, an important author of twenty-four poetic works, believed that emancipation would come from Sahajanand, who is the perfect teacher and manifestation of Krishna. Whoever comes to him is promised salvation from miseries. Even at this early date in Sahajanand's career, some followers believed that at the death of followers who have faith in him, Swaminarayan will come to transport them to his abode, where they will reside as released souls. The last chapter of *Yama Danda* is a song of thanksgiving for the one who brings this emancipation.

At several points during his preaching followers came to the realization that Sahajanand was a manifestation in human form of god. So, it is said: "The sadhus and devotees seated in the assembly realized that the form of Shree Krishna described as remote in *akshardham* had manifested before them presently as Shreeji Maharaj, son of Mother Bhakti and Father Dharmadeva. No one transcends Him. He is the Divine

Form for our worship and He is our preceptor also" (*Vachanamritam*, Vadtal 18). The development of insight to recognize this mystery was the path of spiritual development followed by a number of his disciples. Some were aided by being placed in a trance state in which they were enabled to "see" the truth, and these events are the most characteristic of the miracles attributed to Sahajanand during that period. Those who had not developed to that point of spiritual insight often opposed the doctrine.

A merging of the images and stories of Swaminarayan and Krishna has occurred. The story of the announcement of the coming birth of Krishna in the *Srimad Bhagavata* is repeated in the story of the birth of Swaminarayan. The deity told Narayana that he had already thought of manifesting himself for the salvation of the earth. Bhakti and Dharma were to be the parents of the coming manifestation, and other eternally released souls were to be his companions. Uddhava, a cousin, was the first of these companions to come and herald the coming of Krishna (Parekh 1980: 3f.). As this story is superimposed on the career of Sahajanand, Ramananda is identified as Uddhava. The Brahmin parents of Sahajanand were given the names Dharma and Bhakti, and images of them, a holy family, are found in the temples. Mallison has indicated that the name under which Krishna is worshiped in the temple at Dwarka, Ranachboda Chhogalo, was attributed to Sahajanand by Muktananda Swami, and that the characteristic dress of the images of Swaminarayan in the temples resembles that of Krishna at Dwarka (Mallison 1974: 83 n. 1). Thus, many satsangis consider Swaminarayan to be equivalent to Krishna, and this equivalence is demonstrated in the multivalence of myths and symbols.

Swaminarayan as the supreme person

While no statistical proof is available, interviews with members of the various groups show that most followers believe that Swaminarayan is the single, complete manifestation of Narayana or the supreme person, and, as such, is superior in power and efficacy to all other manifestations of god, including Rama and Krishna. According to those who hold this position, Swaminarayan was not an incarnation of Krishna, as some believed, but was the full manifestation of Purushottam, the supreme person himself. Among some followers it is thought to be incorrect to equate Swaminarayan with other avatars. This is the import of a banner displayed in the temple at Nairobi on the occasion of the celebration of the bicentenary of Swaminarayan's birth: "God is one and unparalleled."

Thus, a reordering of divine beings is suggested. The deities (*ishvara*) are involved in the functions of creation, sustenance, and destruction of the universe. They are involved in the flux of the world (*maya*) because they are attached to the activities of cosmic creation. The avatars have been sent into the world by Purushottam, and they manifest themselves at his will. His powers emanate through the avatars for the execution of assigned duties for human emancipation. Not all avatars manifest the same level of perfection of the supreme person, according to this interpretation. As we have seen, preference is given to those in human form, and among these, to Rama and Krishna. Superior to all, however, is Swaminarayan, thought to be the perfect and complete manifestation of Purushottam in his human form on earth.

Purushottam is the supreme person, and here, as in the teaching of Ramanuja, Purushottam is both a divine name and a metaphysical definition of god (Carman 1974: 159). Ramanuja accepted three eternal entities: the self (jiva), the deity (ishvara), and the principle of flux (maya). Sahajanand said five eternal entities exist: self, deities, maya, the abode of god (akshar), and the supreme person (purushottam). He taught that the supreme person is the only unconditioned ultimate reality and that all other entities, though separate realities, are contingent on the will of the supreme person. He added that the abode of god (akshar) and the supreme person (purushottam) are the only realities that transcend the flux of the world (maya) and are unaffected by it.

Sahajanand also agreed with Ramanuja, against Shankara, that the supreme person is not formless. In fact, he taught that god always has a divine form, and that to deny that god has a form is to commit the unredeemable sin of blasphemy (*Vachanamritam*, Gadhada 1, 71). Indeed, his eternal form is that of a human being, albeit a supreme being. The advantage to the devotee of the divine reality in human form is that he is always available for worship as well as meditation. A famous passage records the description of the form of Purushottam given by Swaminarayan:

Within this shining light I see the image of God as extremely lustrous. Even though the complexion of God is dark, with the extreme luminosity emanating from Him, He appears fair. He is almost human in shape with two hands, two legs, and has a fascinating charm. He does not possess four hands or eight or a thousand hands. He is perfectly like a human being and a young person. I see this image of God either seated or sometimes standing or moving. (*Vachanamritam*, Gadhada 11, 13)

5 Image of Swaminarayan

A constant image in the description of akshardham is light and great luminosity. The divine form of god is described as emitting light from every particle of his body equivalent to the light of millions of suns. Perhaps this is the background for the reference to Surya in the conversation with Bishop Heber and of the iconography of the picture "of a naked man with rays proceeding from his face like the sun" which Swaminarayan gave to Heber and identified as "the picture or form in which God dwelt in his heart" (R. Heber 1846 II: III).

Those in the fellowship who believe in the identity of Swaminarayan with Purushottam follow the logic to affirm an identity of the human form of Swaminarayan, as perceived by the wise devotee, and the form of Purushottam in akshardham (see plate 5). On those occasions when

Sahajanand intimated this to his early disciples, he faced opposition. He recognized that it was a difficult doctrine, easy to misunderstand, and that it would cause many to leave the fellowship. Nevertheless, he felt that failure to perceive god in human form would result in a failure to gain redemption from the bondage of the world. Therefore, he taught, "The divine form of Lord Purushottam visible here before you and the divine form seated in His divine abode akshardham are one, and there is absolutely no difference in these twin forms" (*Vachanamritam*, Loya 18 and Gadhada iii, 38). Professor Yajnik suggests that one who knows the essence of god's nature does not make any kind of ontological distinction between god himself and his manifestation on earth (Yajnik 1972: 93). One who meditates on the human form manifest on earth will see the divinely resplendent form of god in akshardham and will transcend the flux of the world and rebirth because both Purushottam and akshar are beyond maya (*Vachanamritam*, Gadhada ii, 13).

Swaminarayan taught that god created man in his own image. Emancipated souls also secure for themselves a similar divine body. The fundamental difference between these two kinds of bodies is that the limitations and imperfections essential to the human body are not attached to the divine body. Thus, according to the teaching of Swaminarayan, the resemblance between man and god is not due to the fact that men can conceive god only in the image of man. On the contrary, it exists because man is the crown of creation and has been made in the image of god. Thus, anthropology and theology are complementary, and what we find here is not so much an anthropomorphic conception of god as what Yajnik called "a theomorphic conception of man" (Yajnik 1972: 71). The goal in the sect is to realize that the god who manifests himself on earth in the human form of Sahajanand is the highest supreme reality and that he is the cause of all avatars.

The main criterion for the preferential ordering of the avatars mentioned above is the degree of revelation brought by each concerning the human form of god. Even if, as some may say, every avatar comes from Purushottam and possesses the inexhaustible powers and infinite value that belong to the nature of god, there are differences of purpose and effect in manifesting the true form of god. Thus, Swaminarayan indicated that though the avatars in the form of fish and tortoise are manifestations of god, "I do not have much liking for them" (*Vachanamritam*, Loya 14, trans. Yajnik). He conceded that god may have appeared in times past as a human being with four hands or eight arms so that ignorant beings could clearly distinguish him from other human beings. Devotees do not despise the images of such deities in other temples, but they recognize that god is like a human being, two-armed, and the spiritually wise person will meditate on this human form of god. Still, even though he appeared as human, true devotees are warned not to equate the human form of god with other human beings or to take other human beings as god.

The difference between human beings and the divine manifestation is that the former have bodies and certain personal characteristics caused by the actions of previous births, whereas the latter takes on a body with ordinary human characteristics by his own free will and has no attachment to it whatever. Still, he does not allow his divine characteristics to overshadow the human characteristics. According to the teaching of Swaminarayan, god even in human form is totally divine and bereft of all human instincts. He said: "The appearance of human instincts in Him is like the magic feats of the great wizard which cannot be fully comprehended by the human mind" (*Vachanamritam*, Panchala 7 and Loya 18). The common illustration is that when god manifests himself on earth in human form and rides a horse, ordinary men think that the horse supports him, but in reality he is the support for the horse. The devotees who see this have come to true knowledge.

It follows that god is not attracted to the world and he would not care to remain in it even for an hour except for his concern to save his devotees. A problem is caused, however, when god in human form exhibits such human instincts as passion, anger, enjoyment of taste, affection, valor, hunger, and partiality. There are many examples in the stories about Swaminarayan. Followers believe that he was unaffected by any of these emotions or feelings. Swaminarayan was criticized because he received large gifts from his followers and dressed and traveled as a Maharaja even though he had taken the vows of renunciation of the world. He responded: "I display the feeling of affection for you all, accept the various sumptuous meals that are offered by you, sit on high pedestals, accept the rich dresses, ornaments and garlands of flowers – all this I do, not for any enjoyment for me, but for your emancipation only" (*Vachanamritam*, Gadhada 1, 18). Therefore, the devotee who has the knowledge that the human form of god is not the earthly bodily form is not led astray when he sees these various human characteristics – good or bad health, success or failure, happiness or melancholy moods. Nor will he ever find fault with the human form of god, because god is beyond the flux of the world and its restrictions and limitations.

Since the supreme person is not bound to any rule, he can appear in human form directly or he can manifest his powers gradually in chronological order according to his desire. This is the explanation for the perception that Sahajanand developed through the stages of life. There was, however, no fundamental change in him; any perception of change is attributed to the condition of the observer. Thus, if it is true that the supreme person in his abode has a form like a human young person, that is also the true form of his earthly manifestation. Any perceptions of change from childhood to youth to mature manhood and perceptions of weaknesses accompanying these changes are illusion. It is this illusion that is removed from those who have come to understand the teaching of the sect that the most perfect manifestation of god is Swaminarayan, who appeared as completely human between AD 1781 and 1830 in Gujarat. It is said that those who are devoted to him and meditate on his human form come to see his perfect form in his eternal abode.

Thus we have seen that at least three levels of understanding of the relation of Swaminarayan to Purushottam and Krishna are found in the literature of the group and in responses of devotees to questions on the subject. Those who hold each position claim that it represents the accurate understanding of Sahajanand's teaching. One can speculate about the source of these differences. One theory is that there was some development in Sahajanand's understanding so that he began as reformer of ascetic practice and of Krishna worship and came at the end of his career to believe that he was the full manifestation of Purushottam. A similar theory is that although he had a clear vision of his true nature at all times, there was a progressive development in his teaching as his hearers were prepared to receive more complete understanding of his nature. While it seems clear from the literature that he tempered his teaching to match the receptivity of his hearers and was reluctant to speak openly about his identity with Purushottam except to his closest disciples, there is no convincing evidence to support a theory of progressive development or systematic progression in his teaching from beginning to the end.

Members of the group argue that from the moment of birth Sahajanand was the full manifestation of Purushottam and understood himself to be such. Therefore, they affirm that the difference of interpretation that is observed in the literature was not due to a development in his understanding or teaching from first to last, but was due to a difference in understanding on the part of individual disciples according to their spiritual development. This becomes a circular argument, impossible of solution.

THE COSMOLOGICAL SCHEME

As followers conceptualize the sacred cosmos, the deities and manifestations of god have separate heavenly abodes or states. These can be pictured and spoken of as locations, but they are states of existence. The highest abode is akshar, or akshardham in the impersonal form, and it is in this state that the supreme person is thought to reside with his devotees. Many believe that Swaminarayan is the lord of akshardham as Purushottam Bhagavan and that he manifested himself from there in the human form as Sahajanand. Some believe that Krishna and Rama are not direct manifestations of the highest form, but of other eternal entities. They are said to preside over much lower abodes, Goloka and Vaikuntha respectively. Others believe that Krishna and Rama were indeed manifestations of the supreme person, though at a lower level, and Krishna's residence is Goloka and Rama's is Vaikuntha. The deities in non-human form preside over other, lesser abodes. Thus, a hierarchy of states or abodes exists with akshardham as the primary state. This seems to be consonant with Swaminarayan's teaching in the *Vachanamritam*:

The other cosmic gods like Shiva and Brahma are not the forms for meditation as they cannot spiritually lift up a *Mumukshu* [aspirant]. Rama and Krishna who are the incarnations of the Divine form of Narayana, the Ultimate Purushottam, are the divine forms for meditation. The spiritually wise, however, visualize the divinity of Vaikunta, Goloka, Shwetdweep, Brahmapur, etc., which are the divine abodes of Narayana, in such places where Rama and Krishna had moved in their human forms. The divinity of Lord Purushottam in the forms of Shree Rama and Shree Krishna, whose forms emanate from Lord Purushottam, who shines with such lustre greater in intensity than the lustre of millions of suns, moons, and fire, is visualized by the spiritually wise in their incarnated forms of Rama and Krishna. (*Vachanamritam*, Loya 11)

Akshardham is the highest abode, and Purushottam, who is described as the resplendent form of god, is thought to transcend akshardham and to be the cause of all the avatars.

Ramanuja allowed for some distinction within ultimate reality, and Swaminarayan elaborated on this duality by indicating that two entities, Purushottam and akshar, are eternal and free from the illusion of maya. Akshar is the eternal abode of Purushottam and has an impersonal form. Though there are mythological references to akshar as a location, the philosophers of the sect explain that it is first of all an eternal principle. The emphasis in the sect on these two principles stands as a further modification of Ramanuja's modified non-dualism.

Van Buitenen traced the history of the concept of akshar to its earlier Sanskrit philosophical meaning of "syllable." Increasingly, he explained, akshar lost its more ancient sense of "syllable," but retained the connotations of the "first and fundamental principle of the cosmic order." He quoted from Yajnavalkya's discourse: "If one does not know this akshar, then one's oblations, sacrifices and austerities for many thousands of years in this world will come to an end; and when one departs from this world without knowing the akshar, one is miserable" (van Buitenen 1959: 183). Sahajanand referred in the *Shikshapatri* to a commentary on *Yajnavalkya Smriti* as a guiding authority for his followers (97). In the philosophy of Swaminarayan also the akshar has the character of a cosmic principle and is the intermediary of the activities of the supreme person. In the understanding of the schools of Ahmedabad and Vadtal dioceses the akshar is the abode of god where Purushottam is always present. These two eternal entities are in communion, the first dependent on the second, but they are eternally distinct. An elaborate theory of the relation of the akshar to Purushottam was developed in the Vallabhacharya sect. According to this theory, the akshar is the abode of the supreme person and appears in various forms according to the different aspects of the latter (Bhatt 1953: 347–59 and see Marfatia 1967: 37–42, 300–2). The Swaminarayan teaching may have developed out of and as a response to this earlier teaching.

A further elaboration of the doctrine of the akshar forms the central and unique teaching of the Akshar Purushottam Sanstha. This community believes that Swaminarayan taught that akshar is an eternally existing spiritual reality having two forms, the impersonal and the personal. The impersonal form is essentially that described above. The impersonal akshar is everywhere; there is not an inch of space without akshar. Yet it is formless. It is the eternal abode of god and ultimately the abode or state of all released souls. Various images are used to illustrate this reality: for example, pure consciousness, divine lights. The personal form of akshar is thought to be that person who is the perfect devotee and eternal companion of Purushottam in whom Purushottam dwells in his totality. That person can be spoken of as the abode of Purushottam (*Vachanamritam*, Gadhada I, 21, 41).

The personal form of akshar is also considered to be an eternal soul, eternally free from the power of maya. There are, in the metaphysics of the sect, other eternally released souls, but none beside akshar has the impersonal form. The terms "purushottam" and "akshar" are Vedic and philosophical in origin, but puranic illustrations are given to describe the relation between the two. The gods of the puranas are always accompanied by their chief devotees, often the female consorts. In Ramanuja's commentaries on the puranic stories Shri is the divine companion of Vishnu; she is the mediatrix for the devotees on earth of the divine grace of god. Though there were many female companions of Krishna, Radha was considered to be the perfect devotee. Those who wish to come close to Krishna must cultivate the devotional qualities of Radha and approach Krishna through her. In the theology of the Akshar Purushottam Sanstha the personal akshar functions in ways similar to that of Shri in the philosophy of Ramanuja or of Radha in the puranic stories of Krishna. These may be transformed into symbols or prefigurations of the relation that exists between Purushottam and his primary devotee in the form of the akshar. Thus, in addition to Purushottam, there is a second eternal entity free from the flux of the world, eternally dependent upon Purushottam, and always at his service at his feet in akshardham.

The major split in the movement developed over the teaching about the personal form of akshar. Swami Yagnapurushdas gained a following for his teaching concerning the personal form of akshar and his identification of this personal form with Swami Gunatitanand (AD 1785–1867), a close companion and disciple of Swaminarayan. Swami Yagnapurushdas taught that Purushottam is always accompanied by his perfect devotee and supported his position with interpretations of the *Vachanamritam* (Gadhada I, 71, III, 26 and Vadtal 5). Since the time of Swaminarayan, he has always been present to his devotees in his perfect devotee in whom he resides and through whom he administers his grace to his devotees to lead them to akshardham. Thus, according to this theory, god continues to manifest himself to his devotees in human form through his perfect devotee. The majority of the sadhus in Vadtal would not accept this teaching, which they thought was novel and heretical. They refused to worship what they considered to be a human being. The name of the Akshar Purushottam Sanstha suggests the primary theological emphasis of the group which separated from the Vadtal diocese.

Members of the old school of Ahmedabad and Vadtal teach that the name Swaminarayan represents one entity, Purushottam. Members of the new school of Akshar Purushottam Sanstha teach that the name represents two entities; Swami stands for the akshar represented by Gunatitanand and his successors, and Narayan stands for Purushottam or Sahajanand. Although they now write the name as one word in common with members of the old school, members of the Akshar

Purushottam Sanstha affirm their allegiance to both when they chant the mantra "Swaminarayan." All followers wear as a sign of the sect a mark in the shape of a U made of sandalwood paste with a red dot of kumkum powder in the middle, but the new school teaches that one is Swami and the other Narayan. Similarly, all followers wear a double-strand necklace of wooden beads, but some followers suggest that these stand for the two primary principles of the theology.

Thus, according to this theology, an unbroken line of perfect devotees appeared as manifestations of akshar through whom the supreme person manifests his grace to people on earth. These men are viewed as the leaders and inspired teachers of the Akshar Purushottam Sanstha, and the official list, the guruparampara, provides an authentication of the office through Gunatitanand back to Swaminarayan himself. A tradition presented by the new school, but repudiated by the old, states that Sahajanand said at his first meeting with Gunatitanand: "This Mulji is the incarnation of Akshar Brahman, my abode, and will in future profusely display by his talk and discourses the greatness of my form" (H. T. Dave 1974: 89). Indeed, it is said that Swaminarayan wished to install an image of Gunatitanand in the temple for worship, but there had been so much opposition to his action of placing his own image in the temple, he knew that there would be no understanding or acceptance if he did so. The result, according to members of the new school, was a kind of "messianic secret," an "akshar secret," if you will. Swaminarayan showed in a number of ways his regard for Gunatitanand as the abode of god in personal form. The few enlightened ones understood the mystery, but the majority were not sufficiently mature to understand.

Nevertheless, according to the teaching of the Akshar Purushottam Sanstha, the akshar has been manifest in a line of perfect devotees. "God-realized," "god-intoxicated," and "Brahmanized" are the most common adjectives attributed to them. Pictorial images of the individuals of the hierarchy appear in the temples of the Akshar Purushottam Sanstha. Gunatitanand is generally in the central position with Swaminarayan; his successors are at the side with the picture of the current leader prominently displayed. Statues of the hierarchy began to appear in temples in the 1990s. They are believed to be at the same time the perfect manifestation of the abode (akshar) of god and hence objects of devotion and the perfect example for other devotees to show them how to serve god.

There is only one manifestation of akshar visible at a time through whom Swaminarayan continues to manifest himself. The current representative of this spiritual hierarchy is a sadhu, Swami Narayanswarupdas, popularly known as Pramukh Swami. He is the spiritual guru for all members of the Akshar Purushottam Sanstha, and he is the administrative head of the institution as well. Reference was made in the previous chapter to his administrative activities, and though they are in fact inseparable from the theological affirmations about his person, the emphasis here is upon his position as the current manifestation of akshar.

He appears as a fully human individual, and seems to have all the characteristics of human existence. At the same time, he is believed to be the form of the eternal abode of god not bound by maya. As is the case in the doctrine of Christology, it is not easy to explain how these two functions are combined in one individual. His name as a sadhu, Narayan Swarup Das, is illustrative. Narayan and Swarup are names for god; Das means "servant." Followers believe that he is the perfect servant of god, and, as such, he is totally filled with god and therefore worthy of reverence and worship. One disciple gave the explanation, "The body is Pramukh Swami; the rest is Swaminarayan himself."

During an interview at Sarangpur on 2 March 1980, Pramukh Swami discussed his understanding of his identification with akshar. He indicated that one who has a constant awareness at every moment of being the akshar of Purushottam, the manifestation of the abode of god, is the form of akshar. He came to this awareness at the moment when he met his spiritual guru and predecessor in the spiritual hierarchy, Swami Yagnapurushdas. He said that without this constant knowledge of oneself as the abode of god, one would not be able to do all the work that is required of him. He is sustained by concentrating upon Swaminarayan and remembering him. Because of the identification with akshar, he feels a constant union with Swaminarayan. His aim is to be aware at every moment of the requirements of following the commands of Swaminarayan; even the smallest of the requirements of the *Shikshapatri* are observed. He related an illustration given by Gunatitanand. A fish can go anywhere in the confines of water, but if it leaves the water, it dies. He said that if he withdrew for a moment from his perfect service to Swaminarayan, he would be like a fish out of water. Though to an outsider the requirement that he always conduct himself as the perfect devotee would seem to be a heavy burden, Pramukh Swami said that as long as he is in communion with Swaminarayan it is not so.

The problems in perceiving the relation of the eternal and finite in the manifestation of the divine in human form discussed with respect to

Sahajanand are also found in the manifestation of the akshar. Pramukh Swami seems to show himself to be a man with the limitations and illnesses of human existence. His disciples explain that he behaves as a man because most people would not be able to stand his full revelation. Even though his disciples believe that he has complete knowledge of everything that is going to happen, he nonetheless asks, as one devotee observed with some amusement, for advice and explanation. The problem in the Indian context is not to explain the sinlessness of the incarnation of god, but to explain the complete knowledge of the akshar manifested in human form without which, devotees suggest, the sinlessness of god cannot be visualized. It cannot be said that the guru is merely a channel for divine grace which is passed through him. It is believed that the guru is absolutely divine and cannot be said to be in any way ignorant. It is explained that the technique of the guru is such that even if he realizes that he is flooded with divinity, he attains the greater state beyond knowing this (Brent 1972: 207). Some devotees affirm that by his grace they have perceived in Pramukh Swami the perfect form of akshar through whom they have been led to a true knowledge of the supreme person.

Only one personal manifestation of akshar is thought to exist at a time, and although each shows different personal characteristics depending upon the requirements of the times, those in the spiritual hierarchy share the same divine attributes. Current devotees have three gurus in living memory – Shastri Maharaj, Yogiji Maharaj, and Pramukh Swami – but they see in the present guru the remanifestation of those who have gone before. This attribution of unity is a great aid in the transferral of allegiance and loyalty at the time of succession. Clearly the most critical times in the history of the Akshar Purushottam Sanstha are those points when the guru dies and a new one is acclaimed. Only one visible manifestation is recognized at a time, but it is believed that the future guru is present, but not yet publicly designated. Pramukh Swami said that he came to feel himself to be the akshar at the point when he first met Shastri Maharaj (see plate 6). He did not succeed Shastri Maharaj directly, but became the guru only after Yogiji Maharaj had held the position. When Yogiji Maharaj died, the prominent sadhus acclaimed that Pramukh Swami is the form of akshar and affirmed that Yogiji Maharaj had indicated by many actions and words, not understood completely until after the fact, that Pramukh Swami was chosen.

Pramukh Swami's successor has not been designated. Pramukh Swami says, however, that he has already decided who the successor will

6 Pramukh Swami and sadhus at temple in Mehalav, the home village of
Shastri Maharaj

be because "Brahman knows Brahman." He knew the moment the
perfect follower entered the fellowship and maintains a special relationship with that individual. No open announcement is made at this point,
but in various ways he is marking out the person who will follow him.
It seems possible that the ultimate meaning of his actions will become
clear to his followers only after his death. Active members, even
members of the central committee, feel that it would be wrong for them
to concern themselves with the succession; they discourage speculation
on the matter. Premature announcement about the succession might
create confusion and lack of focus on current tasks. Still, the belief is
that there will be a continual succession of manifestations of the akshar

because god will always manifest himself in his abode – the perfect devotee.

Disciples believe that in AD 1781 and 1785 the two principal eternal entities appeared on earth at the births of Sahajanand and Gunatitanand. Members of the fellowship, even those who do not accept the authority of Gunatitanand as the personal form of akshar, affirm that with Sahajanand other individuals came from akshardham in human form to assist him in his work. These are the eternally released souls (muktas) who reside in akshardham. They are believed to operate according to the direction of the supreme person and not according to their own will or according to previous karmic acts. Other Vaishnava theories of the avatars contain the element that whenever god appears, the eternally released souls come to serve him. Lakshmana, the brother of Rama, came to assist him. Arjuna is supposed to have been the bosom friend of Krishna in an earlier age when they had the names of Nar and Narayana. It is said that Uddhava, the cousin of Krishna, was sent in the form of Ramananda Swami to prepare the way for Swaminarayan. Thus, there were muktas who were sent from akshardham to assist Swaminarayan in his work. He explained: "When God descends on earth for the redemption of the jivas and assumes human form, His divine abode Akshardham, the released jivas and His full-fledged lordship, all descend on earth, but they cannot be seen by those who have not the divine vision" (*Vachanamritam*, Gadhada I, 71).

Some of the chief companions of Swaminarayan are identified as muktas. Ramananda, Gopalananda, Muktananda, and others appeared in human form, but actually they were and continue to be released souls in akshardham. In this they are similar to akshar and Purushottam, but there are fundamental differences. Akshar and Purushottam are divine; even when they manifest in human form, they do not lose their divinity, nor do they forget their identity with the divine form. The released souls who are sent lose their powers and forget their true identity. God wills it so in order that they can perform their specified tasks. During one gathering at Gadhada it was reported that Swaminarayan allowed some of his disciples to remember their true form, but after a moment he returned them to their stations on earth. No list exists of all the released souls thought to have appeared even though their presence is believed to have been essential to the growth and development of the sect. Even the released souls could not remember their true form or identify themselves. Nevertheless, the belief is that the eternally released souls continue to manifest from akshardham and assist the success of the movement. There is the feeling that the fellowship is surrounded by a great cloud of witnesses who give active assistance.

SCHEME OF DEVOTIONAL DEVELOPMENT

The devotional scheme reflects the inner world of the spiritual development of the devotee in which he moves through stages to a higher understanding. Sahajanand's contemporaries can be categorized as having reached different stages of spiritual development. Opponents are judged demonic. Bishop Heber, who described Sahajanand as "a middle-sized, thin, plain looking person, about my own age, with a mild and diffident expression of countenance, but nothing about him indicative of any extraordinary talent," represents another level. Those with little understanding viewed him as a holy man and ascetic reformer. Spiritual advancement led to the understanding that he was a manifestation, if only of Krishna. A higher state was the perception that he was equal to Krishna. Stories recount the experience of some devotees who came to the realization that Swaminarayan was the manifestation of the supreme person. The highest spiritual attainment is thought to be the ultimate vision, seen through the earthly human form, of his divine form seated in the eternal abode, which leads to ultimate release in akshardham. Ambiguities in the literature are explained as resulting from differences in levels of spiritual perception. The teaching is that the full manifestation of Purushottam was present in Swaminarayan; perception of difference or change was in the eye of the beholder. Thus, it is understandable that members of the religion hold different views about the nature of Swaminarayan.

The majority of followers accept Swaminarayan as the highest manifestation of divinity and believe that final emancipation in akshardham is possible only through faithful devotion to him. There are instances in his teachings when he indicated, sometimes hesitantly and indirectly in the face of considerable opposition, that he was the manifestation of this ultimate reality. The focus here is not upon Krishna or upon Swaminarayan as a manifestation of Krishna, but upon the eternal reality which exists beyond the flux of the world.

And then hinting at the esoteric truth he [Swaminarayan] said, The image of God seen in the divine light within is Me. However, if you cannot quite digest this truth, you may at least feel sure that I see the image of God in the light emanating from the form of akshar. If you have the conviction within you of this sacred truth, you will remain attached to me with ties of love and wilt as such be redeemed. Shreeji Maharaj thus revealed before His devotees though indirectly that he was God-Purushottam. Hearing this story, all the devotees and paramhansas could comprehend the significance of the image of God in the divine light, Maharaj himself. (*Vachanamritam*, Gadhada II, 13)

Swaminarayan became the object of worship and meditation as the perfect manifestation of god in human form.

The stated purpose of his manifestation is the redemption of many souls and the establishment of moral and social order. He manifests himself as both redeemer and reformer, but the emphasis in the literature is upon his work of redemption. The main function is to fulfill his devotees' earnest desire to have intimate and direct contact with god. He subdues his divinity and supernatural powers so he may seduce his devotees with his virtue and goodness as he mixes freely with them. It is felt that the virtues and attributes of god are better visualized when he reveals himself in ordinary human form because the divinity which radiates through the human form attracts the sense organs and the minds of men and leads the devotees toward perfection (*Vachanamritam*, Gadhada I, 49 and Karivani 5). From the standpoint of society at large he is a reformer come to establish the dharma of moral and social order, but from the perspective of the individual he is a redeemer come to lead the individual to the perfection of his divine abode. Without knowledge of the divine form of god attained by devotion, a person faces rebirth in the abode of other spiritual beings or again in this world. Sahajanand taught that if god wants to enter into relationship with human beings to save them from ignorance and suffering, he must assume ordinary human form and not reveal fully his supernatural and divine power (*Vachanamritam*, Gadhada I, 63). Therefore, he appeared in human form.

The paradox set forth in the literature of the satsang is that whereas the human form of god in the world is identical with the form of supreme person in akshardham, most persons do not see or recognize this pure form. Because of ignorance, they perceive him in a form susceptible to change, pain, old age, and death. The finite human form is at the same time a barrier that must be transcended by the true devotee with knowledge and also an attraction to the unlearned devotee. That devotee is led to a more perfect knowledge through his attachment to the imperfectly perceived human form of god. Sahajanand taught that when Purushottam appears on earth, he assumes a physical body and human characteristics and he uses those characteristics for the emancipation of his devotees.

The ultimate goal, then, is not to act like a god in human form but to realize the unity of the human form of god on the earth and in akshardham. There is the warning that those who try to behave as Swaminarayan did, for example, a sadhu who accepts lavish gifts and eats food for enjoyment, invite punishment. The important difference between an ordinary human being and a manifestation of god is that the latter is not bound by his actions. He is an eternally released soul who is essentially moral and eternally free. When it is said that he is free from his actions, it means that his actions are beyond the impact of ignorance and are under the complete and conscious control of god. A prime example of an action done by an earlier avatar but not to be followed by ordinary persons is Krishna's sexual conduct with the maidens. Such action would be an abomination if done by the sadhus of the Swaminarayan group, but it is interpreted as an essentially free and moral act when done by the avatar. The injunction, "Don't do as I do, but do as I say," is perfectly legitimate within this system.

True devotees will be led by their contact with the human form of god to transcend with their mind the appearances of ordinary human characteristics and will come to see the divine form of god which is identical in akshardham and on earth. In the process the individual will overcome his attachment to the world and will be prepared to be released by Swaminarayan's grace from the attachment to the flux of the world (maya) and the cycle of rebirth (*samsara*). The reward is that at the time of death Swaminarayan comes to take his devotees to his permanent residence in akshardham. There the transformation of the devotee will be complete, and he will have a form, both human and divine, like that of Swaminarayan. In the iconography of the sect which pictures the residents of akshardham, there are no differences between the forms of the souls of devotees released from earth, the souls of the eternally released souls (muktas), and the divine form of Purushottam. The emancipated souls secure for themselves this divine form, and it represents the highest state of spiritual development.

The distinctive belief of members of the Akshar Purushottam Sanstha is that contact with the manifestation of akshar on earth is essential for one to reach Purushottam. As Shrivaishnavas approach Vishnu through Shri, so followers come to Swaminarayan through the perfect devotee, who is the abode of god. Only after the devotee has reached Swami, which is akshar, can he reach Narayana, who is Purushottam. The akshar, as one of the succession of "god-realized" saints, is the representative of god on earth; he gives the perfect example, speaks with the authority of god, and receives the reverence and worship of the devotees. He is accepted as the perfect ideal for emulation by all spiritual aspirants.

Members of the old school believe that Swaminarayan is present in the images, when properly installed by the acharya, and in the sacred scriptures which he left. Members of the new school believe he is primarily present in the person of the guru and also in the images and sacred scriptures. The guru is spoken of as "the sacred texts personified" because he lives in harmony with all the precepts of the scriptures given by Swaminarayan. He also has authority to interpret, revise, and apply traditional rules for living. Without such a guru, it is said, there can be no satsang. It is only through association with the akshar who has come to earth in a personal form that one can get rid of his vices, baser instincts, and the clutches of maya and thereby gain release (R. Dave 1978: 10).

Pramukh Swami is revered by members of the Akshar Purushottam Sanstha as the first disciple, most strict in his observance of the commandments, most active in propagation of the religion, the best interpreter of the meaning of the scriptures, and most effective in eradicating the ignorance that separates man from god. In short, he is the devotee who exemplifies all the ideals of the religion. He has totally renounced the world so that he can be completely devoted to god. Thus, viewed from one perspective, he holds his position because of his devotion and attainments. No other person is thought to be so worthy as a devotee.

Every morning Pramukh Swami performs the morning worship before a small image of Swaminarayan, the *thakorji*, which he carries with him at all times. As many male devotees as are in the area sit around him to observe his acts of worship. To an outsider in this and all other circumstances he appears as an outstanding and very devoted ascetic, a perfect servant. It is clear, however, from the attitude and comments of those gathered around him that they consider him to be divine and that they offer reverence and worship to him. On some special occasions the waving of the light and the chanting of the hymn is performed before him by a lay devotee. Followers say that he is divine, the abode of god, or the manifestation of akshar, and that "he should be worshiped with the same form of worship which one offers to the images in the temple." Indeed, devotees observe many of his daily activities, such as eating and walking, with a reverential demeanor. The devotee is urged to meditate on the guru and all his activities, and this kind of mental worship of the guru leads the disciple to god.

The paradox is that Pramukh Swami is revered as the manifestation of the eternal akshar even though he does not claim divinity for himself or demand such honors. His role forbids such claims because pride, self-praise, and ostentation are forbidden by the rules of conduct for sadhus. When I asked him if his physical body is divine, he said that it is not his place to say. He seems never to praise himself or to demand worship. He maintained that his purpose is not to lead people to worship him, but to point them to correct worship of Swaminarayan. He worships Swaminarayan and gives reverence to his predecessors. The image of Swaminarayan is always before him, and he directs the worship to the image. All garlands and gifts presented to him are first presented before the image. When there is the chanting of the list of the spiritual hierarchy, the guruparampara, he stops with the name of his immediate predecessor, Yogiji Maharaj, or chants "Narayana" while the other devotees shout "Pramukh Swami Maharaj." Followers see this as an evidence of the humility and self-denial that are appropriate to a devotee, a covering of his true radiance, and this inspires them to shower him with even greater honor and worship.

This structure for understanding spiritual development leads to a somewhat ambiguous position regarding devotion to other deities and avatars. The teaching of the group follows the general Hindu tendency to tolerance. The rules of the *Shikshapatri* forbid followers to criticize deities or to listen to such criticism (21), and require that devotees bow down with due reverence when they pass by the temples of Shiva and other deities (23). Nevertheless, the teaching makes a clear distinction between these deities and the ghosts and spirits who are thought to cause evil. According to the rules, in the case of some affliction, formerly attributed to an evil spirit, the follower is permitted to chant verses to Vishnu and Hanuman, but under no circumstances is he or she to chant verses of the inferior deities (85). Devotees are said to be freed from the superstitious attachment to these deities, and Parekh reported that there were many instances when new converts threw away the images of those inferior deities when they entered the satsang (Parekh 1980: 96). They prefer not to associate with those deities for whom animal sacrifices are performed. In general, the gods and goddesses and the teachers of other religious sects are to be respected and a sort of homage may be paid to them, but for those within the satsang, Swaminarayan is the full manifestation of Purushottam and he is the perfect object of both meditation and worship. The lesser deities and avatars can be seen as part of a progressive revelation which culminates in the revelation of Swaminarayan. While there is no great attempt to convert people from the worship of other gods, as distinguished from superstitious attachment to spirits, no surprise is expressed when devotees of other gods transfer primary allegiance to Swaminarayan. It is thought to be the culmination of the spiritual quest.

ICONOGRAPHIC SCHEME

The architectural plans for temples and the placement of images are discussed in the next chapter. Here it is important to note that the way a person sees the images in the Swaminarayan temples is determined by the way the image fits into the theanthropic, cosmological, and devotional schemes outlined above. The iconographic scheme belongs to the same conceptual framework. The ceremony for the installation of the images in the temples builds to a climax when the supreme person or the manifestation of the supreme person at whatever level takes up permanent residence in the image in the temple or shrine. Thereafter, the image is the appropriate object of devotion by the followers because it is a manifestation of the eternal reality which, nonetheless, is never absent from the heavenly abode or state. When the followers enter the main shrine of the Swaminarayan temples, they see only a human face of god. In none of the Swaminarayan temples known to me do images other than in human form appear in the central shrines.[3]

The images in the temples built by Sahajanand are evidence of the priority of Krishna. The first temple he constructed, built in Ahmedabad in AD 1822, houses the images of Nar-Narayana, forms of Arjuna and Krishna, in the central shrine. The shrine on the worshiper's left has images of Krishna and Radha; the one on the right has the holy family, Harikrishna and his parents, Dharma and Bhakti. All of the temples constructed during his lifetime house images of Krishna in some form, and all the temples constructed since have such images; in the temples of the dioceses of Ahmedabad and Vadtal they are usually in the central shrine. A result of the emphasis upon the human form of god is that the images in the central shrines of the Swaminarayan temples are all statues of human form. The daily rituals performed in the temples enact the events of the daily life of god in human form and encourage meditation on the human form of god. Shrines to gods in other than human form, Hanuman and Ganapati, are found in almost every temple, but they are subsidiary shrines at the entrance to the

---

[3] An exception may be the temple at Sarangpur in Saurashtra associated with the Vadtal temple. The Hanuman shrine is most prominent and popular because on Saturdays persons come for healing of mental and other disorders. One suspects, however, that the ritual center of the temple complex is an image in human form.

temple. Hanuman and Ganapati are thought to provide protection and prosperity, but the higher goal of emancipation is thought to come only from the god who is in human form.

The images of Sahajanand were not placed for worship in the earliest temples that were built. Some present-day followers explain that he wished to install images of himself in those temples, but did not do so because of the opposition it would have aroused. It is even said that the images of Krishna in Ahmedabad and other temples are in reality of Sahajanand, but they were called Krishna because of the feelings of some disciples. Yet, by AD 1825 he was able to install an image of himself in the temple constructed in Vadtal, albeit only in one of the side shrines. The carved wooden images in Vadtal and Ahmedabad are supposed to bear a physical resemblance to Sahajanand.

Swaminarayan is the focus of the ritual of the fellowship; Krishna, though always present, takes a subordinate position. The images similar in form to images of Krishna, and perhaps originally identified as such, are accepted by most followers as representations of Swaminarayan. The most striking examples of this are the images, often in a side shrine, of Bal Krishna or Ghanashyam. The child is on his knees on the floor reaching out with a ball-shaped object in his hands. In association with Krishna the ball is of butter which Krishna has taken in one of his pranks. Devotees often identify the images as the child form of Swaminarayan. One night he took the moon in his hand to play with it and the ball of butter with the Krishna image becomes the moon of the Ghanashyam story. One devotee indicated that the images with the leg crossed in the characteristic pose of Krishna are actually representations of Swaminarayan. He said that when the early temples were built, Swaminarayan installed images with the leg crossed to avoid disputes with followers who had not yet recognized the truth that Swaminarayan is the human manifestation of the supreme reality, Purushottam.

The image or picture of Swaminarayan occupies the central position in the main shrine of all the temples associated with the Akshar Purushottam Sanstha. The images of Krishna and Radha are in a side shrine, but there is no uncertainty in the teaching of this wing of the movement that Swaminarayan is the premier form of the supreme person, and that Krishna is subordinate to him. Pramukh Swami referred to several accomplishments of Swaminarayan which indicate his superiority to other manifestations. First, he installed an image of himself in a temple and consecrated it for worship; no other avatar did this. Then too, whereas other avatars including Rama and Krishna resorted to killing persons like Ravana, who were representations in human form of evil forces such as lust, anger, and greed, Swaminarayan was able to release men from these evil forces without resorting to violence (*himsa*). Therefore, his work was more fundamental and of greater importance than that of other manifestations. Reference was made to the large number of ascetics whom he consecrated during his ministry and to the fact that he was able to place persons immediately into the samadhi state in which they could see god. These are taken as evidence of his superiority.

The group teaches that one reaches Purushottam most effectively by means of contact with the personal, human manifestation of the akshar. Thus, in the temples associated with the Akshar Purushottam Sanstha, the image of Swaminarayan is flanked on the right by the image of Gunatitanand. Gopalanand Swami is often, but not always, present on the left side to represent all aspirants. Followers affirm that the living guru, Sadhu Narayanswarupdas, possesses all the qualities of Gunatitanand as perfect devotee and is the abode of the supreme person. Therefore, they consider him to be an appropriate object for worship, meditation, and devotion, a living icon. Whenever the images of Radha and Krishna, Narayana and Lakshmi, and Nar and Narayana appear, they are thought to represent the two realities. Even when there is only the one image of Swaminarayan, it is said that akshar is present in the heart of Swaminarayan. This is what one sadhu referred to as their "philosophy in idols." The whole theology of the personal akshar in the new school was summarized by one sadhu in the words of Jesus, "He who has seen me has seen the Father." He who has seen the akshar has seen Purushottam. Therefore, both are entitled to worship and devotion (*Vachanamritam*, Gadhada III, 26).

Clifford Geertz suggests that "what we call our data are really our own constructions of other people's constructions of what they and their compatriots are up to" (Geertz 1973: 9). These four schemes – theanthropic, cosmological, devotional, and iconographic – and their interrelation as we have described them constitute such construction. A danger exists of mistaking the lines drawn with ink and words in the diagram for the hazy world inhabited by the devotee where images and symbols overlap in ways that cannot be diagramed or placed on a chart. Still, references to elements from these four schemes were mentioned in the conversation between Bishop Heber and Sahajanand Swami, and they permit us to understand the connections between some of what appear to be isolated phenomena in the experience of devotees. "It is," as Geertz remarks, "like trying to read (in the sense of 'construct a reading of') a manuscript – foreign, faded, full of ellipses, incoherencies, suspicious emendations, and tendentious commentaries, but written not in conventionalized graphs of sound but in transient examples of shaped behavior" (1973: 10).

Bishop Heber's discussion with Swaminarayan focused, however briefly, on the central doctrine of the Swaminarayan fellowship. Heber said that he could not accept what he understood of this doctrine of the human face of god. Some accounts of the meeting between Bishop Heber and Sahajanand circulated within the satsang indicate that Heber was so favorably impressed by the ethical teaching and theology of Sahajanand that he decided that it was not necessary to send Christian missionaries to Gujarat. Undoubtedly Heber was favorably impressed by the ethical teaching and social impact of Swaminarayan, but he was disappointed by the theology because it did not approach the monotheism he had been led to expect. He concluded: "On the whole it was plain that his advances towards the truth had not yet been so great as I had been told" (R. Heber 1846 II: 111). Later developments show, however, that Heber had received a brief introduction to a doctrine of the human face of god, in harmony with traditional Hindu philosophy and theology, which provides a theological basis for the movement and an object of personal devotion for millions of Gujaratis, many of whom have migrated to Bishop Heber's homeland to establish there temples housing the images of Swaminarayan in human form.

CHAPTER FOUR

The sacred world

An ancient Harappan town and port have been uncovered at Lothal in Gujarat, now far removed from the river or the sea. The site and the unearthed artifacts are reminders that Gujarat is an ancient land and that elements of what we call Hinduism have been present from the beginnings of the cultural history of India. The face of Gujarat has changed, however, as each new social and political force has moved across the land. New cities, new avenues of transportation, new forts, and new boundaries have appeared as the old were covered with sand and debris and provided the foundation for the new.

New religions and cultural movements have helped to change the landscape of Gujarat. Members took down old shrines and monuments and built new shrines with the stones. Not only the physical surroundings, but along with them the mental universe inhabited by the people was changed. Members of the various Hindu groups in Gujarat in the eighteenth century inhabited a Gujarat with boundaries of time, space, and social status only partially identified by marks on ancient maps for pilgrimage centers and sacred temples. The Jains occupied the same physical territory, but a different world. Then the Muslims moved across the area, but they set apart different locations and people as sacred and, therefore, "saw" their surroundings differently. So, for example, the sacred map of the Muslims in Gujarat is oriented westward, toward Mecca. The orientation is mental and social, not physical, and it is part of the sacred world inhabited and shared by those who are members of a religious group. Each religion presents a particular constellation of things set apart as sacred which locate the religion in a social and historical tradition. Members inhabit a sacred world.

One function of a modern reform movement in Hinduism is the rebuilding of the sacred world experienced by followers. Members of the Swaminarayan sect claim that at a critical time of social change and of the breakdown of the old world-view, Swaminarayan took the best of

the religious tradition of India and constructed a new and more adequate sacred world. Thus, they say, in the past two centuries in the face
of increasing secularization and the weakening of religious devotion, the
Swaminarayan religion has provided a revitalization of the experience
of sacred person, sacred space, and sacred time by associating these with
the life and theology of Swaminarayan.

Milton Singer tells that whenever Madras Brahmins wished to introduce him to some aspect of Hinduism, they took him to see some cultural performance (M. Singer 1972: 64). These observable performances
became the basis of his analysis of the cultural system. Similarly, whenever members of the Swaminarayan religion wished to illustrate some
aspect of their religion during my fieldwork, they took me to meet and
interview a holy man, invited me to journey with them on pilgrimages to
sacred temples or shrines, or asked me to watch them celebrate some religious festival. These sacred persons, sacred places, and sacred festivals
are the phenomena which provide a starting point for understanding the
religious experience of the followers of the Swaminarayan religion.

SACRED PEOPLE

The primary religious impetus for the Swaminarayan reform movement
was the experience and belief that the sacred was manifest in the person
of Sahajanand Swami. The emphasis upon the human form of the
supreme person resulted naturally in the belief that the manifestation of
the divine or the sacred is primarily through persons. So it is that some
persons who appear to be perfectly ordinary are perceived to reveal the
sacred. A long tradition of veneration of holy men has been present in
Hinduism. From the time of the *Vedas* it has been believed that the one
who knows Brahman is Brahman. Yet some suggest that one of the moti-
vating reasons for the reforms initiated by Swaminarayan was that the
ideal of the holy person as the mediator of the sacred had been greatly
tarnished by the disreputable conduct of persons in the guise of the
saints. Although there is no structural necessity that the sacred be associated with morality, in the Swaminarayan movement the unity of the
two is preserved, and persons have been designated as sacred, beginning
with Swaminarayan and continuing to the present. Contact with a
sacred person is an important step, and some think the essential step, in
religious development.

The experience of the sacred person by members of the fellowship is
characterized by both attraction and separation. The individual wishes

to come into close contact with the sacred person because such contact is thought to lead to spiritual growth and salvation. Thus, the sacred persons in this tradition are not removed into isolated retreats, but come into regular contact with the lay members of the fellowship. They live in cities, travel to the villages, and communicate freely with both members and nonmembers. The major restrictions on association are concerned with the avoidance of close contact with members of the opposite sex. Still, the sacred persons are separated by distinctive dress, by rules of conduct, and by rituals of respect which set them apart from the average person.

The leaders: a householder and an ascetic

The leaders of the two major divisions of the Swaminarayan movement are viewed as sacred persons. In the previous chapters we have seen how the acharyas of Ahmedabad and Vadtal and the leaders of the Akshar Purushottam Sanstha have been set apart by their administrative responsibilities and in the literature and theology of the sect. Our purpose here is to record some of the rituals of respect which set them apart as sacred. Then we will turn to the ascetics, both male and female, who occupy the status of sacred persons.

Tejendraprasad Pande is Acharya of Ahmedabad because he is the most direct descendant in the line from Ayodhyaprasad Pande, the adopted son of Swaminarayan. The symbols which visibly designate him as such, the symbols of his office, are his manner of dress, the large golden parasol and silver mace which are carried by his attendants, and the silver couch (gadi) on which he sits during formal occasions in the temple in Ahmedabad (now called Amdavad). From this exalted position he presides over all the major functions and festivals of the temple. He goes to the temple every morning, except when he is on tour, and takes his place before the assembled ascetics and laymen on the silver couch. He is raised above all others in attendance, including the mahant of the temple and the sadhus, and he is the center of attention even though he is a householder. In the evening hours he makes himself available to his followers in a reception room at his residence some distance from the temple. His official dress is the same as that worn by his ancestors as shown in the pictures displayed in the temples. The attractive red turban is the primary symbol of his office which he received at the time of his father's death. He wears a white dhoti and a silk jacket, and carries a silk cloth folded over his shoulder. When he walks in the open, he is covered

7 Acharya Tejendraprasad Pande with satsangi

by the gold-colored umbrella. His attendant carries the mace. Great deference is shown him when he appears as the acharya in the temple or at festivals in Amdavad or at the other temples in his diocese. Male devotees approach him with respect, touch his feet with their foreheads or hands, and speak to him privately *sotto voce.*

An important official function of the acharya is the ceremonial tour to the villages to visit and bless the disciples. Acharya Tejendraprasad spends several days each month on official visits called *padhramani* (see plate 7). The schedule of these visits is carefully planned, and most villages have a sort of religious holiday to honor the occasion. On a typical visit the acharya is met at the entrance to the village by officials and leading devotees according to the prescription in the *Shikshapatri*: "On hearing of the arrival of the Acharya, my disciples should proceed up to the outskirts of the town to receive him with respect, and on his departure should accompany him to the outskirts to bid him farewell" (72). Then he rides through the gaily decorated streets on a cart or wagon, accompanied by musicians, men dancing in front of the vehicle, and women following behind dressed in their finery with the auspicious water pots and coconuts on their heads. There is much noise and rejoicing in a festive display. He goes first to the temples and shrines of the village to perform an act of worship.

During the day, the acharya tours the homes and businesses of all the devotees in the village, which in some cases involves several hundred brief visits. He enters the home and takes his seat at the place of honor. The male head of the household shows respect by waving a camphor light before the acharya with appropriate chanting. Women members of the household observe from a distance. The devotee places red kumkum powder on the acharya's forehead and in turn receives the mark from him. The acharya performs the ritual of waving the light in front of the images in the home shrine. Although the acharya is usually accompanied by several sadhus, it is he who performs the ritual acts of blessing the devotees and their homes and businesses. His official manner is friendly, but somewhat aloof and reserved. Generally a gift is "placed at the feet of the acharya" which goes into the treasury of the diocese. A lay devotee travels in his party to receive, record, and give receipts for the gifts. Entire villages and individual families send invitations to the acharya to be present for special events because the visit and blessing of the acharya are thought to be especially auspicious.

Usually in the evening a public meeting is held at the local school or some other appropriate place. The acharya occupies the place of honor surrounded by the symbols of his office. Elements in the programs vary, but may included devotional songs, dramatic or musical presentations by young people of the village, speeches by leading men of the village, and greetings from honored guests. The sadhus give religious discourses, and the acharya gives a brief speech. The villagers respond with the announcement of the amount of the gift or pledges which have been given to mark the occasion. In one small village the amount was 150,000 rupees. At the conclusion of the public meeting the acharya with his party departs for his lodgings or his residence in Amdavad.

Such visits are important in raising large sums of money for the work of the institution. Larger gifts are given when the acharya visits than when the sadhus visit to request the annual donations of the villagers. The visits are more important, however, in designating the acharya by the rituals of respect as the sacred person who is the primary leader of the old school of the Swaminarayan movement and the sole focus of its unity, at least in the Ahmedabad diocese. Acharya Tejendraprasad has been more effective in the exercise of this aspect of his office than have been other acharyas, and this accounts for the relative strength and growth of the sect in his diocese and its affiliates abroad.

Members of the Akshar Purushottam Sanstha speak respectfully of the Acharya of Ahmedabad, but the sacred person who is their undisputed religious leader and the object of the rituals of respect is Sadhu Narayanswarupdas, called Pramukh Swami. He is the administrative president of the organization (see chapter 2), and the theology of the group presents him as the manifestation of the eternal divine abode of the supreme reality (see chapter 3). Biological descent from Sahajanand Swami is not claimed; his exalted status, and that of his predecessors, as the most sacred individual in the sect is the achieved status of conduct as the perfect devotee. Places, objects, and dates associated with the lives of his predecessors are treated with respect, and Pramukh Swami receives the attention and respect which set him apart as one who is sacred.

Pramukh Swami's manner of dress does not designate him as the spiritual leader. He wears the saffron-colored clothing common to the ascetics of the new school. His daily conduct is similar to that of the other sadhus, but all of his activities take on special importance because of his position. Devotees explain that they willingly serve him when in his presence and meditate on his daily activity when absent from him. A regular publication from the temple at Amdavad, *Padrika*, gives a detailed account of his schedule, travels, and activities, and it is read in weekly satsang meetings in India and abroad. Followers believe that they are closely associated with him in all that he does.

All sadhus and devoted laymen perform a prescribed ritual of worship in the morning, usually privately in their rooms, but in the case of Pramukh Swami the ritual becomes a public ceremony. Some sadhus and male devotees sit in the presence of Pramukh Swami in the attitude of worship as he performs the worship before the small metal image of Swaminarayan that is always in his presence. During the ritual he places some relics from Swaminarayan – a piece of his clothing, one of the beads from his necklace, and a small bone chip – in water with some rose petals. The holy water is then distributed to persons who want it to aid in healing or in overcoming some other adversity. The use of holy water from the temples to impart some blessing is common in this and other Hindu sects, but the water used in Pramukh Swami's worship is believed to be especially auspicious and potent. The ambience of the ceremony in which he worships god, and the persons gathered around show reverence to him, marks him as the sacred person *par excellence* for this group. Indeed, many of his daily activities, such as his morning exercise or eating meals, are occasions of both reverence and instruction as sadhus and male householders respectfully observe and listen carefully for his comments and instruction.

Other sadhus travel to the villages on preaching and collection tours and make the padhramani visits to the homes of followers, but the tours of Pramukh Swami, in India and abroad, have special significance for believers. In the first decade after he succeeded Yogiji Maharaj in 1971, he undertook regular tours to more than 4,000 towns and villages, visited over 67,000 homes, and performed the installation ceremony (pran pratistha) for images in seventy-seven new temples associated with the group. He also undertook foreign tours in 1974, 1977, 1980, and 1981. As health problems have developed – he eventually had cardiac by-pass surgery in New York in 1998 – his two-week visits to major temples have become more formal, and followers have been encouraged to come to the temples to receive darshan and guidance. Other sadhus, especially the most prominent (sadgurus), continue the padhramani visits to villages and homes.

Followers seek out respected sadhus for individual advice on the naming of children, marriage and divorce, career decisions, and business decisions, as well as on spiritual matters regarding theology and discipline, but Pramukh Swami's advice is definitive. (See Williams 1985 for a discussion of the guru as pastoral counselor.) The theological support for his role as spiritual leader and counselor comes from his designation as the abode of god in the akshara doctrine. Constant communication is thought to be an essential aspect of the guru–disciple relation. Hence, he receives many letters, faxes, and telephone calls each day, and several sadhu-secretaries respond to each message as he directs. The anomaly is that he gives advice to followers in all manner of mundane affairs related to family, business, personal striving, and pleasure even though as a sadhu he has renounced attachment to all these things. He explains that the purpose of giving such advice is not to establish the devotees in business or to enable them to become wealthy, but to relieve them of anxieties about mundane affairs so they can attend to their spiritual progress (personal interview, 23 July 1985). When asked about his understanding of this role, he replied that he came to the awareness of being the manifestation of the abode of god when he met his spiritual guru and predecessor in the hierarchy, Swami Yagnapurushdas. He said that his constant rapport with god provides the basis of the advice he gives so that, when asked for advice, "it is just there." He says that he is always sure of the correctness of the advice he gives because god's inspiration is always there. He seems to be firmly established and psychologically secure in his role.

The sadhus

Swaminarayan sadhus represent a type of ascetic affiliated with modern *bhakti* (devotional) movements in Hinduism, whose activities contribute both to the growth and to the development of the religious institution and to the salvation of its members. The old school continues to follow the traditional practice of having three classes of male ascetics. The first class are initiates from the Brahmin caste, and are called brahmacharis, a specialized use of the term. They are marked as different from other ascetics by wearing a white cloth around their waist and legs and a saffron cloth or shirt on their upper bodies. Their residence in the temple is separate from that of other ascetics, and they eat out of a different kitchen which maintains their ritual purity as Brahmins. Their special responsibility is the care of the images of the gods in the temples, which requires such purity. Leaders report that currently there are fewer Brahmins who are presenting themselves for initiation as ascetics.

The second class of male ascetics are the sadhus who are from the non-Brahmin, twice-born castes. They all take the sacred thread as a part of the initiation and wear it for the rest of their lives. They wear saffron clothing, top and bottom, and reside together in the temples, either in a kind of dormitory, or in apartments with other sadhus who are disciples of a senior ascetic whom they regard as their preceptor (guru). It seems that those who present themselves for initiation as sadhus in the old school are in the main young boys from poor, large families, some of whom are on occasion "donated to the temple," or they are school graduates who have difficulty finding employment. Some concern is expressed by leaders regarding the commitment and ability of the future generations of sadhus. Those who are initiated undertake a variety of activities of teaching, tours of villages, preaching, and study, and it is from their numbers that the mahants of the temples of the Ahmedabad and Vadtal dioceses are chosen.

Initiates from the lower-caste Shudras make up a third class called parshads, palas, or bhagats. They wear white clothes and live under a less strict discipline, a sort of semi-asceticism. All young men pass through the probationary period on the way to full initiation, during which they wear white clothes and undertake the manual labor appropriate to the parshads. Those from the lower castes, however, have this status permanently. They do not receive full initiation as sadhus, and they never wear the saffron clothing which signifies renunciation of the world. The parshads are assigned the heavy manual labor of cleaning and maintaining the temples and related buildings. Because they follow a less strict rule regarding conversation with women and contact with money, they conduct some of the business of the temples. In earlier, more lawless times they acted as guards for the temples and bodyguards for the acharya. The attendants and household servants of the acharya come from the group of parshads. When the question is asked about those from the lowest polluting castes and Untouchables, the response is that young men from those castes do not present themselves for initiation.

In 1999 the number of male ascetics under the Ahmedabad diocese had increased to 765, comprising 25 brahmacharis, 650 sadhus, and 90 parshads (Ahmedabad Acharya, personal communication, 12 January 1999). The number of brahmacharis and parshads had decreased dramatically since 1980, but the number of sadhus had increased. The Vadtal diocese had more male ascetics, totaling 1,468, comprising 35 brahmacharis, 829 sadhus, and 604 parshads (Vadtal Acharya, personal communication, 20 January 1999). The program of the old-school sadhus follows the pattern of the earlier generations and involves administration of the temples and occasional visits to the villages associated with each temple. The number of ascetics is sufficient to continue that program, and there seems to be little effort made to attract young men into the community of ascetics. Unless needed for the programs of the temples, a larger number of ascetics could be viewed as a burden because provision for their livelihood is the responsibility of the diocese.

The Akshar Purushottam Sanstha began with six sadhus in 1906, and the number grew to about 50 in 1951, to 150 in 1971, then to 200 in 1980. The number increased dramatically to more than 625 in the final two decades of the twentieth century (Ishwarcharandas Swami, personal communication, 25 January 1999). That increase in the number of sadhus, many of whom are university graduates, both reflects and propels the growth of the sanstha. Two decisions by leaders of the new school have made significant changes in the structure and functions of the group of ascetics. Shastri Maharaj made the decision after his departure from the Vadtal temple in AD 1906 to abolish the distinction between the Brahmin ascetics and the others, so there are now only two classes, the sadhus in saffron clothing and the parshads or bhagats in white. Although there are some Brahmins among the sadhus, they are not set apart from the others by dress, residence, or provision of food from special kitchens. Neither is there any differentiation of tasks or responsibilities.

Yogiji Maharaj made an equally significant decision to abolish some of the distinctions between the sadhus and the bhagats. About 1955 he decided that the bhagats should follow the same strict rules of discipline as the sadhus and have virtually the same duties. All wear the sacred thread. These revisions of the original pattern were accepted because the word of the living abode of the supreme person is believed to take precedence over the written regulations. He did not abolish the category of bhagat, however. During the probationary stage prior to final initiation, all wear white clothes until the preceptor decides that some are ready for the final initiation. In the past, ascetics from the lower castes were permanently in white. However, a significant reduction of status differentiation has occurred. The bhagats live under the same rules as the sadhus and engage in preaching, administration, and service common to the sadhus. Some are very highly regarded and occupy positions of power and authority in the fellowship. The main difference in duties has been that the bhagats did not cook food for the deities or other ascetics, and they did not perform the rituals for the images in the inner precincts of the temples.

A major step in the removal of caste distinctions among ascetics was taken at the bicentenary celebrations of the birth of Swaminarayan in April 1981, when 207 young men took initiation at Ahmedabad. Without prior announcement to the followers, Pramukh Swami took the occasion to give *bhagavti diksha* to approximately twenty ascetics from low castes who had previously been permanently in the white clothing. Castes such as blacksmiths and barge men were represented. He performed the initiation ceremony for them, gave them new names and saffron clothing, and by that act abolished for the Akshar Purushottam Sanstha the caste-related category of ascetics permanently in white. Henceforth, the period as bhagat has been temporary, only a preparation for final initiation as sadhu. Thus, all distinctions among the castes, except for the Untouchables, has been removed in the corps of ascetics. The initiation produced great excitement among those present in Ahmedabad, and it was hailed as "a revolutionary act."

There are visible signs which enable the viewer to distinguish ascetics of the new school from those belonging to the old. All sadhus and bhagats of the new school have their head shaved once a month on the thirteenth day of the bright half of the lunar month. A small tuft of hair is left at the crown of the head, what one sadhu jokingly referred to as their "sacred antennas." Ascetics of the old school generally have a larger, thicker tuft of hair. Some elect to allow their hair to grow, which is permitted with the provision that they must also let their facial hair grow. Some younger sadhus of the old school have adopted machine-made, stitched clothing colored by a relatively light orange dye. They seem to follow individual preference in the style and thickness of their clothes, some of which are made of light and relatively transparent material like that worn by laymen. Sadhus of the new school are uniform in their dress, and take some pride in following the prescriptions to wear two plain, unstitched pieces of cloth, sufficiently heavy not to be transparent, and colored by the dust of the prescribed stone, which makes their clothes somewhat darker in hue. Sadhus of the new school travel in pairs and are fairly strict in observance of rules about maintaining distance from women and avoiding contact with money. The custom has developed in the old school, partly because of court judgments, of giving the ascetics a monthly allowance of 120 rupees for clothing and sandals. Thus, they are permitted to handle money. Mahants who are charged with the administration of temples and some other senior ascetics handle considerable amounts.[1] The ascetics of the Bhuj temple in the Kutch region of the Ahmedabad diocese resemble the ascetics of the new school in dress and conduct. They have maintained the traditional ways in part because of the isolation of Bhuj. It is very difficult for them to travel to the urban centers of Gujarat, where they would be influenced by other ascetics and modern ways. They do not travel away from Kutch except to Amdavad for initiation and on official business.

All ascetics in both groups are Gujaratis, but a surprising and growing number, including several prominent sadhus in the Akshar Purushottam group, are from the Gujarati communities in East Africa, England and the United States. Many sadhus of the new school have had a Western-style education through university level, and Pramukh Swami now tells young men who seek initiation that they should finish their education before they present themselves for initiation. Laymen take great pride in referring to those who have left promising careers in medicine, teaching, engineering, or business to renounce the world and take initiation as ascetics.

Yogiji Maharaj seems to have been especially effective in talking with young men about the religious life and in challenging them to become ascetics. Two initiatives taken by him have led to the rapid growth of the

---

[1] See paragraphs 30–3, 41–2 of Exhibit 908 in the Court of City Civil Judge, Fourth Court at Ahmedabad, Civil Suit No. 136 of 1963 decided on 4 April 1973. The comments about the financial affairs of the ascetics come in the context of a suit against Acharya Narendraprasad of Vadtal.

number of ascetics. He developed the practice of having young men spend their school vacations traveling in the villages with him or observing the festivals at the large temples. Many sadhus report that they accepted his challenge because they were drawn to him "as an idol of love" during these vacation visits. These times became a kind of holy apprenticeship for the ascetic life. Pramukh Swami continues this practice, and it has resulted in an increased number of young men presenting themselves for initiation. A second initiative of Yogiji Maharaj was the establishment of a youth organization. He instructed young men devotees in Bombay (now Mumbai) to begin a youth organization with regular Sunday sessions in 1952. From that original group several university students and graduates entered the order of ascetics. The youth organization has grown from that beginning and has been and continues to be the primary recruiting ground for new ascetics and for lay leaders of the Akshar Purushottam Sanstha.

Initiation
Formerly in the old school the initiation of ascetics was performed on the anniversary of the birth of Swaminarayan, the ninth day of the bright half of Chaitra, but now it occurs on any of the Ekadashi days, the eleventh day of either half of the month (Ghurye 1964: 209). Though the regulations allow men between the ages of ten and fifty to be initiated, most initiates are in the period of young manhood. In the old school a youth is accepted for training by a senior ascetic and enters the probationary period in white clothes. He is under the discipline and tutelage of the senior ascetic and undertakes the duties appropriate for a parshad as he prepares for initiation. When his preceptor thinks that he is ready, the youth is taken to the acharya of his diocese, Ahmedabad or Vadtal, for initiation. Often he remains in the temple or residence of the senior ascetic as his disciple. Instruction by the senior sadhus continues in the traditional gurukul pattern of apprenticeship in which the students live with and serve the guru while they receive their education and spiritual formation. Gradually they are given additional responsibilities within the guru's circle and among his followers. The disciples often take over responsibilities of the guru or separate to establish their own circle of sadhus and followers within the temple or diocese. In the 1990s the Ahmedabad acharya opened schools for a few sadhus in his previous residence in Shahibaug in Amdavad and in the town of Jetalpur.

The Akshar Purushottam Sanstha has evolved a different type of training for the sadhus. Some prominent sadhus remember with some nostalgia their experience of being among the first large group of 51 young men to be initiated as sadhus in 1961 by Yogiji Maharaj. There was no formal training program. They lived together in three rooms in the Dadar section of Bombay when there were few disciples, little material support, much opposition and harassment from neighbors, and considerable privation and hard work. They say that "Yogiji Maharaj was the training program," and their travels with him were a "mobile training school." Throughout the 1970s Pramukh Swami continued that pattern. New initiates regularly traveled with him and listened to his discourse and conversations in a kind of "holy apprenticeship." When the 207 young men were initiated in 1981, Pramukh Swami established a more formal Sadhu Training School, the Sant Ashram in the temple at Sarangpur, a small village in Saurashtra. He explained: "I cannot take a coach-load of sadhus with me as I travel through the villages. The villagers could not cope with large numbers." "Moreover," he said, "because the movement has grown so rapidly and there is a great demand for sadhus to go into the villages to teach the people, it is necessary that sadhus be given complete training quickly" (Personal interview on 14 August 1990).

A second Sadhu Training School is under construction at Sankari near Surat in South Gujarat. Growth in the number of students and a recurrent water shortage at Sarangpur that complicates administration of the Sant Ashram are reasons for creating a new ashram. Sankari is the town where Pramukh Swami dedicated his first temple after Yogiji Maharaj died. Rapid growth in numbers of satsangis, concurrent economic and educational development in Gujarat, changes in technology and means of communication, and the need for leadership for a transnational organization caused a structural change from the traditional guru–*sishya* relation to a modern form of training. (For details of the Sadhu Training School see Williams 1998.)

Young men who contemplate becoming sadhus talk with the sadhus in their local temples, perhaps also with Pramukh Swami, and begin to restrict their activities to conform to those of the ascetics: reduced contact with relatives, avoidance of unnecessary contact with women, not eating in public places, a regimen of fasting, and avoidance of movies and secular dramas. The current regulation is that they must be eighteen years old, and Pramukh Swami regularly advises that they complete their secular education, some through university and professional schools, before they present themselves for initiation. Each must obtain a recommendation from his local sadhu and the written permission of his parents, but Pramukh Swami decides when each enters the Sant Ashram and how long his training period will be.

A probationary period of six months to a year is necessary to test the commitment of entering students, during which time the student moves into the ashram residence, has his head shaved, wears a white dhoti and shirt as uniform, and eats out of a bowl. At this stage he still has the freedom to meet with relatives, even females, and to go home to attend marriages and festivals.

The sadhak stage: Sadhaks are instructed to concentrate on the regular discourses and on service in the temple. The regular temple schedule calls for five formal acts of worship during the day, each session followed by a discourse. Sadhaks undertake a series of bi-weekly examinations on the sacred texts, and they meet in small groups to discuss with the teaching sadhus both the lifestyle of sadhus and the difficulties they face in attaining a truly spiritual life. They also prepare to take a series of four examinations on aspects of Swaminarayan Hinduism that are given annually to householders throughout the satsang. Each student must pass these examinations during training at Sarangpur. They also begin a fifteen-day rotation of jobs – making garlands, cleaning the kitchen and dishes, cleaning toilets and baths, gardening, and other tasks in the temple.

Parshad and sadhu stages: It has been customary since 1992 to conduct initiations in November/December on Pramukh Swami's birthday. A young man approaching parshad status visits his parents for a few days prior to initiation. After *parshadi diksha* he faces four or five years of training at Sarangpur. He dons the white clothing of a parshad for the first eighteen months, and then, when Pramukh Swami decides, he receives full initiation as a sadhu. At that time he changes into saffron dress. Parshads and sadhus reside together in the ashram. The rest of their lives are public; they live together and their personal affairs are open books. Training continues in three areas: academic study, practical experience in various forms of service (*seva*), and spiritual development. They study a set curriculum of Hindu and Swaminarayan scriptures and philosophy, devotional music, public speaking in three languages (as they say: Gujarati, the regional language; Hindi, the national language; and English, the international language), Sanskrit, priestly skills, and world religions. Service includes both the regular assignments of tasks in the temple and special training in tasks common to sadhus. Sarangpur is called "a warehouse of saints" because 200 saints are stationed there, so they go to assist other temples during busy times such as Diwali, Pramukh Swami's birthday, and other festivals. Teaching sadhus oversee the spiritual formation of the students, and two senior sadhus travel to Sarangpur regularly to meet with the students, give discourses, answer questions, and deal with problems. Pramukh Swami gathers all the sadhus who can be spared from the temples to an annual "Saint Shibir," a convention where only parshads and sadhus are present so he can discuss with them activities of the sect and the work and spiritual development of sadhus. When the teaching sadhus think that a sadhu is ready, Pramukh Swami assigns him to a temple and a specific task, and he begins what is planned as lifelong service to his guru and Swaminarayan institutions.

The rituals of initiation (bhagavati diksha) are much the same in the old and new schools; the major difference is that the central part of the ritual is performed by the acharyas in the old school and by Pramukh Swami in the new. The elements and pattern of the ritual are common to the initiation of ascetics of other Hindu sects. The initiate bathes and has his hair cut prior to the ceremony. A Brahmin specialist performs the appropriate Vedic ritual and recites the Sanskrit verses for the occasion. The initiate performs the worship ritual of waving the light and places the red kumkum mark on the image of the deity and on Pramukh Swami or the acharya. As a mark of acceptance, Pramukh Swami or the acharya applies the red mark on the forehead, places the sacred thread of the twice-born over the shoulder, wraps the new upper cloth to be worn by the ascetic around his body, and places the turban on his head. The initiate receives the mantra, "I take refuge in Swaminarayan." The bowl from which he will eat, wooden for sadhus and metal for bhagats, is placed before him. Finally, he receives a new name, which marks the dramatic change in his status. Thus a person renounces the world, possessions, family, and ego and has his status transformed into that of a sacred person.

Activities of the sadhus

The distinctive clothing marks them as sacred persons, and through several rituals of respect the lay devotees indicate acceptance of that designation. Male devotees prostrate themselves before the prominent ascetics. The ascetics are given places of honor in gatherings, places removed and elevated from ordinary persons. Physical contact is thought to be auspicious. As the ascetics leave the shrine area of the temple after the worship rituals, it is common for male devotees to line the steps in order to touch the feet of each ascetic in a gesture of respect. In the Ahmedabad and Vadtal dioceses individual ascetics have groups of lay followers, in some instances numbering in the thousands, who revere the ascetic as their guru.

Signs of status differentiation are present in provisions for residence and food, and some senior, saintly, or scholarly ascetics, along with the mahants of the major temples, are treated with great respect. Pramukh Swami is the current preceptor for all followers of the new school, and no ascetic has individual disciples. Nevertheless, there is some evidence of status differentiation. The mahants of the major temples are called sadgurus and occupy seats of honor and receive acts of respect from followers in the territory of their temples. On public occasions and when eating, the prominent ascetics sit closer to Pramukh Swami on elaborately decorated, raised platforms. There is a paradox involved in the respect shown to the ascetics. With his name each claims the role of a servant. They engage in status-denying acts of lowly personal service for male devotees such as cooking and serving at meals or cleaning the temples, but the more they engage in these acts of selfless service, the more they are objects of these rituals of respect.

All the ascetics have accepted the same vows of renunciation and they follow the same discipline. These will be the subject of chapter 5 (on ethics and the duties of each class of devotees). However, the work undertaken by the ascetics is as varied as the conjunction of their personal abilities and the needs of the institutions dictate. Some ascetics are engaged in the study of Sanskrit and sacred texts, and some are sent to Varanasi or other centers of sacred learning for study. The ascetics cannot study in secular schools or universities because that would involve association with women. Their study is useful to the fellowship because they publish articles and pamphlets based on their study. They design and paint some of the pictorial images used in the temples, and they compose sacred songs and perform concerts of devotional music in public gatherings. Of course, the most important task is to care for the images of the gods in the shrines of the temple, to perform the rituals, and to give religious discourses for visitors to the temple.

The ascetics go out of the temple, always in pairs, for tours of the villages where they visit homes of devotees, collect the annual contributions from the harvests of the villages, and preach and give religious discourses. Some ascetics spend most of their time visiting the villages in the territory associated with the temples to which they are assigned. On special occasions the ascetics are sent out to the villages on evangelistic campaigns called "awakening the masses" (*janjagruti*). The ascetics of the Akshar Purushottam Sanstha have been particularly energetic in this activity and have eighty groups of sadhus assigned to tour the villages of Gujarat.

As a result of the centralization of organization and modern program developments, some ascetics of the Akshar Purushottam Sanstha have responsibilities for the general programs of the institution. Administration has been centralized in Amdavad. Ishwarcharandas Swami has been with the institution since birth and is the primary central administrator after Pramukh Swami. Under his guidance other sadhus oversee the 1,900 centers in India, educational and medical institutions and trusts, publications, children's and youth activities, women's work, volunteers, and major building projects. Several sadhus travel with Pramukh Swami and serve as a personal staff and secretaries. The prominent ascetics, along with some of the more influential householders, form an informal cabinet which aids Pramukh Swami in the planning and implementation of the programs of the institution. As the institution grows in size and complexity, and as the demands on the time and energy of Pramukh Swami increase, the delegation of responsibilities and the assistance of these prominent ascetics become more important.

The ascetics are free to leave the order at any time, and there is some attrition from the ranks of both groups. Those who leave simply put on regular clothes and take up normal life in the world. It is, of course, more difficult for older ascetics who have for a long time separated themselves from their families and their former occupations to change their status. No trustworthy estimate exists of the percentage of those who are initiated who turn back, but the number seems to be relatively small. Some leave the group without permission, on occasion to attempt to establish a splinter group; others receive the permission of the leaders to return home and remain active participants in the fellowship.

It is possible to expel an ascetic for misconduct. In the new school, Pramukh Swami is the only person who has the authority to make the decision to expel a person. The decision of Pramukh Swami in such a matter is ratified by the central committee of the religious trust. In the old school, the authority for final discipline rests with the trustees, but it is difficult to exercise. Care must be taken because the act of accepting a young man for initiation involves an implied contract that the institution will provide for his livelihood as an ascetic, a minimum of room and food. This contract, now considered legally binding, can be broken only with due process; otherwise the institution could face a lawsuit.

When an ascetic dies, the final rites are performed by his fellow ascetics. The body is washed with cold water and anointed with a mixture of honey, curd, milk, sugar, and ghee. After this cleansing, the body is dressed in ascetic clothing with a new necklace of beads (*kanthi*), sacred thread, and sect mark (*tilak*). Then the body is wrapped in a bedsheet to be carried to a special cremation ground reserved for the ascetics. Fellow ascetics join the procession chanting sacred verses. The ascetic who cares for the images in the main shrine is prohibited from taking part because viewing any part of the ceremony makes him ritually impure, and thereby makes it impossible for him to perform the rituals for that day. The body is placed on the funeral pyre facing north, and the chief ascetic of the temple, the kothari or mahant, performs the ritual of lighting the fire. The *Dharmamrit* prescribes that the body be burned, be placed in a river to go to the sea, or be left in a cave; cremation is the usual method of disposing of the body. This marks a difference from other Hindu sects, in which the preferred practice is to bury ascetics. It is believed that faithful devotees will be taken to the abode of god (akshardham) immediately at death, and the ascetics pray that the deceased will gain that release. Then they return to the temple and take a purifying bath. The objects which the deceased used in his morning worship are given to another ascetic or are ritually disposed of by being placed in a river or body of water.

Female ascetics

Among the persons set apart as sacred in the fellowship are the female ascetics of the Ahmedabad and Vadtal dioceses, but they are now fewer in number. These women, called Samkhya Yoginis, receive initiation from the wives of the acharyas and follow a strict ascetic rule. They wear dark red clothes and live in a haveli, a separate precinct of the temple. The old temple in Amdavad has a huge haveli, originally the residence or palace of the acharya, but currently only twenty-two women ascetics are permanently in residence in the temple. Only the Bhuj temple has a large ashram housing 300 women ascetics, including a large number of young women. The 440 female ascetics in the Ahmedabad diocese serve in the separate shrines for women, perform initiation for female devotees, and conduct some religious discourses for women (statistics from the acharya's wife, communicated by the Ahmedabad Acharya, 12 January 1999). Just as female devotees show respect to male ascetics by avoiding contact with them, so male devotees show respect by avoiding the female ascetics. Women devotees show respect to these women who have renounced the world, but no male researcher is permitted to observe their daily activities. The Vadtal diocese has approximately 115 female ascetics (Vadtal Acharya, personal communication, 20 January 1999). There are a few elderly, respected women associated with the Akshar Purushottam Sanstha who live according to strict ascetic vows, but no initiation of female ascetics is permitted. The tradition is that Swaminarayan only reluctantly allowed for the women ascetics to reside in the temple at the urging of Jivuba, the sister of the Prince of Gadhada. James Burgess reported that 150 women ascetics were present during the life of Swaminarayan; they resided at Gadhada, as did 300 sadhus and 300 brahmacharis (Burgess 1872: 333).

At the level of the individual believer, these sacred persons function to aid in the attainment of the goal of spiritual development and release. At the institutional level the union of the sacrality attributed to the persons and the administrative power exercised by them undergirds the structure of the institution. Different groups within the religion experience different persons as sacred, even though there may be some overlap. Where there is some opposition, as between the ascribed, hereditary status of the acharyas and the achieved status of pious ascetics, tension and even division result. Nevertheless, those who think of themselves as members together of a religious group share the experience of the same group of sacred persons because they inhabit one world together.

SACRED SPACE

The act of paying respect to the feet of holy men and to their footprints has been common in Indian religions from the time of the Buddha. The "holy footprints" of Swaminarayan are in evidence all over Gujarat and have changed the sacred geography of the region. He traveled widely throughout Gujarat, and at many places associated with events of his life, markers have been erected to remind pilgrims of the event and to designate the space as sacred. James Burgess reported: "After the death of Swami Narayan, his disciples erected *chauras* or stopping places, and monuments to his memory, in all the villages, and beneath all the trees where he had at any time made any stay. There they worship him" (1872: 335). Hundreds of these monuments still stand. Generally they are raised platforms about chest high with a flat surface about four feet across. Embossed on the top are stylized replicas of the soles of two feet. Usually the footprints are beautifully carved in marble and have on them the various signs of divinity. Such signs are, according to the tradition, to be found on the body of the manifestations of god. Around the monument, sometimes raised from the surrounding ground, is a walkway to permit circumambulation of the "holy footprints." Most monuments are covered by a protective umbrella-shaped roof.

Monuments

These monuments are found in different types of locations to commemorate events in Swaminarayan's career. Some are out in the open under trees or beside rivers or ponds to mark places where he regularly took rest on his journeys. One marks the location of his meeting in Rajkot with Governor Malcolm. The monument at Dabhan is a reminder of one of the early sacrifices (yajnas) performed by Swaminarayan to protest and counter the practice of animal sacrifice; it is inconspicuous out in the middle of an open field, and it seems to be rarely visited. The monument in the courtyard of the house of Dada Khacher in Gadhada has been incorporated into a large temple complex, and many pilgrims regularly visit it. Stories are associated with these monuments, and inscriptions on the monuments give the details. Most devotees know the stories and recount them to their children and to visitors. A tour around Gujarat to visit these monuments becomes a movement back through the calendar of sacred time as the stories recreate the events that took place in the early nineteenth century.

The ritual of a visit is simple. Devotees circumambulate the monument in a clockwise direction with their right hands touching the marble footprints (see plate 8). On some occasions there is the repetition of the Swaminarayan mantra. The number of circumambulations varies, as does the demeanor of the worshipers. Some carry on conversation as they move around; others are silent; some repeat the mantra. Women perform the circumambulation of these monuments, but not when male ascetics are present. During the visit, a retelling of the story or conversation about the event associated with the place keeps the tradition alive.

Visitors are taken to other locations which are associated with events from his life. In the temples built during his lifetime the rooms where he stayed are preserved in their original form. They have become religious museums with clothing, furniture, and other objects preserved for viewing by pilgrims. One villager proudly displays for visitors a pair of wooden sandals used by Swaminarayan. Footprints on paper or cloth are preserved in the temples and in homes. One disciple repeated a common Hindu saying: "The feet of the preceptor and the head of the devotee

8 Sadhus circumambulating a memorial with sacred footprints

complete the connection of man with god." This reference to the act of touching one's head to the feet of the preceptor in a ritual of respect indicates the reason importance is attached to these sandals or prints. The room in Vadtal where Swaminarayan composed the *Shikshapatri* and the veranda at the small village of Kariyani where he delivered some of the discourses in the *Vachanamritam* are preserved and marked as sacred. Thus, the career of Swaminarayan and the places associated with his life have transformed Gujarat with a new set of sacred shrines.

One sign of a division in a religious community is that followers in the separate groups inhabit different sacred worlds. They set aside different locations as sacred space; they worship at different temples; they visit different sacred shrines. Even though the sacred space of different groups may overlap, as in the respect given to the Ganges as a sacred river by all Hindus or the pilgrimage occasionally made to Swaminarayan's birth-place at Chhapia in Uttar Pradesh by followers of different groups, each separate group has its own sacred map. Thus, the ascetics of the Akshar Purushottam Sanstha worship at the temples dedicated to Swaminarayan in the Ahmedabad and Vadtal dioceses, when permitted, and pay respect to all the shrines and monuments associated with his career; they never-theless have their own temples and sacred places that are holy because they are associated with persons or events important in the development of the new school.

Memorials in the same style with raised footprints have been placed at locations associated with events in the life of Gunatitanand Swami and his successors. The small village of Bhadra in Jamnagar district is the native place of Gunatitanand, and it is a village full of stories associated with sacred sites. A temple was built in 1968 at the place of his birth by the Akshar Purushottam Sanstha. As a result, the number of pilgrims has increased dramatically, and now over 100,000 people visit the small village each year. A shrine marks the location where Swaminarayan called Gunatitanand to leave his occupation and become an ascetic. Nearby is the place on the Und River where Swaminarayan bathed and delivered religious discourses. This is reported to have been one of the favorite spots of Yogiji Maharaj, to which he often came with his sadhus. A small shrine room is preserved in a residential hut in the village where Swaminarayan resided for one month with a carpenter family. The room is kept as it was for pilgrims to visit. This shrine is associated with the Ahmedabad diocese, and the picture of Acharya Tejendraprasad is prominently displayed. Nevertheless, members of the new school visit the home as a part of their pilgrimage; it is a part of their sacred world as well. The sacred space in Bhadra is an example of the fact that several layers of historical tradition may be associated with the same sacred place, and though not at Bhadra, in some other places mythological traditions are also present. Thus, the locations in Bhadra are associated with events in the career of Swaminarayan, Gunatitanand Swami, and Yogiji Maharaj.

A characteristic of the theology of the Akshar Purushottam Sanstha with its designation of Gunatitanand Swami and his successors as manifestations of the supreme reality is that it encourages the multiplica-tion of sacred places for the fellowship throughout Gujarat. The birth-place of each becomes a place of religious interest and pilgrimage. Rooms in the temples where each stayed and objects used by each are treated as holy. Monuments are built at the places of cremation, such as

9 Swaminarayan temple in Mehalav

shrines that mark the place opposite the Sarangpur temple where Shastri Maharaj was cremated and at Gondal where Gunatitanand Swami was cremated. In January of 1999 Pramukh Swami opened a large temple complex in the small village Mehalav, where his guru, Shastri Maharaj, lived (see plate 9). A huge festival on his birthday recounted the life and work of Shastri Maharaj. Such places are revered by members of the Akshar Purushottam Sanstha, but not by members of the old school. In addition, the new school has its own temples throughout Gujarat.

The largest monument and the most popular tourist/pilgrimage center in Gujarat is the memorial to Sahajanand Swami, called Akshardham, which was dedicated in 1992 at Gandhinagar, the capital city of the State of Gujarat (see plate 10). In 1998 Akshardham attracted over 2.3 million visitors from 74 countries. A gold-leaf-covered statue of Sahajanand is in the central rotunda, and images of other deities and sacred people decorate the building, but it is not a temple. One wing of the complex contains large exhibition halls with the latest technology to teach visitors about Indian culture, Hinduism, and Swaminarayan precepts. Another wing houses the Akshardham Center for Applied Research in Social Harmony. The complex contains gardens, restaurants, a theme park, and a bookstore. Nineteen sadhus are assigned to

10 Memorial shrine at Akshardham

Akshardham and 350 people serve on the staff, many of them full-time volunteers. The monument has been very effective in attracting positive attention and new satsangis to Swaminarayan Hinduism: so successful, in fact, that similar monuments are planned for New Delhi, Mumbai, London, and Edison, New Jersey. Such monuments combine the traditional attraction to sacred sites and the rich experience of pilgrimage with modern modes of information technology and tourism to create a powerful communication medium.

Temples

Temples belonging to both the old school and the new are of two types (see plate 11). The larger, more important temples have metal or marble images in the three central shrines and are called *sikhara mandirs* because they have three large domes or spires (sikhara) over the central shrines. The mode of architecture, even in the newer temples, is what Mallison identifies as the colorful indo-mughal style in vogue in Gujarat during the nineteenth century (1974: 457). Sadhus serve as temple priests (*pujari*) in the central shrines of the Swaminarayan temples that have images of metal or marble. Therefore, it is necessary to provide residence halls for them. The temples which have no metal or marble images have pictures

11 Kalupur temple in Amdavad

in the central shrine and are called *hari mandirs*. Ascetics need not be in residence in these temples; the daily rituals are performed as needed by a Brahmin or other qualified householder. Thousands of such temples and shrines are in Gujarat. Some are large and well appointed; others are small rooms in very small, poor villages. See figures 2 and 3.

Worshipers enter the temple compound through a gateway which is often marked by a tall and elaborately decorated temple tower. They remove their shoes at the entrance or before they enter any of the buildings in the compound. The older temples and those in villages have large open compounds; some are able to accommodate several thousand people. The newer temples in urban centers typically have less space. The shrine which houses the main images of the gods occupies a central place in the compound, and the primary purpose of the devotee in coming to the temple is to see the images, "to have darshan of god."

The shrine building is so constructed that those entering ascend stairs to the main shrine on the upper floor. Some devotees touch each step with their hand as they ascend in a gesture of respect for the sacred place. The building has large domes and spires reaching toward heaven to remind the devotees that at the sacred place of the residence of the gods the plane between the earthly and the divine is broken. Thus they are reminded that the purpose of their visit is to aid their own spiritual

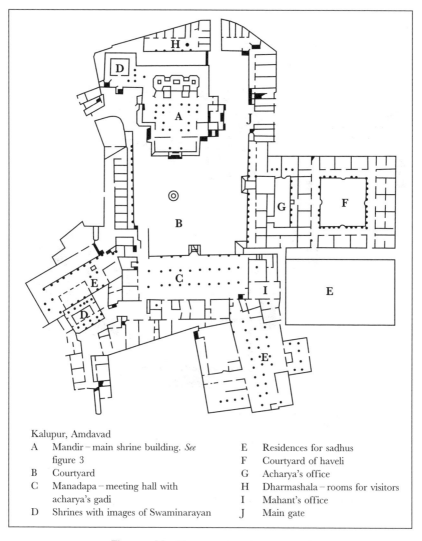

Kalupur, Amdavad

A Mandir – main shrine building. *See* figure 3
B Courtyard
C Manadapa – meeting hall with acharya's gadi
D Shrines with images of Swaminarayan

E Residences for sadhus
F Courtyard of haveli
G Acharya's office
H Dharmashala – rooms for visitors
I Mahant's office
J Main gate

Figure 2 Nar-Narayana temple compound

ascent. One layman remarked that the temples are constructed in the shape of the summit of the mountains with the highest spires suggesting the world of the sky; a touch of the infinite is brought into the mundane world. Inside the domes on the tops of the pillars are statues of eminent men who assisted Sahajanand in his work. All over the temple are the various designs taken from the lotus flower to suggest that life is very fragile but still blooms. The lotus flower grows from the mud and attains

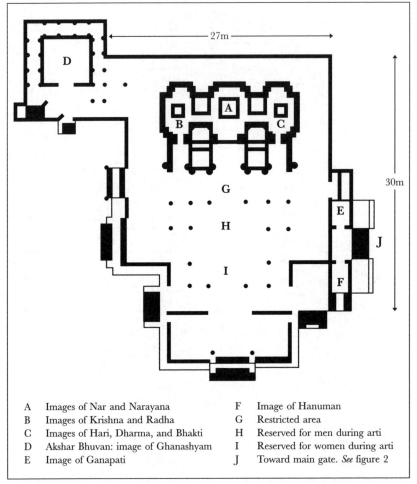

A	Images of Nar and Narayana	F	Image of Hanuman
B	Images of Krishna and Radha	G	Restricted area
C	Images of Hari, Dharma, and Bhakti	H	Reserved for men during arti
D	Akshar Bhuvan: image of Ghanashyam	I	Reserved for women during arti
E	Image of Ganapati	J	Toward main gate. *See* figure 2

Figure 3 Mandir (main shrine building) of Nar-Narayana Kalupur temple, Amdavad

the quality of detaching itself from the surrounding mud which sustains it. The silent message given is: "Remain detached and yet bloom."

The worshipers come first to the two shrines of Hanuman and Ganapati (Ganesh) before they reach the main shrine area. The shrine with the image of Ganapati, the elephant-headed son of Shiva, is on the right, and the shrine of the monkey god Hanuman is on the left (see plate 12). Devotees stop at each to make an offering and to have darshan of these before going into the location of the main deities of the temple. The explanation for the presence of these two shrines at the entrance to

12 Image of Ganapati (Ganesh)

the main shrine area is that worship at these shrines prepares visitors to go on to the main shrine with the proper attitude of mind. Ganapati is the deity who is associated with the preservation of health and physical well-being and with the creation of material prosperity. Hanuman and his warriors overcame the evil powers of the demons and saved Sita in the *Ramayana*; thus, he is thought to be responsible for protecting the individual and his or her possessions from all evil. These are concerns appropriate to the daily affairs of householders, but are secondary to the concern for spiritual growth and salvation. Therefore, the ideal is that as the devotee enters the temple, he pays respect to and makes requests of these gods concerning worldly affairs appropriate to them so that he can enter the main shrine free from anxieties about material affairs and can concentrate on his spiritual development.

Swaminarayan sadhus cannot act as priests (pujari) at the shrines of Ganapati and Hanuman, even though they serve as priests in the central shrines, because Hanuman and Ganapati are at the entrance where women pass by regularly and worship and where offerings of money are left. The Shiva *linga* is in the Ganapati shrine, and women bring water and milk from home to be poured over the lingam. The priest in charge must be able to receive it, offer it, and return the vessels to the women. Similarly, oil is offered at the shrine of Hanuman, especially on Saturday, which is the day dedicated to Hanuman. The Hanuman shrine in one temple of the Vadtal diocese located at Sarangpur is more prominent than the other images. It is reported that the Hanuman image was installed by Gopalanand Swami, and that when he touched the image with a rod, it came alive and moved. This story has become the charter for a healing ritual performed there. Persons with mental illnesses and other disorders come to the temple on Saturdays to be touched by the rod, now covered in silver, in the hope that they will be healed. In most cases a Brahmin householder is hired by the temple administrator to act as priest at these shrines, to care for the images with the appropriate rituals, and to be available to assist the devotees with their offerings.

The next act of the worshiper, to be repeated after darshan is completed, is to circumambulate the main shrine area a number of times. Circumambulation by devotees is common to most Hindu temples. Some people take special vows to do this a specified number of times. Some repeat the Swaminarayan mantra as they go. Most large Swaminarayan temples have wide porch-like walkways around the shrine area, often decorated with exquisite designs of inlaid marble. Around the shrine area are many statues of the great saints and teachers of Hinduism and pictures depicting events from the mythical past or from the career of Swaminarayan. Pictures or statues of leaders of the Swaminarayan movement are displayed. Devotees are urged to remember these heroes and to show respect to them by bowing as they move around.

They then enter the main shrine area, which is divided into sections by low railings. The size of each section is determined by the prescribed pattern of temple construction on a grid with the size of each square ideally determined by the total space covered by the temple. At the back an area is reserved for the women. There is a strict separation of men and women during the public acts of worship; when rituals are in progress the women stand behind the railing. At other times they enter the men's section in order to get a better view of the deities with their elaborate clothing and adornments. When the acharya's wife and the female ascetics enter the shrine for darshan, as they do in Amdavad every morning about nine o'clock, all men are excluded from the area. At the railing between the two sections are metal collection boxes in which both men and women place their offering of money and grains. Men gather in the section in front of the railing to view the images and prostrate themselves flat on the floor with their hands extended toward the images. Some men undertake a specified number of prostrations and repeat the Swaminarayan mantra as they perform them. In front of the men's section, nearest to the doors of the main shrines and enclosed by a metal security barrier, is a smaller space reserved for the ascetics and special guests. The ascetics enter this area for darshan and perform their prostrations there. The acharya enters this area in the temple in Amdavad to perform his acts of worship.

All focus on the three doorways which open into the most sacred space where the images of the deities reside. The doors are of elaborately carved wood covered with silver, and they are closed at night and during the afternoon rest period. A curtain is pulled across the doorway at other times to preserve privacy when the priest is performing his service to the deities. During most of the day the doorway is open so the devotees can view the images. The priest responsible for the care of the images, and his assistants must be very careful to observe the rules regarding ritual purity.

There is great variety in the form and identity of the images in the various temples. Differences exist between the old-school temples and those of the new school. Even within the diocese of the old school, the identities of the central shrine images differ. The two images in the central shrine of the old temple in Amdavad are of Nar and Narayana (see plate 13), but images of these two are not found in the central shrine of any other temple, including other temples in the Ahmedabad diocese. The shrine on the left, as the worshiper looks at it, contains Krishna and Radha. On the right is a form of Krishna with his parents, Dharma and Bhakti; these may be viewed as images of Swaminarayan and his parents, who have assumed the status of Dharma and Bhakti. Between the central shrine and the one on the right is an opening containing the ceremonial sleeping couch of the deity. The central shrine images at Vadtal are Narayana and Lakshmi along with the Ranachhoda form of Krishna, the form found at the famous pilgrimage center at Dwarka. In some of the temples the side shrine contains an image of Swaminarayan with Krishna and Radha. The acharya has the authority to determine which images of

13 Images of Nar-Narayana in Kalupur temple in Amdavad

the deities will be consecrated in the temples. Once the decision is made, the images of metal or marble are prepared according to the traditional prescriptions for craftsmen concerning size, design, and detail.

The central shrines of the Akshar Purushottam temples reflect the theological emphases discussed in the last chapter in what one sadhu described as "philosophy in stone," and many contain marble images of the same figures. The middle image is Swaminarayan; on the left as seen by the worshiper is the image of Gunatitanand Swami, taken to be the personal manifestation of the divine abode of god (akshar); on the right is Gopalanand Swami, another of the faithful companions of Sahajanand who is taken as a representative of the released souls (muktas) who assisted Sahajanand. The height of the images of Swaminarayan is a standard sixty-four and a quarter inches because it is believed that this was his actual size. The hand gestures of the images are in the traditional patterns (*mudra*): the left hand of Swaminarayan is in the blessing gesture; the left hand of Gunatitanand is in the preaching gesture; and the left hand of Gopalanand is in the service gesture. The small metal images of Swaminarayan which are carried by the sadhus when they travel to the villages are kept in the shrines to be served by the priests.

No such uniformity is found in the images of the side shrines of Akshar Purushottam temples. At Amdavad, Swaminarayan, Krishna, and Radha are on the left. On the right is a metal image of the child Ghanashyam in a crawling posture with one hand raised holding a metal orb – or it could be Krishna, depending on what the worshiper "sees." Behind the image is the sleeping couch. Also in this shrine are several pictures; from left to right these are of Pramukh Swami, Shastri Maharaj, Swaminarayan and Gunatitanand, Yogiji Maharaj, and Pragji Bhakta. Metal or marble images of the successors of Gunatitanand Swami do not appear in these main shrines.

The decoration in these shrines is opulent. The raised platform on which the images stand is intricately decorated with inlaid marble designs. Behind the images is a carved backboard plated with silver or gold. Carved posts support the elaborate canopy which covers the images. The images themselves are dressed in clothing of the finest design and cloth. Ornaments of gold and costly jewels, donations from faithful devotees, adorn the images. The treasury of the temple contains a large and varied wardrobe, and the priests change the dress and ornaments every third day. Special festivals and seasons require specific dress, as is noted below. Some criticism has been made of the new school because the images of Gunatitanand and Gopalanand are dressed in opulent clothing even though their regular apparel was the dress of a sadhu. The explanation is that their eternal form in akshardham is what is portrayed, and that the pictures of the companions in the eternal abode found in the old-school temples, specifically a wall mural in the Amdavad temple, also show them in elaborate dress. The primary reason the devotee comes to the temple is to see the sacred images, and it is an impressively beautiful sight even for one who is not a member.

The worshiper may go to other locations in the temple complex where there are images of the deities. The most famous image in the separate shrines of the old temple in Amdavad is the wooden image of Swaminarayan thought to bear a close physical resemblance to Sahajanand Swami. Other shrines have the single image of Swaminarayan, including the shrine reserved for women in the residence of the female ascetics within the temple compound. There are also separate women's temples in some towns. In temples of the Akshar Purushottam Sanstha there are separate shrines which contain images of Swaminarayan, his close followers, and his family. In Gondal an image of Gunatitanand Swami is placed over the spot where he was cremated, and pilgrims flock there to make this one of the larger pilgrimage temples. A shrine with the image of Shastri Maharaj was consecrated at Sarangpur in 1981 at the place of his cremation, and daily rituals are performed there just as in the main temple. A temple with a shrine to him was dedicated in Mehalav on 22 January 1999. On a typical visit to the temple complex the devotee circumambulates one or more of the shrines and views the images in the sacred precincts.

Some devotees remain in the temple to hear the reading of portions of the sacred scriptures and religious discourses given by an ascetic or learned householder. The larger temples have an assembly hall where the discourses are delivered. Women may listen from a reserved area at the rear of the hall, or they may go to another area of the compound to listen to religious discourses given by women leaders. If the crowds are too large for the assembly hall, as on important festival days, the open space of the courtyard is used.

Mention has been made of the fact that rooms, furniture, clothing, and objects associated with Swaminarayan's career, or in the Akshar Purushottam tradition with Swaminarayan, Gunatitanand Swami, and his successors, are carefully preserved in the temples. The Acharya of Ahmedabad regularly makes a donation of relics from Swaminarayan to new temples associated with the diocese, and they are displayed in a prominent place – perhaps a footprint, a *puja* article used in daily worship, a turban, or piece of clothing. Thus, portions of the older temples are religious museums which preserve a slice of Gujarati culture from the early nineteenth century. Architectural styles, examples of craftsmanship, and other artistic work are preserved. The collection of clothing worn by Sahajanand Swami, given by princes and wealthy followers, surely matches in beauty and historical value some of the material exhibited in the famous textile museum of Amdavad. But the material is preserved in the temples because of its religious value. Devotees hope to receive the special blessing obtained by seeing or touching objects made sacred by contact with Swaminarayan.

In the larger temples the deities share their residence with their servants, the ascetics, so there are residence halls within the compounds. These range in architectural style from elaborately carved and painted wooden buildings from the early nineteenth century to modern, functional dormitories of concrete; in size from large buildings with separate apartment complexes which would house several hundred ascetics to small buildings with two or three rooms to house a few.

A striking feature of the Swaminarayan temples are the guest houses (*dharmashalas*) which are provided for visitors. Overnight accommodation is provided for members upon request in simple but comfortable rooms. Food and lodging are provided for individuals or families who wish to make a visit to the temple on their travels or who are making a religious pilgrimage to visit the main temples. It is not uncommon for newly married couples to make a pilgrimage to visit one or more of the important temples, a religious version of the honeymoon. Provision is made for large numbers of persons who come to the temples for festivals lasting several days. No charge is made for the accommodation; nevertheless, most visitors make a donation. Small temples may have only two or three guest rooms, but large temples such as the old temple in Amdavad or the Akshar Purushottam temple in Gondal have several buildings with the capacity to house hundreds of pilgrims. The Akshar Purushottam temple in Amdavad constructed an eight-story dharmashala that houses a modern medical facility on the ground floor where pilgrims can obtain a complete physical examination. During major festivals at Gondal when several thousand persons attend, the buildings of a residential boys' school across the road run by the Akshar Purushottam Sanstha are used to house some of the overflow. New buildings are being constructed at many temples, mainly to accommodate the increased number of pilgrims.

The temples have kitchens, dining rooms, and large storerooms for grains and foodstuffs. Some have cattle stalls for tending milch cows which provide milk for the temple, and one temple has a large prize-winning herd. Food is prepared for the deities, the resident ascetics, and the visitors to the temple. All food prepared in the temple is first offered to the deities, if only in small symbolic amounts, and is then eaten by devotees as holy food (*prasada*). Part of the food, especially the sweets, is taken home from the temple to be shared with members of the household. The food services of some of the temples are large and complex, routinely feeding as many as two or three hundred resident ascetics and almost as many visitors. As with the Benedictine monasteries, the rule is that any person who comes and asks is housed and fed without charge. Obviously there are some social constraints which make it impossible for the temples to become the permanent residence for the impoverished. On some festival days several thousand pilgrims are fed in the temple. The foodstuffs are provided by the 5 or 10 percent tithes of the harvest which are donated and stored in the temples.

Temples derive additional income from farms which have been donated. The temple at Atladara near Vadodara (previously called Baroda) has about forty acres of land nearby where rice, grains, and fodder for the livestock are grown. Although the property is managed by the temple, the ascetics do not work the land. In earlier times some of the temples owned large farms, perhaps as large as a thousand acres, but the Land Reform Acts of the mid 1950s and subsequent government regulations forced the temples to sell the land. Temples in towns and cities have property, some adjacent to the temple compound, which is rented out to shopkeepers, and the income is used to support the work of the temple.

When sadhus go out from the temple to visit the villages, public meetings are held in the evening at the village shrines or in a devotee's house. The ascetics stay in the temple or in the home of a devotee. If they stay in the home of a devotee, the family vacates the house so no women are present. Sadhus are permitted to eat food from Brahmin houses even if cooked by women provided it is served by men. If the food is prepared by Vaishyas, it must be prepared with milk rather than water. Otherwise, the sadhus cook their own food. While in the village they visit homes, give talks in the school, talk with individual devotees, and collect the tithes. A householder accompanies them to accept the gifts or pledges and to give the receipts. They may stay in a village three or four days, depending on the size of the village and the number of disciples there. During the monsoon season, when people are not so busy, they conduct a program of scripture reading (*parayana*) which lasts for several days. These visits by the sadhus are the primary means for attracting and instructing new members and maintaining close personal contacts with the villagers. When the devotees travel to the main centers, they are, in effect, returning the visits of the sadhus.

Temples can be places of quiet and meditation, but the main temples are full of activity. Most have reception rooms and business offices where a householder handles the details of the business of the temple and gives a receipt for contributions. The records of the temples are audited by the central committee and are open for government inspection. Depending on the location and special responsibilities assigned to the temple, other facilities are in the compound: offices, workshops, wells, flower gardens to provide flowers for the garlands, power plants, and even a threshing floor in one. Some of the temple complexes now contain modern office buildings that are headquarters for extensive institutional development around the world.

Thus, the chief ascetic of the temple oversees a large and complex institution. The work of the mahant resident in the large Akshar Purushottam temple at Gondal may be taken as illustrative. He was initiated from a Brahmin family in 1953. He has been at Gondal for forty-one years, assigned to visit villages for the first period and then appointed kothari for a decade. Then he was elevated to mahant of the temple so he could devote his time to giving spiritual discourses. Gondal is an important temple with the largest guest facilities because it is the place of cremation of Gunatitanand Swami and Yogiji Maharaj. More pilgrims visit this temple than any other. Hence, the temple feeds 200,000 persons in a year, sometimes as many as 10,000 in a day at festival times. The mahant oversees the work of the ascetics assigned to the temple. Some act as priests at the shrines, and others make tours of the villages. Two hundred and fifty villages are assigned to this temple. The kothari is responsible for all the affairs of the temple: construction, maintenance, farming, program planning, museum, residential school, daily accounts, and the worship schedule. The annual income of the temple is more than 600,000 rupees from donations and the farm. Great stores of foodstuffs are gathered to feed the large number of pilgrims. He is responsible for the work of the paid employees of the temple, who include two shepherds, two pursers, one driver, three night watchmen, and two cooks. In addition, there are a dozen men, some retired from successful careers, who donate their full-time service to the temple. He serves on the central committee of the Akshar Purushottam Sanstha.

Swaminarayan temples are found outside Gujarat, especially in the urban centers of Bombay, Delhi, Calcutta, and Madras (now called Chennai), where there are large concentrations of Gujaratis. Both the old school and the new school have temples with resident ascetics in Bombay to serve a large Gujarati population. Kutchi satsangis associated with the Bhuj temple dedicated a hostel near the airport in Mumbai in 1999 to provide a convenient stopping place for satsangis visiting

Swaminarayan sites in India and abroad. Thus, the sacred space of Gujarat is extended. Many of these temples outside Gujarat are hari mandirs without metal or marble images. The pictures are worshiped with the same rituals as the images in the larger temples except that where a full-time priest is not available the daily schedule is abbreviated. Generally a householder performs the rituals and leads in the gatherings on Sunday evening. Akshar Purushottam temples prominently display the pictures of Gunatitanand Swami and his successors. Some small village temples have had these pictures added to the shrine area to signify a change in allegiance from the old school to the new. In such cases, if the villagers are divided in their will, a court case concerning possession and rights in the temple is possible. In most cases an amicable solution is found.

Home shrines

No account of sacred space in a Hindu sect can neglect the important place of the home shrine. For most Hindus who are householders the home shrine may be at least as important as the temple. It is even more important for most devout women. Householders who are devotees of Swaminarayan have home shrines, some as extensive as a whole room set aside for that purpose, others as simple as a niche in the wall or a small cabinet under a table (see plate 14). Most kitchens have small shrines. These home shrines have pictures of the deities and sacred persons similar to those in the temples. The existence of these home shrines represents an ancient and powerful form of sacred space.

A devoted Swaminarayan businessman in Mumbai keeps one room of his home for a shrine room. One wall holds pictures and images. The shrine is eclectic in character; most prominent are figures associated with the Swaminarayan sect, but pictures of other deities and sacred persons are present. Many are associated with the Vallabhacharya sect worshiped by his mother when she lived with them. A rug, a reading stand, a small library, and other articles used in worship are kept in the center of the room. The man and his wife perform the morning worship every day before breakfast. The ritual is similar to that performed each morning by the sadhus. The husband reads sacred texts for almost an hour and fulfills special vows to chant and memorize selected portions of the texts. After he comes home from work in the evening, he returns to the shrine room for a shorter period of meditation and worship. Such shrines are present in most homes, but the pattern, length, and care of

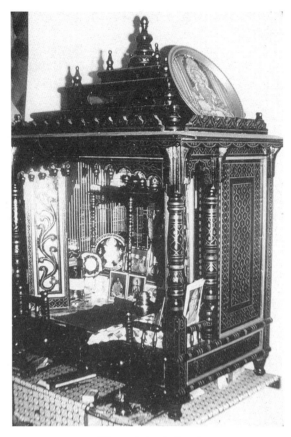

14 Home shrine in London

the program of worship depend on the level of devotion and individual proclivities of members of the household. In remote places and in foreign countries the home shrines are the only places available for worship.

It is customary in many homes that all food is first offered at the home shrine, if only in symbolic amounts, before it is eaten. Many followers take the vow to avoid insofar as possible eating undedicated food from outside the home or temple. The Mumbai businessman eats only a morning and an evening meal on work days because he will not eat undedicated food from a commercial establishment. Food is prepared at home and dedicated at the kitchen shrines for long trips. Thus, the home shrines are very important for the worship, devotion, and eating habits

of many devout followers. Other members are less strict in their observance, however.

Not all space is the same. Religious persons experience some locations
as qualitatively different from ordinary space because they are associated
with the appearance of the divine. Gujarat is experienced as a holy land
because of the new association of places with the life and work of
Swaminarayan. These are thought to have left the marks of the sacred
across the land. The memorials, temples, and shrines are reminders of
that space where the individual comes into contact with the divine. It is
a part of the mental universe of the believers. In its physical shape it can
be as magnificent as the ornate pilgrimage temples or as common as a
niche in a mud wall, but observation of the actions of people as they
approach these places confirms that they are indeed sacred space.

SACRED TIME

Devotees of Swaminarayan follow a religious calendar which leads
them to share the major sacred festivals with other Hindus, but which
also sets aside times for the celebrations unique to this group. In the festivals the participants recover the sacred dimension of existence by
learning how the gods or the mythical ancestors created man and
taught him the various kinds of social behavior. In the Swaminarayan
fellowship, the daily, monthly, and annual cycles of celebration enable
the devotees to celebrate events from the primordial past of Hindu
mythology and the historical events from the career of Swaminarayan.
The function of the annual cycle of rituals and festivals is not just historical, however; the cycle of rituals and festivals propels individuals
and the institution forward and always focuses attention on the next
event. At these sacred times the profane passing of time is transformed
by contact with the divine. See table 5.

Swaminarayan accepted the traditional Hindu lunar calendar of
the Vaishnavas which has 354 to 360 days, with 30 lunar days to a
month. The lunar month is divided into two fortnightly halves. The dark
half follows the full moon and is a relatively inauspicious time. The
bright half follows the new moon. The ritual year begins with the new
moon of Chaitra. He told his followers to conduct their rituals and
festivals according to the prescriptions of Vitthatanath, the son of
Vallabhacharya: "Shri Vitthatanathji, son of Shri Vallabhacharya and
the exponent of Vaishnavism, has prescribed the days of Vratas, and my
disciples should observe these Vratas and perform festival duties accord-

Table 5. *Events from the annual ritual calendar*

Month	Day		Event
Chaitra (March–April)	9th	bright	Swaminarayan's birth Ramanavami Gadhada assembly
	15th	bright	Hanuman's birth
Vaishakha (April–May)	3rd	bright	Akhatrij (begins hot season)
	12th	dark	Yogiji Maharaj's birth
Jyeshtha (May–June)			
Ashadha	2nd	bright	Chariot festival
	11th	bright	Dev-Podhi (monsoon vows begin)
(June–July)	Full	moon	Gurupurnima
	2nd	dark	Swing festival
Shravana (July–Aug.)	8th	dark	Krishna's birth
Bhadrapada	4th	bright	Ganapati's birth
(Aug.–Sept.)	11th	bright	Ganapati's procession
	1st	dark	Shraadha
Ashwina	Full	moon	Gunatitanand Swami's birth
(Sept.–Oct.)	15th	dark	Diwali
Kartika	1st	bright	New Year's Day (Annakuta)
(Oct.–Nov.)	11th	bright	Dev-oothi (monsoon vows end)
	1st or 2nd	dark	Dhanurmas begins
Margashirsha (Nov.–Dec.)	8th	bright	Pramukh Swami's birth
Pausha (Dec.–Jan.)	Full	moon	Gunatitanand Swami's initiation Dabhan assembly
Magha (Jan.–Feb.)	5th	bright	Shastri Maharaj's birth *Shikshapatri* completed
	8th	bright	Gopalanand Swami's birth
Phalguna (Feb.–March)	15th	bright	Pragji Bhakta's birth

ingly; they should religiously adopt the practice of adoration and worship of the Lord as laid down by Shri Vitthalanathji" (*Shikshapatri*, 81, 82). Thus, the daily rituals and the lunar monthly calendar follow the pattern of the Vallabhacharya sect and coincide with those of other Vaishnavas.

The daily schedule of the temple revolves around the service of the deities and, as in other Hindu temples, is patterned after the manner in which a monarch would be served. The deities are awakened, bathed, fed, and dressed by their servants, the priests. In the evening the images are prepared for rest. The food which is offered to the deities becomes sacred food (prasada) and is distributed to the devotees as an auspicious gift. There are five times during the day when the ceremony of waving the lamps before the images (arti) is performed. The exact time varies between seasons because it is regulated by the rising and setting of the sun. A typical schedule would be as follows: Mangala arti at 6 a.m., Shanagar arti at 7.30 a.m., Rajbhoga arti at 11.30 a.m., Sandhya arti at 6.30 p.m., and Shayan arti at 8.30 p.m. Worshipers enter the temple in greater numbers at these times. As the priest waves the lamp before the images, beginning at the central shrine, the worshipers stand in the appropriate space with their hands in a gesture of respect. A bell hanging in front of the shrine and a drum are struck to create a loud noise as the worshipers chant the arti chant, "Hail to Sahajanand Swami . . .," which was composed by Muktananda Swami. (See chapter 3 for the text of the chant.) After the chanting is over, the worshipers prostrate themselves before the images and take their leave. During the middle of the day the deities are given rest, and the doors to the shrine are closed. At about 4 p.m. they are awakened, offered sliced fruits, and made ready for the visits by their followers. The fruit used in the ceremony, now considered to be holy prasada, is distributed to persons all over the temple compound. By following the daily ritual, the devotee can visualize and participate in the daily activities of the gods.

The month is divided into the two phases of the moon, bright and dark. The images of Swaminarayan are dressed with golden crowns on the full moon day because he is supposed to exercise his rule on that day. On the new moon day each month the images are dressed like warriors with weapons and shields in their hands and a crown – not necessarily of gold – in place of the turban. A knife is placed at their waists. The weapons symbolize that god protects his devotees from evil powers which are believed to be more active during the dark half of the moon. The eleventh day of each half of the month is Ekadashi, when there is a mandatory fast for all ascetics and when householders undertake fasts as well. The images are dressed in finery and golden crowns, and devotees make special efforts to visit the temple. Every month the birth of Swaminarayan is celebrated on the ninth day of the bright half. It is also a fast day for ascetics. In addition to these regular observances, the times of eclipse are given religious significance, and the images of the gods are clothed with silk garments. All activities are suspended during the eclipse except for the chanting of the Swaminarayan mantra and the singing of devotional songs. Afterward the sadhus bathe with their clothes on, a complete purification, and dress again in clean clothes. Devotees donate new cloth pieces on the occasion. The temple priest bathes and then changes the clothing of the images in the shrines.

Though there are some differences between the annual ritual calendar of the Ahmedabad and Vadtal dioceses and that of the Akshar Purushottam Sanstha, most festivals are observed by both, and we can follow the annual cycle of festivals which they observe at the same times. The ritual calendar begins with the celebration of the birth of Swaminarayan on the ninth day of the bright half of Chaitra (March–April). The date is also the birthday of Rama, Ramanavami, and a public holiday, so there is a grand festival. The birth is supposed to have taken place at 10.10 p.m., so the celebration of those gathered in the temple reaches its climax at that most sacred time. The best red garments and the golden crown are placed on the image of Swaminarayan that day, and the finest foods are offered and then distributed to the devotees. The day is spent in chanting the Swaminarayan mantra, singing devotional songs, and listening to religious discourses. A small image is placed in a decorated cradle, and at the time of the birth the rocking of the cradle is begun. The image remains in the cradle until 10 a.m. of the fourteenth day of the bright half of the month. Especially large gatherings were held to celebrate the bicentenary of the birth of Swaminarayan on 12 April 1981. The birth of Hanuman is celebrated on the fifteenth day of the bright half of the same month by devotees who offer a special item of fried food at the Hanuman shrines.

The observance of Akhatrij to mark the beginning of the very hot season comes on the third day of the bright half of Vaishakha (April–May). From this day the priests begin to apply sandalwood paste to the images because it is thought to be very cooling. It is applied every morning and removed in the evening at 5.30 p.m. The paste is used to create artistic decorations on the images so that it could be said that the images are clothed with the sandalwood paste. This practice lasts until Dev-Podhi, the eleventh day of the bright half of Ashadha (June–July), which marks the beginning of the four months of the monsoon season. The period of the monsoon is traditionally a period of rest, and ascetics and householders take special vows which begin on this day.

The full moon day of Ashadha (June–July) is Gurupurnima, when devotees gather to offer devotion to their preceptor (guru). This festival is celebrated in the old-school temples and by other Hindus as well, but it is one of the most important of the festivals in the Akshar Purushottam Sanstha. On that day several thousand followers gather at the temple in Bochasan in the presence of Pramukh Swami to express their devotion to him. The Swing Festival begins in this month on the second day of the dark half of Ashadha and lasts for a month into Shravan (July–August). Swings are elaborately decorated for the gods, and people come to the temple to see the deities on the swings.

Shravana is said to be a very holy month; one reason is that the birthday of Krishna, the Krishna Janmashtami, falls on the eighth day of the dark half of the month. The pattern of the ritual is similar to the celebration of the birth of Swaminarayan, which is another indication of the close relation of these two figures in the iconography, theology, and ritual of the sect. The birth is celebrated at midnight with great devotional fervor of singing and chanting. Scenes which depict the birth of Krishna are erected. The small image is placed in the cradle to be rocked over a period of several days.

The birthday of Ganapati is observed in the month of Bhadrapada (August–September). On the fourth day of the bright half of the month a small image of Ganapati is placed in the central shrine to mark his birth. It is the only time the image of Ganapati is placed in the central shrine. Seven days later a procession (Jal-zilani) takes the images of Ganapati and Swaminarayan out of the temple to a nearby river or pond. The image of Ganapati is placed in a small boat, and the ceremonial waving of the lamps before the image (arti) is performed five times. In the evening the image of Ganapati is immersed in the water and cucumber is distributed to the devotees as holy food (prasada). On the way back to the temple the image of Swaminarayan is carried to the houses of some of the devotees for a visit. When they return to the temple, devotees listen to religious discourses and offer new clothing to be used by the ascetics.

The Shraadha ceremony begins the first day of the dark half of Bhadrapada and lasts for fifteen days. It is a kind of All Saints celebration during which the famous pious devotees and released souls (muktas) from the past are remembered and their deeds are celebrated. Each day is assigned to a hero of the past, and during that day the individual is remembered and honored in the temple rituals.

Diwali, the festival of lights, is an all-India festival observed by most Hindus. It is celebrated in the Swaminarayan temples in Gujarat on the fifteenth day of the dark half of Ashwina (September–October). Surrounding this festival there are a number of rituals. On the thirteenth day of the dark half of Ashwina the ornaments of the deities are washed and cleaned, and coins are placed before the images. During this period businessmen bring the new account books which are to be used in the new year to the temple for blessing. Thereby prosperity is assured for the new year. During the evening of Diwali the account books are offered worship with full Vedic rites and then signed by the chief ascetic of the temple. Pramukh Swami is at Gondal to sign the account books, and many businessmen send their books to him there. Now, because of government requirements and tax regulations, the financial year of business firms does not coincide with the sacred year, but the books are blessed and kept until the new financial year begins. The day after Diwali there is an Annakut festival when a mountain of several varieties of food is placed before the images. Beautiful rose garlands are placed on the images. It is believed that what is offered to god in this period will be bountifully returned to the devotee by Swaminarayan in the new year.

New Year's Day is the first day of the bright half of Kartika (October–November). Large crowds gather at the temples early in the morning because people believe that they should begin the year with darshan of the deities. New ornaments and garments are offered on that day, and the best golden crown is placed on the image of god. The first two rituals of waving the lamps (arti) come earlier on that day, at 5.30 and 6.30 a.m. The devotees make a special point of greeting the sadhus and of receiving their blessings. The chief ascetic of the temple delivers the morning discourse and distributes holy food (prasada) of sweets to all who visit him.

The eleventh day of the bright half of Kartika, known as Dev-oothi, marks a change of season which comes at the end of the monsoon. Because the monsoon season is a period of rest for the deities as well as for the devotees, this celebration traditionally marks the return to activity. In the villages people engage in the agricultural tasks of the growing season. In the evening after 4 p.m., the food offering to the images in the temples is raw vegetables, which are then sold to devotees after the evening ceremony of waving of lamps (arti).

A month-long celebration of Dhanurmas begins on the first or second day of the dark half, depending on a solar calculation, and lasts into Margashirsha. According to the puranic stories, Krishna began his studies on this day, so the images in the Swaminarayan temples are dressed and decorated as students. The images hold pens, slates with slogans written on them, and school books. The arti schedule is revised so that the first three are performed at 5.30, 7.00, and 8.00 a.m. The image of the deity is offered breakfast between the first two, and lunch between the second and third. After the third arti he is supposed to be in school, so some food items which children like to take to school, for example, dried fruits and chocolates, are left before the image. Articles appropriate to students are placed there every day except Sunday, which is the day of rest. Musical instruments are placed in the shrine on that day.

Each temple has in its sacred calendar the annual celebration of the anniversary of the dedication of the images in the temple (pran pratistha). In the morning the image of Swaminarayan is offered a bath of five items poured over it: milk, honey, curds, sugar, and ghee. These are poured over the image by the chief ascetic of the temple while the sadhus chant sacred verses. Afterward the ascetics join in giving the bath with the five items and water. Then male devotees are permitted to go into the shrine in order to participate in the bathing ceremony – this being the only occasion when it is allowed. Householders are permitted to approach the images only if they are dressed in the traditional dhoti, a plain cloth wrapped around the waist. After the washing, new garments are offered to the image of Swaminarayan while devotional music is sung and dedicated food is distributed to those present.

The rituals discussed thus far are common to the temples of both the old and the new schools. They follow the lunar calendar, the agricultural cycle of wet season and dry season, and a cycle of births of mythical figures and Swaminarayan. The Akshar Purushottam temples observe festivals unique to them which are primarily concerned with the births of the preceptors. One of the largest celebrations of this sect is the birth anniversary of Gunatitanand Swami, which is observed on the full moon day of Ashwina (September–October) at Gondal. A meeting is held in the evening, during which five artis are performed interspersed with devotional songs and discourses. A special type of holy food (prasada) made with parched rice, milk, and sugar is distributed. The Akshar Purushottam Sanstha conducted extensive celebrations of the bicentenary of Gunatitanand Swami's birth in 1985. The birth anniversary of each of Gunatitanand Swami's successors is included in the sacred calendar: Pramukh Swami on the eighth day of the bright half of Margashirsha (November–December); Shastri Maharaj on the fifth day of the bright half of Magha (January–February); Pragji Bhakta on the fifteenth day of the bright half of Phalguna (February–March); and Yogiji Maharaj on the twelfth day of the dark half of Vaishakha (April–May). On the day of the birth of Shastri Maharaj there is also the celebration of the birth of Nishkulanand Swami and Brahmanand Swami, two close companions of Swaminarayan. On that day Swaminarayan also finished the composition of the *Shikshapatri*, and that event is celebrated. Hence, the dedication of a temple in Mehalav on Shastri Maharaj's birthday in 1999 incorporated all these sacred times.

The birth of the living preceptor, believed to be the manifestation of the abode of god (akshar), is celebrated with great fervor. On the eighty-fifth birthday of Shastri Maharaj the devotees arranged a gift of his weight in gold. He refused to allow himself to be weighed against gold, so his weight was matched in sugar, and that amount of gold was given. The birth of Pramukh Swami in November/December is celebrated by large gatherings that stretch almost to breaking point the infrastructure that supports them.

The ritual calendar of the Akshar Purushottam Sanstha is not static. As new places are being added to the sacred map by the addition of birthplaces of the preceptors, so the sacred calendar is being enlarged. A relatively new celebration has been added, largely through the efforts of householders without official sanction. Gunatitanand Swami was initiated with a large sacrifice (yajna) at Dabhan in Kaira district on the full moon day of Pausha (December–January). The place is marked by one of the monuments with "holy footprints" described above. About fifteen years ago a few devotees began the practice of going there on that day for a religious gathering and picnic. The event now attracts over 10,000 people and has a fixed place in the ritual calendar. Another localized celebration is that of the birth of Gopalanand Swami at Torda/Todala in Sabarkantha district on the eighth day of the bright half of Magha. Some festivals are celebrated with more attention and pomp in some districts than in others. The major calendar is set, but there are variations in the regional calendars and in the calendars of individual temples. This allows for the growth of the sacred calendar as new celebrations are added and regional celebrations become more universal in their appeal.

Swaminarayan began the practice of pilgrimage and holding large gatherings in his presence at festival times. The *Shikshapatri* has the injunction: "My disciples with means should celebrate the religious festivals in temples with great pomp and enthusiasm" (156). When the fellowship grew so large that members could not attend all the functions, he sent a circular letter instructing them to attend two annual meetings, one at Vadtal in central Gujarat on the eleventh day of the bright half of Kartika (October–November) and the other at Gadhada in Saurashtra on the ninth day of the bright half of Chaitra, the birthday of Swaminarayan (Parekh 1980: 83). The two assemblies are now held each year at Vadtal and Ahmedabad in the presence of the acharyas of the respective dioceses. In addition to these two prescribed dates, the members of the Akshar Purushottam Sanstha observe as major gatherings the Gurupurnima in Ashadha (June–July) and the birthday of Gunatitanand Swami in Ashwina (September–October). Evidently Swaminarayan's intention in calling these gatherings was to bring members together from various areas to create strong bonds between devotees and a sense of unity of the fellowship. Such religious gatherings have also had a larger social impact of reducing regionalism and aiding in the more general unification of Gujarati culture and language. Before the regions of India were linked together during British rule by the railroad and the telegraph, they were tied together by the stream of pilgrims visiting the holy places. One should not overlook the importance of pilgrimage and these gatherings within Gujarat in helping to produce a strong sense of ethnic identity which led eventually to separate statehood and now unites Gujaratis in many countries.

The Akshar Purushottam Sanstha has developed the practice of assigning the celebration of the major festivals to the major temples where Pramukh Swami is in attendance. At such festivals there is a ritual conjunction of sacred person, sacred time, and sacred space. The birthday of Swaminarayan is assigned to Amdavad, Gurupurnima to Bochasan, the birthday of Krishna to Atladara in Baroda, and the Jalzilani to Sarangpur. Thus, the movement of the pilgrims through the sacred calendar takes them around the sacred places associated with the life of Swaminarayan. The travel plans of Pramukh Swami are made so that he is present at these temples during the festivals. Thousands of devotees gather on these occasions from all over Gujarat and from abroad to spend the festival time in the sacred space of the temples in the presence of the sacred person whom they believe to be the manifestation of the divine abode of god. The union of these three – sacred person, sacred space, and sacred time – makes participation in the festival a powerful experience in the lives of the devotees.

Pilgrimages are a unifying activity for all of India. It could be argued that in pre-modern times the practice of sacred pilgrimage – an erstwhile tourism – was one of the major forces for preserving what cultural identity and bond of unity existed. Certainly the practice of pilgrimage throughout Gujarat helps to unite all devotees of each sect into a more unified group. The success of the Akshar Purushottam Sanstha in moving the festivals around to the various areas of Gujarat and giving them focus through the presence of Pramukh Swami reinforces a greater centralization of power and stronger sense of unity in this group than seems to be experienced in many other Hindu sects.

Members of different religious groups inhabit different sacred worlds. Members of the sect set apart different persons as holy and sacred, perhaps judged by different criteria, they visit different shrines, and they follow different sacred calendars. We have seen that the sacred worlds may overlap, as when followers of Swaminarayan observe with other Hindus the birth of Krishna or Diwali or when members of the two schools celebrate the birth of Swaminarayan. Still, members of a religious group share with one another a sacred world which provides them with a frame of reference, discourse, and communication. They inhabit the same world at a level more fundamental than the profane world, and this is what unites them into one fellowship.

CHAPTER FIVE

Dharma: the disciplined life

Bhaktimata and Dharmadeva are the names given to the mother and father of Swaminarayan. The mother represents the devotion and worship (bhakti) that is the heart of the religion, and the father represents the discipline of moral conduct (dharma) that gives it shape. Images of Bhaktimata and Dharmadeva stand together in the shrines of the temples as symbols to devotees of the necessary harmonious union of intense love for god and religious discipline.

The devotion of love for god in complete surrender to him has been the heart of the religion. Krishna gave the central injunction in the *Bhagavad Gita*: "Abandoning all other duties, come to me as thy sole refuge; from all evil I shall rescue; be not grieved" (18:66). Swaminarayan prescribed acts of public and private devotion for his followers which include singing devotional songs, serving the images in the temple, prostrating themselves before the images of god, listening to religious discourses, and mental worship in the form of remembering god. The poet saints among his companions sang of the joys of following the devotional path. The sect is firmly a part of the bhakti movement in Hinduism. Swaminarayan warned, however, against the dangers inherent in those forms of devotion that permitted or even encouraged a lack of discipline. He attacked the erotic imagery and symbolic acts associated with some debased forms of Krishna worship. Moreover, he attacked those who believed that their intense devotion to god raised them above the constraints of ordinary morality. He taught that it is impossible for a true worshiper to be immoral and indicated that one who cannot walk upright on the level plane will not be able to climb the steep mountain of true devotion. Thus, devotion is wedded to the discipline of moral conduct.

The emphasis on discipline rather than the merely devotional aspects of the religion brought the new teaching to the attention of British observers. Although Bishop Heber and others were not persuaded by the philosophy and theology, they commented favorably on the reformation of character and conduct inspired in devotees. Few of the ethical injunctions were new; most were derived from the ethical manuals and law codes that make up the *dharmashastras* of traditional Hinduism. The novelty and power appeared in the ability of Swaminarayan and his followers to inspire a mass movement which attracted to the ancient disciplines persons, many from the lower classes, who had not previously been observant. He formed them into a modern sect in which the disciplined life was warmed by the fires of devotion. Swaminarayan was an example of the "world renouncers" whom Louis Dumont calls the "creators of value" in Hinduism. The unique position of Swaminarayan as renouncer gave him the license to put everything into question, to revise elements of the discipline, and to become the founder of a new sect (Dumont 1970: 46).

The moral code in the Swaminarayan religion is status-specific: some rules are applicable broadly to all members of the fellowship, but many duties are different according to place, time, age, and social and economic position. Thus, the *Shikshapatri* contains rules for conduct for the various classes of persons – householders and ascetics, men and women, Brahmins and Harijans, married women and widows – all according to their station (120). The rules are adapted to the circumstances of each group.

Swaminarayan replaced the four stages of traditional Hindu life in which a man was successively student, householder, retired, and ascetic with the two patterns of the disciplined life, the ascetic (*nivrtti*) and the householder (*pravrtti*). Thus, as in other modern sects of Hinduism, a devotee normally does not move through the four stages, but selects in accordance with his natural inclinations the path of the householder, who conducts the affairs of family life and business, or the path of the ascetic, who renounces the world. Whether one becomes a householder or an ascetic is less significant than that one follows carefully the discipline of the path of his choice. Both the householder and the ascetic are able to attain the goal of redemption through devotion and discipline. Both are waging the battle to overcome the same enemies and to reach the same goal. As one ascetic explained, "The ascetic fights against temptation and vice from behind the barricades erected as a part of renunciation; the householder must fight the same battle from an exposed position."

THE ASCETICS

Swaminarayan initiated men to be sadhus, reformed the institution of asceticism which had fallen into some disrepute, and established the rules for the order. Thus far we have discussed the role of ascetics as religious specialists, sacred persons, administrators, and teachers. The primary goal of the ascetic, however, is to attain salvation by following a discipline of renunciation of the world. Swaminarayan left guidance for the ascetics of various classes in the last section of the *Shikshapatri* (175–202). He described the path of renunciation in that section of the *Satsangijivan* known as the *Dharmamrit* under the five basic vows of the ascetic: (1) absolute celibacy and the avoidance of women; (2) separation from family relationships; (3) detachment from sense objects, especially those of taste; (4) non-avarice and holy poverty; and (5) restraint of the pride of ego. The ascetic discipline of the world renouncer as described in the *Dharmamrit* in the Swaminarayan religion can be summarized under these five vows.

The vow of celibacy

The first vow requires absolute celibacy and the avoidance of women. An ascetic walking down a village lane keeps his eyes downcast, and at the approach of a woman tries to maintain a safe distance of twelve to fifteen feet from this threat to his celibacy. If the woman is a member and the lane narrow, she will face the wall and cover her face with the end of her sari to achieve the invisibility that will assist the ascetic to maintain his discipline. Swaminarayan ascetics strive for a celibacy that is both physical and mental; they avoid sexual contacts and they attempt to avoid lust. Their celibacy is hedged around by many regulations concerning separation from women and from any other objects of sexual desire.

During his period of spiritual vagrancy Sahajanand Swami followed the rules of strict celibacy, which he internalized as an abhorrence of women as objects of sexual desire. The disciples of Ramanand Swami reported with approval that at his arrival in Loj his celibacy was so pure that he became ill whenever a shadow of a woman fell upon him. One of his first acts when he became leader of that group of ascetics was to forbid even the most minor contact between the ascetics and women. Later in his career, even after his leadership in the religion required some associations with women, he established rules to protect the celibacy of his disciples. Eight major restrictions are named which effectively remove women from the conscious world of the ascetic. These eight outline the ideal of self-control and strict physical and mental separation from women which even the most zealous ascetics say is very difficult to maintain.

(1) The ascetics do not look at any part of a woman's body. Therefore, even though the ascetics live in active temples in the cities and travel to villages to teach, they avoid eye contact with women. They say that even in the temple, where one is aware that women are present, some awareness is necessary in order to avoid contact – but direct gazing at a woman is to be avoided. It is especially dangerous to look at the eyes, breasts, navel, or genitals of a woman, so ascetics must avoid any place such as a bathing area or dressing room where that may be possible. Women devotees are instructed to assist the ascetics and other men by separating themselves and dressing modestly at all times. Ascetics are forbidden to look at or touch a picture or a statue of a woman. The magazines in the library of the temple are censored so that no representation of a woman remains to tempt. One exception to this regulation is the representation of the goddess. Sadhus care for the pictures and images of the goddesses in the temples. Otherwise an ascetic may touch a woman only in life-threatening circumstances for the purpose of saving a life.

(2) Ascetics do not talk to women even for the purpose of teaching religion. Verbal intercourse may create attachments which lead to sexual intercourse, so it must be avoided. They cannot engage in conversation with women, send or receive a message, or even communicate over the telephone. Women attend meetings where ascetics lecture and preach, and even though the women sit at the back or over to the side, they pay close attention to the lectures. The ascetics, however, consciously lecture only to the men. They are taught that it is a failure of mental discipline if they speak or lecture to men with the intention to instruct or impress the women who may be present. Under no circumstances will an ascetic receive instruction from a woman. Women do not lecture or speak in meetings where ascetics are present.

(3) The regulations forbid ascetics to sit on the same mat with a woman. This simple rule from two centuries ago is variously applied today. For example, one legalist asked if an ascetic is permitted to enter an airplane that has carpet covering the passenger area. Once the first-class compartment was reserved for ascetics, but that created a stir of negative publicity. It was decided that such carpeting is not "the same mat" for the purposes of this regulation. Women remain in a separate room when ascetics visit the homes of householders. Ascetics do not ride in a car with women, though some accommodation is made when they travel in large commercial vehicles. At public meetings they sit on a platform not contiguous with the area set aside for women and oriented so that they do not directly face women.

(4) Sadhus live apart from women, eunuchs, and animals. The residence for male ascetics in the temple is remote from the haveli where women ascetics reside and from the dharmashalas for pilgrims. Women are not permitted to enter the area reserved for ascetics. When ascetics enter a room recently occupied by a woman, they purify the area by sprinkling water over the floor. Clothes, utensils, and even ritual objects, such as the *Shalagrama* stone representative of the deity, that have been used by women are not used by ascetics. Sadhus are instructed to have nothing to do with men who dress in the apparel of women. The sacred scriptures contain prohibitions of homosexual activity, masturbation, and any form of sexual contact with animals. Stories exist about disciples of Swaminarayan who went so far as to make themselves eunuchs so their parents would give permission for them to take initiation. While the stories contain an element of praise for their devotion, the act of self-mutilation is forbidden. Ascetics must overcome sexual desire by mental discipline.

(5) Ascetics remove themselves so far as is possible from all forms of sexuality. They are warned not to go near couples while they engage in sexual intercourse even if there is a partition separating the ascetic from the couple. They do not observe married couples and do not participate in any religious rituals such as marriages or sacrifices (yajnas) which require the participation of husband and wife. They do not watch animals in the act of mating. Secular dramas, movies, and many forms of secular literature are avoided because these may cause the ascetic to concentrate on women and sexuality.

(6) Because the primary human sex organ is the brain, ascetics must avoid thinking about or creating mental images of women. They try to avoid recalling previous experiences of sexual activity. They must undergo a prescribed penance even if involuntarily they have a dream in which women or any sexual activity appear.

(7 and 8) In short, the ascetic avoids all those activities and situations that could lead to sexual arousal. Swaminarayan prohibited those things which were thought in his time to excite the passions. Therefore, ascetics do not take hot baths, and they do not allow their bodies to be pampered with oil massages. They avoid those foods which they believe arouse the passions.

The goal is to control the body and the mind to such an extent that there will no longer be any sexual desire. Wisdom in this matter consists in realizing that "the woman who attracts attention is made up of bones, blood vessels, spittle, blood, mucus and feces; she is simply a collection of these things, and there is nothing to be attractive" (*Dharmamrit*, 2). They believe that the correct understanding of the nature of woman that results in overcoming sexual desire is a major step toward that understanding of the true nature of reality that leads to the renunciation of the world.

Vow to renounce family ties

The second vow of the sadhu is to sever all ties to his family. On the evening before the young man is initiated he meets his parents and siblings for the last time as a son and brother. A special poignancy exists in the farewell of the mother and sisters because never again will they be able to communicate with their loved one. Thereafter the mother's eyes and thoughts follow her son with a special intensity and pride, but he cannot respond. Because of the nature of this separation, the parents must give their written permission before the young man may be initiated. It is rare that permission is given to the eldest or to the only son.

Renunciation of family ties involves cutting himself off from all social status resulting from birth and from past achievements in the family. Ritually the old man dies and the new individual appears freed from previous social constraints. This new status is signified by a new name. In the new status the ascetic will never return home, talk with or about his parents, accept gifts from relatives, or even refer to his accomplishments prior to initiation. Members of the sect speak with pride about the wealth and educational or professional achievements of those who become ascetics, but the ascetic does not refer to his past life. He is instructed to have the same concern for his natural parents that he has for his parents in previous births. The only relaxation of the rule is that he takes a ritual bath for purification when he receives word that one of his parents has died. Leaders explain that Swaminarayan gave rules to insure strict separation from relatives because family ties are among the strongest of human attachments and thereby men are ensnared in many worldly concerns.

Vow to renounce attachment to objects of the senses

The third vow is to subdue the sense of taste and the attachment to the objects of the senses. According to the psychology taught in the sect the five senses enmesh the individual in the world of flux (maya), so one who renounces the world must control all the senses. Thus, regulations require him to avoid the sweet smell of perfume or the comfort of a soft bed. But sex and food are subjects of the most careful regulation, perhaps because they are so central to life, one to the creation of life and the other to its sustenance. The intake of food is as carefully regulated as contact with women. Regulations regarding eating are thought to aid the ascetic in overcoming the desire for good-tasting food.

The sadhu carries a wooden bowl from which he eats the main meal of the day. Before eating he mixes the food items in the bowl and pours water over them to produce an unappetizing mush. The aim is to make the food unpalatable so that he will not form any attachment to the taste. He eats to provide nourishment, not to enjoy the taste; he eats to live and does not live to eat. In the early days of the satsang the ascetics had to beg for food and prepare it themselves; frequently they went without. Now ample provision is made for the ascetics of the sect. They undertake largely ceremonial begging rounds on only one day of the year.

Ascetics follow the restrictions based on the proposition, "pure food promotes purity of mind and conduct." Meat and meat products require the killing of animals and are very polluting. Some fruits and vegetables, such as onions and garlic, are avoided by ascetics because they are thought to excite the passions. Food prepared from milk, curds, and coconut milk is pure, and ascetics may eat such food from metal plates in the company of householders. Food prepared with water – rice, dal, and chapattis – must be mixed and eaten from the wooden bowl while ascetics are separated from householders. All food for the ascetic must be ritually pure so that it may be offered to god before the meal. All the ascetic's food is thus sacred food (prasada).

Fasting is a part of the discipline. Ascetics regularly fast on five days of the month – the two Ekadashi days which are the eleventh day of the bright and dark halves of the lunar month, new moon day, full moon day and the birthday of Swaminarayan on the ninth day of the bright half. They observe a full fast from the time of the evening meal until after morning worship of the second day. No food or water is taken, and the total fast is an arduous discipline in the Indian heat. If conditions make it necessary, they can perform the morning worship just after midnight and take water. The sick and the elderly are exempt from fasting. Some ascetics accept a voluntary personal discipline of additional fasts, either total or partial, on other days of the month. Because food and water are necessary for the sustenance of the body in the world, the careful restriction of intake is both the means and the sign of renunciation of the world.

A fast is also the primary form of penance, and those who are guilty of impure thoughts and conduct undertake fasts in addition to the five regular fast days. The penitential texts prescribe several types of fasts for misconduct. One fast requires a diet restricted to crushed grain mixed with warm water. The *dharana-parana* fast involves a day of full fast alternating over a prescribed period with a second day when food is taken. In the *chandrayana* fast the intake of food is regulated by the phases of the moon. During the bright half of the month food is increased from one morsel the first day to fifteen, and during the dark half the amount is decreased to the day of full fast. The *padakruchcha* fast follows a four-day schedule in which one meal is eaten the first day, a light meal is eaten before sunset on the second day, food is eaten on the third day only if it is offered without the asking, and a total fast is observed on the fourth day. The *taptakruchcha* fast is the most strenuous – three spoons of water each day for three days, three of warm milk for three days, one of warm milk for three days, one of ghee for three days, and full fast for three days. This fast is prescribed as penance for a homosexual act or sexual contact with an animal. Penance may include rituals of chanting, silence, or reading of sacred texts. The personal guru or other prominent ascetic prescribes the appropriate penance for each sinful act so that the punishment fits both the sin and the sinner. Expulsion is the ultimate punishment for an ascetic who refuses to undergo the prescribed penance. After the ascetic undergoes the penance, however, he is fully accepted by his comrades, and they may never again refer to his lapse. After penance he is as pure as the others.

Vow of poverty

The fourth vow is a holy poverty. Swaminarayan sadhus live a discipline of holy poverty meant to protect them from greed and avarice. Attachment to money and material possessions is viewed as a great hindrance to spiritual development. A variation of an ancient story is used to illustrate the danger. A demon was seeking a place to stay, and a wise man suggested four residences for the demon: a casino, a slaughterhouse, a place of prostitution, and a liquor store. When the demon said that he could not be in four places at once, the wise man gave him a piece of gold and said: "Take up residence in money and you will find all four along with enmity." Therefore, it is said, ascetics do not acquire possessions beyond the bare necessities.

Many sadhus follow a discipline of refusing to touch money. A layman accompanies the ascetics to receive or disperse any funds. A lay business manager administers the financial affairs in the temples of the Akshar Purushottam Sanstha, but he works under the direction of a leading ascetic of the temple. In some temples of the Ahmedabad and Vadtal dioceses the mahants handle money and give a small stipend each month to the ascetics. Critics view this as a serious breach of the discipline and a sign of serious worldly attachments. An anomaly exists in the combination of the power of some ascetics to control the assets of large institutions with the ideal of personal poverty.

Legitimate personal possessions are those alone which are necessary for the ascetic to dress modestly, to eat, to worship, and to study. His clothing consists of two dhotis to wrap around the lower body, two shoulder cloths, two undercloths to cover the genitals, one shawl, one turban, one cloth to filter water, and a cloth for bedding. He must not covet expensive new, fine, gaudily colored or decorated clothing. Eating requires a wooden bowl and a wooden water pot. He carries with him the accessories appropriate for worship, which include a puja cloth, pictures of the gods, kumkum and sandalwood-paste powder, a U-shaped wire for making the tilak mark on the forehead, and a copy of the *Shikshapatri*. Because the sadhu is expected to study the sacred scriptures, he possesses other books, writing paper, and pens. He stores these items in a small open cubicle in the temple or carries them from place to place wrapped in a single dhoti cloth. If he acquires and enjoys any other possessions, he is required to undergo penance.

Even though the religious institution is presently very wealthy, the ascetics are expected to conduct their daily affairs with a disregard for material possessions and luxuries. Unless they are ill or infirm, they sleep on the floor covered with a piece of cloth. They ride in whatever conveyance is offered or they walk. They eat the food donated by the devotees if it is pure. They cultivate the attitude that a piece of gold and a lump of clay are the same, becoming immune to the luxuries of wealth or the deprivations of poverty. One said that his goal is to "collect my inner self as much as possible and renounce everything else." While the sadhu concentrates on mental renunciation, the institution has a legal and moral responsibility to provide for the ascetics, and in a poor land the ascetics are assured of food, clothing, and lodging, however humble. Though many renounce the opportunity for prosperity and comfort, critics note that for young men of meager means, little education, and dim prospects, life in holy poverty can be relatively comfortable.

Vow to overcome ego

Ascetics wrestle with the temptations of concupiscence, rapacity, and worldliness, but the fifth vow requires a battle against the last and most difficult sin, the pride of ego. Worldly greatness, whether of wealth, fame, or spiritual attainments, can bring much misery. Therefore, the ascetic is taught to beware when he thinks that he is attaining greatness. Swaminarayan told the story of a man who began to perform great austerities. A cat came and sat in front of him, and after several days the cat became sleek and fat. The ascetic asked: "How is it that you are becoming fat even though you are also fasting?" The cat replied, "I am your pride; your body has been reduced by your austerities, but your pride has grown." He warned that too humble is half proud.

Swaminarayan taught that pride caused by attachment to ego is the source of many sins. Jealousy results so that the ascetic believes that he is superior to others. Hence, he engages in futile arguments with his colleagues, he fails to show proper respect to senior ascetics, and he haughtily refuses to engage in humble acts of service to other devotees. Anger is a sign that the ego has not been controlled and the anger leads to violence against other men, animals, and living things. Pride makes it impossible for the ascetics to accept with calmness the insults, abuse, and injuries they often receive. Swaminarayan prohibited retaliation (*Shikshapatri*, 201), and indicated that anger and violence can be removed only when overweening pride is subdued. He noticed that pride leads some ascetics to abandon their basic duties on the pretext that they have attained the state of liberation. Therefore, he made obedience to the rules incumbent on all ascetics.

Humility is demonstrated by obedience and by acts of service to the devotees. Although a vow of obedience is not a formal part of the ritual of initiation, the novice expects to obey the commands of his spiritual adviser. Sections of the *Dharmamrit* indicate that vows are to be undertaken with the aid of a perfect devotee. Sadhus of the Akshar Purushottam Sanstha obey the directions of Pramukh Swami. The assigned tasks of the ascetics include the meanest tasks of cooking and cleaning along with the more exalted tasks of the temple priest, scholar, and administrator. Now, as in the days of Swaminarayan, some ascetics engage in hard manual work on construction and relief projects. The suffix for the name of every ascetic is "das," which means "servant," and the ascetic is expected to perform humbly whatever tasks are assigned. Swaminarayan taught that in the past the great saints attained high spiritual status only when they overcame pride, offered their humble service to others, and led the simple life. These remain the ideals of the ascetic life.

Paradoxically the sadhus of the Swaminarayan religion are praised by Gujaratis for renouncing things highly valued in Gujarati society. In a way they provide the mirror image of that society. Couples yearn for children, and family ties in Gujarat are strong and deep. Yet young men renounce family responsibilities to parents and to future generations. Gujarati cuisine is a point of pride, and guests are served a variety of tasty dishes even in the temples. Justified pride is demonstrated by the care with which the food offered to the deities is prepared, even on days of total fast for the ascetics. Yet ascetics destroy the taste before they eat. Likewise, industry and success in business and financial affairs are praised, but the ascetics renounce all possessions. The sacred person renounces those things which are highly valued in the society, even by devotees.

The surprise is that those who have renounced the world and are thus dead to society are the teachers and counselors of those in the world. Laymen take problems and decisions about family and business affairs to their spiritual advisers among the ascetics. Pramukh Swami spends much of his time giving advice to devotees about matters with which as an ascetic he can have no direct contact, for example, business contracts and investments, marriage arrangements, and procreation and the naming of children. The ascetic's position outside society confers the authority and duty to give instructions on how to live in the world. (See Williams 1985.) While scorn and blame are directed against those ascetics who are lax in conduct with women, lazy, venal, and proud, great honor and personal loyalty are given to those known for chastity, poverty, piety, and humility. Though all devotees stress their primary allegiance to Swaminarayan, many prosperous and successful laymen indicate that they were drawn to the Swaminarayan religion by the simplicity, piety, and chastity of the ascetics. They call them "saints." Dumont catches a fundamental dynamic of the Swaminarayan religion with his comment, "the secret of Hinduism may be found in the dialogue between the renouncer and the man in the world" (1970: 37).

HOUSEHOLDERS

Initiation as a lay member of the sect does not require renunciation of the world. The ritual of initiation is simple. One chants the formula, "I give over to Swaminarayan my mind, body, wealth and the sins of previous births." Then water is poured over the right hand and the Swaminarayan mantra is repeated. The novice enters the path of discipline as a householder by taking the five primary vows: not to eat meat, not to take intoxicants, not to commit adultery, not to steal, and not to defile oneself or others. The five vows provide the categories for the summary of the teachings meant to help the householder live a disciplined life in the world.

The first vow begins with the simple prohibition of eating meat and leads to the active practice of non-violence (ahimsa). Devotees give several arguments for strict vegetarianism. Eating meat or eggs involves killing and the destruction of life. Meat is therefore the grossest kind of food and, because the types of food are related to mental states and modes of action, eating meat leads to acts of passion and violence. Vegetarianism promotes the passivity in life that leads to good conduct. Moreover, vegetarianism is recommended as healthful. All Swaminarayan devotees are vegetarians, along with the Jains and most other Vaishnavas of Gujarat, and view the practice as essential for a peaceful way of life.

During Swaminarayan's life some Hindu sects and some lower castes worshiped deities who demanded animal sacrifices. He prohibited his followers from participating in such rituals, from worshiping deities associated with animal sacrifice, and from eating meat even if offered to the gods. He instituted bloodless sacrifices on a large scale, which, he argued, was the correct form of the ancient Vedic sacrifices. By means of such changes in diet and ritual he separated his lower-caste followers from some of the defiling practices of their castes.

The command, "Thou shalt not kill," is taken seriously by devotees. Murder or injury to another living being is a serious sin. Members do not go to the extent that some Jains do in wearing masks, avoiding agriculture, and sweeping insects from the path, but they do avoid violence and murder. They are warned against threatening injury to another person, even with a blade of grass. The prohibition extends to oneself, and suicide and self-mutilation of any kind are strictly forbidden; they are himsa. The prohibition of murder becomes a command to care for other living things. Devotees are permitted to keep cattle and other farm animals, but only if they can provide for them adequately.

Swaminarayan taught that non-violence issues from a calm mind. Devotees are therefore to avoid the anger and hatred that give rise to violence. They are not to exercise undue force on another person even to attain a good end. One leader said that they must not criticize or ridicule another man's religion or convert that person to the Swaminarayan religion by external force, even by force of words, because that would be a form of violence. Implied here is a criticism of the activities of missionaries of other religions, but it is mild and indirect criticism. Non-violence was a central part of the Jain teaching which was widespread in Gujarat even during Sahajanand's time. A century after the beginning of the Swaminarayan religion, Mahatma Gandhi began his movement in India with a program of non-violence among the mill workers in Ahmedabad (now called Amdavad).

The second vow of the householder is to avoid all intoxicating drinks and drugs. Gujarat was a source of opium for the British trade with the Far East, and Swaminarayan spoke against the use of opium and other drugs. Opium and alcohol continue to be problems in the state, even though it was for a long time a dry state because of the influence of Gandhi. Members of the Swaminarayan religion along with the Gandhians support a strict prohibition. A common activity for ascetics and youths of the movement is to conduct anti-addiction drives. Much of the preaching in the villages includes a call to give up drugs and alcohol, which waste meager resources and bring hardships and destitution to the families of the villages. Even when ill and in the hospital, devotees avoid prescription medicines that are addicting. The use of tobacco is also prohibited. Ascetics and some devout members also avoid the use of coffee and tea, even though both drinks are prepared and served in the temples. Devotees do not participate in any religious rituals in which intoxicants are used, and they deny the popular idea that drugs are aids in attaining truth and union with god. Indeed, they argue that drug-induced states are a form of slavery that makes service to god impossible. Only with a clear and free mind, they say, can anyone focus attention on god and live a disciplined life.

The ascetic vow of celibacy has its complement for householders in the third vow, not to commit adultery. Lest there be any temptation, sexual contacts are greatly restricted. Men and women are separated in the meetings and in the temples. Both men and women are expected to dress and conduct themselves modestly so as not to attract the attention of members of the opposite sex. The ribald and immodest behavior of the rituals of reversal associated with the Holi festival are forbidden; Swaminarayan replaced the risqué songs of Holi and marriage songs with devotional hymns. Men avoid conversation with widows and women outside their families. Indeed, a man is not to be alone in a room with a woman other than his wife, not even with a daughter. He is warned not to seek the company of other men's wives, and he is encouraged to view every woman as an elderly woman without sexual attractiveness. Householders who assist with the administration of women's activities of the sanstha are instructed never to meet with women alone. Even within marriage there are restrictions aimed at keeping the sexual urge under control. A devotee and his wife do not engage in sexual activity when she is ritually impure or during the religious festivals of Ekadashi, new moon day, or Swaminarayan's birthday. Marriage is one of the structures of society for the good of man and the protection of woman; thus the institution is protected by regulations associated with the prohibition of adultery.

The ascetic vow of poverty becomes for householders the fourth vow to respect the personal and property rights of others. Theft is a sin. Nothing, not even a flower to decorate the image of god, is to be taken without the permission of the owner. The prohibition of theft is elaborated in the sacred texts to include dishonesty in business affairs. Armed bands of thieves terrorized the countryside during the ministry of Swaminarayan and caused major disruption of the social order, as Bishop Heber and Governor Malcolm testified. The literature of the sect contains many stories of the conversion and transformation of these brigands which are told in the meetings to inspire hearers to stop stealing and to encourage personal honesty. Members explain that as satsangis they share Gandhi's commitment to truth-telling. The rules prohibit the utterance of an untruth or false accusation. Moreover, the devotee must not tell the truth if doing so will bring harm to another person. The vows not to eat meat, not to drink intoxicants, not to commit adultery, and not to steal, along with the elaborations, are similar to the vows taken by Jain laymen (Jaini 1979: 166–78). Reference is not made in Swaminarayan literature to Jain influence, however, because Jain teachers are considered to be non-theists.

The first four vows have remained relatively constant in force and interpretation, but the fifth vow has undergone some reinterpretation. The original form was a vow not to take food or water from any person from a lower caste. The rule is: "Except at Jagannathpuri you shall not eat or drink anything served by a person unacceptable according to caste regulations, even if it is food that has been offered to Krishna" (*Shikshapatri*, 19). The application of the explicit regulation of intercaste dining is a part of the adjustment of the discipline of the sect to the realities of modern caste association, which are discussed below. Now the wording of the vow is often broadened to say that the devotee will never defile himself or others. In addition to rules about commensality, other rules of purity are given. The traditional requirement of a ritual bath before morning worship is extended to include personal cleanliness. An ascetic preaching to a group of farmers in a remote village said that Sahajanand Swami indicated that if he was not successful in getting people to cleanse the outside of the body, there was little hope of inspiring inner purity.

Rules of personal cleanliness, about the disposal of human waste, and about avoiding contaminated water lead to improved public sanitation as well as to ritual purity. Devotees drink only filtered water and milk; therefore, a filter cloth is required for both laymen and ascetics. In some modern kitchens in Britain and the United States a filter cloth is tied over the faucets to satisfy this regulation of ritual purity. Regulations regarding ceremonial impurity resulting from birth and death in the family and menstruation restrict association with other devotees or visits to the temple during those periods.

Eleven basic rules of moral conduct for all householders appear in the literature of the sect: (1) Never kill any living creature or insect; (2) Never seek the company of another man's wife; (3) Never eat meat; (4) Never drink liquor or touch intoxicants; (5) Never touch a widow; (6) Never steal; (7) Never make a false allegation about anyone; (8) Do not commit suicide; (9) Never slander god; (10) Never accept food or water from an unworthy person; (11) Never listen to religious discourses by an atheist or immoral person. Special regulations of the *Shikshapatri* apply to the acharyas and restrict their contact with women who are not close relatives (123–56). Rulers are instructed to treat their subjects as members of their family and to support correct religious practices in their realm (157–8). Issues regarding norms of correct conduct which are not addressed in the *Shikshapatri* or other writings of Swaminarayan are decided by reference to the *Yajnavalkya Smriti* (96).

Four goals for life are established in the ancient Hindu texts. Swaminarayan indicated that these goals are reached by following the discipline he prescribed: "Our followers, both men and women who act according to these directions, shall certainly obtain the four great objects of human desire – the disciplined life (dharma), material gain (artha), pleasure (kama) and salvation (moksha)" (*Shikshapatri*, 205). The pursuit of material gain and pleasure are appropriate to the life of the householder, but the pursuit must be controlled by a moral discipline. Otherwise it would lead man to disaster and cause failure to attain salvation.

Thus, the regulations allow for, and even encourage, the acquisition and sober use of worldly possessions. Casual observers refer to the

Swaminarayan discipline as puritanical because it requires the segregation of the sexes, the avoidance of sexual misconduct, and the avoidance of all appearances of evil. As David Pocock indicates, however, the discipline is puritanical in the classical Weberian sense (1973: 141). The person who follows the precepts regarding honesty, sobriety, careful dealing in business, and avoidance of extravagant and conspicuous consumption becomes a responsible man of affairs. He works hard, lives simply, and shares his possessions prudently.

"A non-satsangi's vices and extravagant expenses equal the satsangi's livelihood." "Kusangina phela n satsangina rotala." This proverb is widely used by leaders to show that the moral transformation which comes through giving up drugs, alcohol, expensive meat, loose women, and idleness leads to economic and social improvement. One leader explained that this is one of the ways that Swaminarayan provides his followers with food, clothing, and shelter. Many devotees give testimonials to such self-improvement and indicate that one of the reasons persons become members is the perception that improved economic and social standing accompanies membership. Certainly many members in India and abroad have become successful businessmen and industrialists, and they invariably attribute this success to "the grace of Swaminarayan." The religious discipline in the *Shikshapatri* contains practical rules for the conduct of business affairs. The devotee must keep a daily account of income and expenses in record books which are blessed in the temple at the beginning of a new year (146). He must take care that expenses do not exceed income (145) and put back some of the profit in money and grain for a rainy day (141). Even in business dealings with kinsmen he is told to prepare a written contract and to have it signed in the presence of witnesses (143–4). He must pay his employees just wages as agreed upon (152) and provide for them generously (67). Each person is to do his assigned task with careful deliberation (66). The discipline encourages good order in business and financial affairs.

Devotees boast that followers of Swaminarayan have a reputation for honesty in business which attracts new business. Because they are hardworking and efficient and do not squander their profits, they invest capital in improvements and enlargements of their farms and businesses. Becoming a member of the sect also establishes valuable associations because there is a tendency to patronize the business of fellow members. Trade and commerce follow family, caste, and sect lines, and as sect ties become stronger they supersede to some degree the economic ties of caste.

Thus, in a religion that praises the world-renouncing ascetic, the acquisition of wealth and the prudent use of capital are justified and viewed as directly willed by god. Success is viewed as the result of his grace. Hence, the emphasis is upon the appropriate acquisition and use of worldly goods. Weber's thesis in *The Protestant Ethic and the Spirit of Capitalism* is supported by many aspects of the Swaminarayan religion, but devotees are not comfortable with the comparison because of the negative connotations of the word "capitalism." Some leaders prefer to emphasize the use of wealth for social welfare and refer to this as a type of socialism. They quote Swaminarayan: "Accumulation of wealth is a great danger; distribution of wealth is a blessing."

Charitable distribution of wealth and the use of time in works of social welfare are praised. Many devotees give a month of the year for activities of the sect. Traditional Gujarati hospitality toward guests and lifelong provision for parents and religious teachers are part of the religious discipline. Moreover, regulations of the sect demand that members give 10 percent of their income to religious and charitable trusts. If one is poor or in debt, he gives 5 percent. This requirement of a tithe is unique in Vaishnava Hinduism. The practice has developed in the Akshar Purushottam Sanstha of devout followers bringing a blank check to Pramukh Swami and asking him to decide what they should give. Wealthy members gain merit and status in the sect by making donations for the construction of temples and other projects of the charitable trusts associated with the Swaminarayan religion. Outsiders, and sometimes the relatives of members, remark that it can be very expensive to be an active member of the sect.

Only improperly might one conclude from the discipline of the world renouncers that they hold the world to be basically evil. The discipline of the householder shows that material existence is not the evil to be overcome, but one must overcome attachment to the things that will perish. Swaminarayan taught that the illusion of creation (maya) is not a source of misery for the true devotee because the householder does his duty to his family and companions with love, affection, a sense of duty, and respect, but without attachment to the results of his activity (*Vachanamritam*, Loya 1, 1). In this way the devotee is able to leave the world from within. Thus, a rich man can be saved. Indeed, life in the world is spoken of as a very great blessing because it is necessary to appear in material human form in order to gain release from the cycle of rebirth. Devotees often comment that at long last, after a cycle of rebirths, they are fortunate to have been born in circumstances that permit them to gain release by becoming devotees of Swaminarayan. They convey the message that this life is the golden opportunity that must not be squandered. Therefore, they devote themselves to Swaminarayan and live the disciplined life of a householder in order to gain release.

WOMEN

As has been said, the Swaminarayan moral code is status-specific and is adapted for persons in different social circumstances. Thus, while it undergirds aspects of social reform, it is based on social distinctions. The attempt is made to reform society without destroying the traditional social structures. Two fundamental social distinctions in Gujarat in the early nineteenth century were that between men and women and that between castes. Swaminarayan initiated reforms in both relationships without totally abolishing sex discrimination or caste differentiation. The interpretation and application of Swaminarayan's reforms raise two hotly debated issues of contemporary social ethics, the position of women in society and the role of caste.

Members are proud of the record of the Swaminarayan religion in the cause of the advancement of women, but are somewhat defensive about some of the practices which seem to restrict the freedom of women and make full equality of leadership impossible. It is ironic that reforms which were meant in one social context to protect women and to provide new opportunities are now criticized by some as insulting and unnecessarily restrictive in the contemporary context.

Swaminarayan taught in Gujarat at a time when women generally had a very low status. The position of women was not uniform in all sections of society because of economic and caste differences. Nevertheless, the unsettled political and social situation made security for the strong precarious and for unprotected women almost nonexistent. Wives and adolescent daughters were relegated to the women's apartments. Formal education was not available. In 1823 not a single female student was in the indigenous schools in Bombay Presidency, and the first effort to establish a school for women was made in Ahmedabad only in 1849 (Desai 1978: 332). Thus, apologists claim that the Swaminarayan religion was progressive in its advocacy of women's rights at a time of harsh discrimination.

Widow suicide and female infanticide were social crimes of the era directed against women, and Swaminarayan joined in efforts to eradicate these evils. These efforts culminated in the Sati Act of 1829, the

15 Image of Lakshmi

Hindu Widow Remarriage Act of 1850, and the Infanticide Act of 1870. Swaminarayan prohibited widow suicide. He encouraged young widows who could not follow the path of chastity to remarry. For other widows he gave regulations for conduct that now seem restrictive, but which nevertheless permitted them a respected and secure place in the social order (*Shikshapatri*, 163–74). The establishment of the group of sankhya yoginis provided the opportunity for socially approved activities for women willing to take the strict vows.

One cause of female infanticide was the great expense involved in arranging marriage for daughters. Some families avoided this threat to the economic security of the family by drowning infant girls in containers of milk. Barbara Miller provides contemporary data to support the hypothesis that when dowry and the overall costs of marriage for daughters are significant, the survival rates of girls will suffer (1980: 95–129). One study made in Kathiawar in 1841 by the Political Secretary, Mr. J. P. Willoughby, shows that the numbers of surviving girls relative to boys grew from a deficit of 159 in 1831–2 to an excess of 32 in 1840–1 (Panigrahi 1976: 66). Swaminarayan prohibited the murder of infant daughters. Moreover, although he did not attempt to abolish the dowry system among followers, he did indicate that he would pay the dowry for families who could not afford to arrange a marriage for a daughter. It is safe to conclude that in the area of Kathiawar and Kutch the teaching of Swaminarayan and British political pressure were effective in the significant reduction of female infanticide.

Rules that enforce separation of the sexes have the manifest function of protecting both men and women from sensual temptation, but leaders explain that the more important latent function is to protect women from exploitation by men. Thus, the regulation that ascetics must avoid contact with women functions to protect women from the unscrupulous use of religious authority. The prohibition of concubinage, prostitution, and adultery strengthens family ties, which provide the main security for women. The argument is advanced that the discipline for the householder makes him a good husband and father and results in improved economic and social security for the women members of the family.

One result of Swaminarayan's regulations is that women conduct their own affairs in the sect. Women have separate temples and meeting halls, and although they "sit in" on the meetings conducted by male ascetics and householders, they also have separate rituals and meetings conducted by and for women. Men are excluded. The acharyas' wives and the samkhya yogini act as religious specialists to initiate and instruct women members. Lay women are increasingly taking positions of leadership in the women's organizations. Women gain experience and leadership skills in public speaking, administration, and teaching through participation in the programs of the women's centers. They organize centers, give lectures, help plan major religious festivals where there are special congregations of women, and publish magazines and journals for women. In 1999 Pramukh Swami dedicated a new office building in the Ahmedabad temple complex as the international headquarters for the extensive programs, festivals, volunteer activities, and publications of the women's wing. Apologists argue that at a time when women were oppressed in Gujarat, membership in the Swaminarayan religion provided significant opportunities for women. They claim that all women, not just those who are devotees, have benefitted from the reforms instituted by Swaminarayan.

Young women now in the group have taken advantage of modern secular education, and some have advanced degrees. They have entered the work force and the professions. Their newly developed skills are being used in the women's work of the sect. Especially in the Akshar Purushottam Sanstha, leaders from this group are gradually replacing the female religious specialists of the traditional pattern, and they provide the role models for the young girls of the next generation.

Women devotees often make the remark that the women are stronger devotees and more faithful than the men. Some mild resentment is expressed over the restrictions, which seem to some to be archaic and unjust. No matter how advanced in learning and piety a woman may be, she cannot exercise authority over men. A woman cannot address an assembly where men are present or even sit on the platform with men. No women are trustees of the religious or charitable trusts, nor do they serve on the managing committees of the major temples. Thus, all the wealth and institutions are effectively under the control of men.

Women religious specialists do not have a status in the religion equal to that of the male leaders. The women are not permitted to approach the acharyas or the ascetic leaders for advice or instruction. While most accept the rationale that the prohibition is necessary to assist the ascetics to maintain their vows of chastity, some women resent not having equal access to prominent religious leaders. Pramukh Swami is respected by women of the Akshar Purushottam Sanstha as the abode of god, and they press as close as they dare for darshan. They do not, however, approach him for advice and instruction as the men do. When a woman has a serious problem which requires Pramukh Swami's attention, she asks a male relative to speak to him about it. One devout woman expressed her belief that women are so spiritually close to god that when one has a problem, Pramukh Swami knows about it and gives the appropriate advice in the course of his public lecture. Nevertheless, women receive what they consider to be the highest spiritual blessings only indirectly.

Some regulations seem to relegate women to an unavoidably inferior position. Concepts of pollution associated with the menstrual cycle lead to the exclusion of women from the temples and from daily worship for several days of the month. Women are protected, but are discouraged from being independent. Daughters are under the authority of their fathers; wives are supposed to serve their husbands in the manner in which they worship and serve god; and widows are to heed the instructions of their nearest male relatives. Boys and young men meet freely in the organizations for children and youth; girls have some study groups and hope after marriage to benefit from religious instruction outside the home in the women's groups. Some regulations regarding modesty, contact with men, and religious duties are parallel to the discipline of male householders, and apologists maintain that the separation is mutual and does not imply inferiority, but there is some justification for the feeling that women are separate and not equal in the sect.

It must be kept in mind that many of the champions of women's rights in India in the nineteenth and early twentieth centuries exercised personal celibacy. Rammohan Roy, Ramakrishna, and Swami Dayananda remained aloof from women. Mahatma Gandhi entered on a vow of chastity early in his marriage. In this respect Swaminarayan is an early representative of the practice of advocacy of women's rights without personal involvement with women. Arvind Sharma suggests, however, that following the rise of the feminist movement in India and among Gujarati immigrants in Western countries, many are inclined to question this practice altogether (1981: 25). The relative position of men and women in the sect remains one of the most serious problems to be faced by leaders as they plan for growth in the urban centers and abroad.

CASTE

Swaminarayan's teaching did not conform to the traditional vertical divisions of the span of human life into four stations (*ashrama dharma*); neither did he leave unchanged the horizontal caste divisions (*varna dharma*). Mr. Williamson, a political officer in Gujarat, reported to Bishop Heber that Swaminarayan had "destroyed the yoke of caste." An early follower of

Swaminarayan told Heber that even though members were from different castes, all were disciples of Swaminarayan and regarded each other as brothers. Heber followed up the point by asking Swaminarayan a question about caste "to which he answered that he did not regard the subject as of much importance, but that he wished not to give offence; that people might eat separately or together in this world, but that above '*oopur*,' pointing to heaven, those distinctions would cease, where we should be all '*ek ekhee eat*' [one like another]" (R. Heber 1846 ii: 111). This ambivalence about caste restrictions in the new sect is reflected in another early report: "People of all castes and persuasions resort to Swamee Narrain . . . Hindoos of all the four classes, Mahomedans, and even Dhers are admitted; but all are seated, and feed [*sic*], according to their castes. The Swamee himself (who is a Brahmin) eats indiscriminately with any caste as far down as Rajpoots, or Katees, but not below them" (n.a. 1823: 348). These early reports indicate a tension between traditional caste regulations and the ties of brotherhood in the new sect.

The tension still exists because the sect cuts across the caste lines of Gujarat and attracts followers from Brahmin, Bhavasar, Charan, Darji, Ghanchi, Gola, Kachhia, Kanbi, Kathi, Koli, Luhar, Mali, Rajput, Salat, Sathwara, Soni, and Sutar castes. Still, for purposes of marriage and commensality it is the caste that is the relevant unit and not the sect. The ties of sect loyalty are not strong enough to dissolve caste distinction completely. Indeed, as Louis Dumont concludes, "A sect cannot survive on Indian soil if it denies caste" (1970: 36). It is a truism that the religious sect in India that attempts to abolish caste becomes a caste. M. N. Srinivas is correct, however, in observing that the feeling of group loyalty and free association within the sect weakens the hold of caste (1953: 33f.). It is significant that obedience to caste regulations is contingent on the authority of the sect, and the leader of the sect who speaks with divine authority is able to change some of the traditional regulations. Thus, the Swaminarayan religion retains elements of caste regulation, but only within a theological exclusiveness which tends to reduce the importance of caste in the eyes of members.

The *Shikshapatri* reaffirms basic caste duties: "None of my followers shall violate the code of Varnashram Dharma and shall never accept any code of behavior other than that sanctioned by the scriptures" (24). Commensality is regulated by the vow not to take food or water from a person of a lower caste. Respect is given to Brahmins, and the sacred thread ceremony is performed by leaders of the sect. Devotees from low castes wear only the red mark on the forehead and not the full sect mark worn by upper-caste devotees. Although there are incidents of intercaste marriage in the urban areas of India, Swaminarayan devotees generally follow caste lines in arranging marriages even though the marriage partner may not be a member of the sect. In marriage, caste ties supersede sect ties.

Some caste distinctions remain in the organization of the ascetics, especially among those associated with the Ahmedabad and Vadtal dioceses. Brahmin ascetics wear distinctive clothing, live in a separate residence in the temple, and eat food prepared by Brahmin cooks in a separate kitchen. The men from lower Shudra castes wear white clothing, follow a relaxed discipline, and perform tasks in the temple appropriate to their caste status. Ascetics of the Akshar Purushottam Sanstha accept one type of food only from Brahmins or other ascetics and another type of food from members of other non-polluting castes, but refuse food cooked by persons from polluting castes.

Recently the Akshar Purushottam Sanstha has removed some of the caste distinctions among ascetics. Ascetics from all castes follow the same discipline and do identical work. They live and eat together in the temples. In 1981 Pramukh Swami decreed that ascetics from the Shudra castes are eligible to receive full initiation as sadhus, so there is now no caste barrier in initiation. Sadhus say that now they don't even know what caste their colleagues once were. Several young men from groups identified by the Baxi Commission as "scheduled classes and tribes" have been initiated since 1981, and a few were *Adivasis* from tribal groups that have attracted the attention of Swaminarayan preachers since the 1970s. The tribal area of Panch Mahal in South Gujarat has become an important center for Swaminarayan preaching and social welfare work, as part of the Hindutva movement popular in Gujarat in the 1990s attempting to counter the influence of other religions that serve Adivasis. These changes in the regulations regarding initiation and the conduct of the ascetics are justified as continuations of the social reforms begun by Swaminarayan.

Nevertheless, untouchability has not been completely removed. Leaders of both groups indicate that Harijans do not present themselves for initiation as ascetics. Some Harijans are devotees of Swaminarayan, and they have a temple for Untouchables at Chhani near Vadodara (previously called Baroda) where Harijans perform the rituals in the shrines. They do not enter the other temples because the regulations call for them to remain in the courtyard and show their respect by having darshan of the spires of the temple. On one occasion at Gadhada the temple officials constructed a platform in the courtyard level with the second-floor shrine area so Harijans could see the images from a distance. Harijans on occasion receive food from the temples, but they eat it in a separate place. Harijans who are followers obey the caste restrictions as part of their duty according to the ancient laws. The secular laws incorporated in the modern Temple Entry Act make it unlawful to restrict the entry of Harijans into any Hindu temple. Although there was initially some resistance to the Act by leaders of the Swaminarayan religion, temple managers now say with a shrug: "We cannot tell who are Harijans." Harijan devotees obey the religious laws; temple officials obey laws of the government in respect to Harijans who come to the temples for worship, food, and lodging.

Although not abolished, some relaxation of caste distinctions occurs in the sect. The theology of the sect maintains that social distinctions are transitory and of only limited significance. Swaminarayan taught: "The garment in the form of body is given to us as either from Brahmin parents or from other castes. Identifying this body with Atman and calling parents of the body father and mother is an indication of a misunderstanding. So long as one carries the ego of caste or stage of life, he does not attain saintliness" (*Vachanamritam*, Gadhada 1, 44). The belief that in akshardham all are one tends to weaken caste restrictions, at least within the satsang. Devotees associate freely in the temples and, with the exception of Harijans at the temples of the Vadtal and Ahmedabad dioceses, all eat at the communal meals. All receive the food offered to the images of god. Some intercaste associations occur in the temples and religious meetings that would not occur outside. A Brahmin college principal said that copy-room workers at the university press regularly engage him in discussions about affairs of the temple or about theology more or less as equals, even though they would never approach him on such familiar terms in the university context.

The preaching of the religion results in changing the conduct of some members of the lower castes with respect to meat-eating, personal and ritual cleanliness, and use of drugs and intoxicants, which traditionally have marked them in their low status. This opens the possibility of some personal upward mobility as the social and moral uplift praised in the sect includes the adoption of certain Sanskrit codes, which removes some of the visible bases of caste discrimination. There is a concerted effort to reform the conduct of Adivasis and members of other scheduled castes and tribes. M. N. Srinivas refers to this when he says that the Swaminarayan sect has contributed to the greater Sanskritization of the

Hindu population in Gujarat (1962b: 154). The Akshar Purushottam Sanstha is constructing a large temple in South Gujarat at Tithal in Valsad district near an Adivasi area where it has instituted significant social and religious activities. A reduction in the effects of caste distinction and untouchability may result. It is too early to judge the long-term effects of recent changes.

Mahatma Gandhi, a son of Gujarat a century after Swaminarayan, did not establish a religious sect, nor was he a member of any sect. Nevertheless, N. A. Toothi concludes that Gandhi was influenced more by the reforms and teaching of Swaminarayan than by any other (Toothi 1935: 279). Toothi may have overlooked the significant influence of the Jain community and teaching on both Swaminarayan and Gandhi (Jaini 1979: 311–15). Gandhi was more radical in his reform of untouchability than the founder or subsequent Swaminarayan leaders. But close parallels do exist in the programs of social reform based on non-violence, truth-telling, cleanliness, temperance, and the uplift of the masses. These elements of a program of social reform are joined with theism and religious fervor and devotion in the Swaminarayan religion. The ideal of renunciation of the world and a strict discipline for life in the world are combined with devotional fervor. Those who follow the discipline believe that at death they will go with Swaminarayan to his abode, a place of release from the imperfections of this world where there is perfect joy.

Devotees undertake the discipline as householders and as ascetics with individual moral seriousness. Birth in human form is thought to be a rare opportunity to gain release from the cycle of rebirths. The vision of Swaminarayan as a social reformer inspires activities of social service by individuals and by the institutions supported by the religious and charitable trusts. Young sadhus sitting in the temple courtyard in the cool of the evening were listening to advice from a retired writer who had been a follower of Gandhi. He urged them: "The times are changing. The government has failed in social reforms and in providing relief and direction for the people. If the religious people fail to lead, who will lead the people? If you cling to the old mythological ballast, you will fail. Swaminarayan was engaged in social reforms and worked for the uplift of the masses. The people are ready for that kind of change; they will listen to you. Go to the masses with a progressive program." If one could read the thoughts of the young ascetics as they listened, he could better predict the future of the Swaminarayan religion in Gujarat and among overseas Gujaratis.

CHAPTER SIX

The sacred thread: transmission of tradition

The sacred thread ceremony marks for the Hindu boy the time when he is ritually admitted to the study of the sacred heritage of his people. As part of the ceremony, the boy's preceptor "opens the books" and, if only symbolically, begins the instruction. Thereafter, the sacred thread worn over the shoulder is the sign that he is a member of the company of those who share the tradition. The thread is a fitting symbol. The heritage of a religious group is the sacred thread which binds the generations together; or rather, it is the rope of many threads which not only binds the generations together but constitutes the ongoing religious culture of a people.

The sacred thread represents the distinctively human capability to create and manipulate symbols in ways that enable humans to communicate complex messages across time and distance. The communication of such human symbols is essential in the formation and preservation of personal and group identities; indeed, essential in the socialization into diverse social and cultural contexts. All human symbols have such power, but religious symbols are especially powerful because they anchor personal and group identity in a perceived transcendent realm. The stability of social and religious groups depends upon sophisticated symbolic systems and intricate communication of messages. Survival depends upon the ability to adapt the symbols and their transmission systems to new cultural contexts. At the beginning of the twenty-first century that adaptation and transmission are occurring in a rapidly changing India and in a highly mobile transnational religious community.

The transmission of this heritage or tradition in any group is a complex social process and is never a private act. A basic presupposition for the study of any religious group is that the existence of the cult implies the possibility, both for the young lad and for the researcher, of becoming familiar with it. This presupposition points to the intricate network of communication shared by the group – a shared verbal language, a shared gesture language, a common message spoken in various ways which gives the group voice and identity.

A logic and coherence are present in the messages transmitted in different modes in Swaminarayan groups. Still, the researcher has some difficulty in understanding the messages communicated in the various modes for three reasons. (1) The communication system encompasses almost everything done by an individual as a member of the group, and much of it is taken for granted so that there is no need for lengthy explanation within the group. The whole group carries the message. (2) Groups are not coterminous. Thus, members of a religious group are members at the same time of different social groups – castes, occupation groups, social clubs – which have specialized traditions. A subgroup within a culture, such as a sect or caste, develops its own configuration of the non-verbal forms of communication which are analogous to dialects in spoken discourse. Moreover, subgroups within a religious tradition preserve somewhat different symbol systems; that is what it means to be part of a distinct religious or social group. (3) The language of acts and gestures by which much information is communicated is almost as complex as verbal language. Outsiders, whether in social location or of historical period, have a difficult task to reconstruct and learn the meaning of these systems of signs.

Although it may be difficult to enter the circle of discourse, means must exist by which contemporaries can become familiar with the ways of any group. Information is communicated to those outside in order to attract new members, and, just as important, to those inside to reinforce participation. One notes that the senders and receivers of messages which are contained in cultural communication are often the same people. As Edmund Leach observes: "When we participate in ritual we 'say' things to ourselves . . . We engage in rituals in order to transmit collective messages to ourselves" (1976: 43, 45). Of prime importance for any religious community is the transmission of the tradition to the new generation of young people so they may know the truths that have been learned, shared, and preserved in the sect. In their work on the sociology of knowledge Peter Berger and Thomas Luckmann have shown that it is precisely by this process of communication that a group constructs and legitimates a "reality" or "world" that is taken for granted by the community. Participation enables members of the group to inhabit the same world of thought and action because they possess the same "language" (Berger and Luckmann 1967). Socialization is the process by which an individual is inducted and sustained in this "reality." Thus, the

Swaminarayan groups constantly transmit messages: internally to instruct, reinforce, and discipline members, and externally, intentionally and unintentionally, to enable outsiders to recognize, understand, and perhaps to join the group.

Jack Goody suggests that three fairly separate complexes of material are involved when one generation communicates its cultural heritage to the next (Goody 1968: 28). The first and most concrete is the shape of the material world, which includes the natural resources, buildings, utensils, and artifacts. Second are the standardized ways of acting, which, he says, are often taught by verbal means, but usually are learned by imitation, for example, ways of worship, correct dress, a sign language. The third complex of traditions is made up of those channeled through words and resides in the particular range of meanings and attitudes which members of a society attach to their verbal symbols. These three interweave to create a coherent set of messages. The message and tradition of the Swaminarayan community are also transmitted through these three complexes of material; they are the means by which the religious sect constructs and legitimates its social world. If the new generation and new converts are to inhabit the same social and religious world, the legitimizations along with their traditional affirmations and theoretical formulations must be taught and learned in the process of socialization.

Members of the Swaminarayan religion, as well as members of other religious communities, often identify themselves as members of a particular sampradaya. They share a heritage handed down by a line of religious teachers, and they are charged with the preservation of the tradition. The transmission of tradition in the Swaminarayan religion has been effective in shaping the thoughts and actions of devotees, confirming them in the world-view of the founder, and forming them into a significant religious community in Gujarat. The sampradaya has an awareness of itself as coming from a founder, in this case Swaminarayan, and of preserving the tradition through the two centuries since his birth. Followers transmit and receive that tradition any time they engage in religious activities in the home, visit temples and shrines, communicate with others using the language and symbols of the group, and participate in Swaminarayan rituals and ceremonies.

MODERN MEGA-FESTIVALS

A significant development in Swaminarayan Hinduism has been the creation of mega-festivals that attract hundreds of thousands of people

– both faithful followers and the idly curious – to religious events that concentrate the transmission of tradition in various media at a single site over a specific period of a few days or a month. Everyday acts, such as a brief meeting between two satsangis, who wear the tilak and exchange the common greeting "Jai Swaminarayan," or a family visit to a temple, are occasions of complex transmission of Swaminarayan Hindu traditions. The communicative aspect of such customary behavior is constant and powerful, but it is intensified at special times in the ritual calendar and at festivals. Pramukh Swami noted that one of the reasons for the rapid growth of the Akshar Purushottam Sanstha during the last two decades of the twentieth century is the success of the mega-festivals (personal interview, Mehalav, 18 January 1999). The Acharya of Ahmedabad also sponsors such mega-festivals in his diocese and abroad.

The mega-festivals have significant effects both internally and externally. Detailed preparation that lasts for several months, even years, mobilizes the volunteer efforts and contributions of satsangis. The festival itself attracts the participation of satsangis from the region where it is held, and also from many other regions and countries. Artisans, musicians, orators, and religious specialists of the highest quality are employed to transmit the religious and cultural messages of the group. Followers are generally proud of what they accomplish, affirm that they learn a great deal about their religion, and are confirmed in their faith. One devotee who took leave from his occupation and donated six months of full-time service for the construction and dedication of the temple in London calls that "the high point of my life" and thereafter sold his business so he could devote all his time to temple service. Many who are not Swaminarayan Hindus participate in the festivals, where politicians, industrialists, and civic leaders are chief guests. That often translates into financial and other types of support. Some who visit the festivals out of curiosity are drawn into satsang activities and become followers. The festivals have certainly contributed to the increasing visibility of Swaminarayan Hinduism in Gujarat and in locations abroad to which Gujaratis have migrated.

Festivals and sacred time are not so much "time outside of time" or a liminal state as they are the energy or engine that motivates a religious person through time toward a defined future. Preparations for the next events in the temple and festival calendar force the individual and the entire group toward a future. Moreover, in preparing for festivals, a new generation of leaders are trained who will be able to take over from the elders. Their transferable skills are used to sustain the Swaminarayan agenda in many countries.

The celebrations of the bicentenary of Sahajanand's birth, which were held in Ahmedabad (now called Amdavad) in April 1981, provided many examples of the ways the religious tradition is transmitted. All branches of the Swaminarayan religion celebrated the event, and most of the larger temples had festivals with tens of thousands of people in attendance. Most devotees thought of the celebration as a once-in-a-lifetime opportunity to demonstrate their religious devotion. The two largest celebrations were held by the Ahmedabad diocese and the Akshar Purushottam Sanstha. Each group constructed a huge, temporary park in Ahmedabad, one in the grounds of Gujarat University and the other near the Sabarmarti River, where for several days the festival was observed. Several hundred thousand people attended the colorful birth festival; over 100,000 people were fed at each location on the major days of the festival. The Swaminarayan Nagars, or parks, were like American state fairs with tent cities, amusement rides, food and display stalls, exhibitions, and entertainment. Nevertheless, the festival was primarily religious, and the basic purpose was to transmit the message of the religion. In that sense it was a media event, and careful attention was given to the communication of the religious message. A similar festival was conducted for a month at Alexandra Palace in London in 1985, attracting broad support among Gujaratis and a great deal of media attention. Many British people gained their first personal contact with Hinduism by visiting the elaborate site. A gold-weighing ceremony was conducted at Ranger Park Stadium at which gold equal to the weight of Pramukh Swami was donated to support the sect's programs. These two festivals became prototypes for the mega-festivals conducted in India and abroad.

In 1986 the Akshar Purushottam held a similar festival in Ahmedabad to mark the bicentenary of the birth of Gunatitanand Swami. The festivals increased in size and importance in the 1990s. The mega-festival was exported to the United States in 1991 as a month-long festival for which the campus of Middlesex County College in Edison, New Jersey was turned into a Hindu temple complex and an Indian cultural exhibition. The next year the dedication of a new type of permanent religious monument and exhibition at Akshardham was the occasion for a month-long festival in Gandhinagar, the capital of the State of Gujarat. Following the festival, the monument remains as a permanent exhibition. Sadhus say that Akshardham extended the concept of darshan by adding *pradarshan*, which refers not to seeing the images of the god but to observing an exhibition. In 1994 the Ahmedabad diocese celebrated the twenty-fifth anniversary of Tejendraprasad Pande's initiation as acharya with a large festival in Ahmedabad. His son, Koshalendraprasad, then a college student, became chair of the planning committee and undertook to strengthen the structure of the diocese, especially among the youths, which both assured a successful celebration and established his new role as leader of the young adults and future acharya. The seventy-fifth birthday of Pramukh Swami was the occasion for a mammoth thirty-seven-day festival in Mumbai that attracted over 8.1 million visitors and for which the organization marshaled over 22,000 volunteers. The enormous success of that festival helped put Swaminarayan Hinduism on the national map and garnered a great deal of support for its programs. The Pramukh Swami Eye Hospital was established in Mumbai with donations contributed at the festival. The custom of dedicating new temples and initiating sadhus on the birthday of Pramukh Swami came together with a festival to dedicate the large temple at Rajkot in Gujarat in November 1999. These festivals combine all aspects of transmission of tradition in a heightened form: communication by physical surroundings, communication by standardized ways of acting, and communication by language.

COMMUNICATION BY PHYSICAL SURROUNDINGS

Archeologists have long known that artifacts and the physical layout of sites reveal interesting messages about a culture if one knows the "language." The messages uncovered by the archeologist are but a small fraction of the information communicated by the material heritage to those who live in a culture. People organize their physical surroundings to communicate messages. Therefore, people are able to "read" their physical surroundings. The communicative aspect of the arrangement of physical surroundings was very much in the minds of those who planned the festivals. The size and scope of the physical layout were intended to communicate a message about the importance and prestige of the religion. Buildings and grounds were arranged on the model of religious theme parks; the intent was that those who visited the park would "see" the religion. The temporary structures were made of bamboo and burlap, and the permanent monuments and temples are covered with images and symbols.

Long lines of devotees approached to worship the images of the deities enshrined there. Cult houses are always centers of communication, even when mute. It has been said that Notre-Dame cathedral in Paris is the

Summa Theologica of St. Thomas Aquinas in stone; the *Summa* could be called the cathedral in words. In the same manner all the temples of the Swaminarayan religion contain messages in physical form. The decorations and murals bear silent witness. The temples and monuments created at the sites of the mega-festivals contain the images of the deities, scenes from the sacred Hindu mythology and Swaminarayan history, and sacred symbols.

The sacred history, especially the story of the life of Sahajanand Swami, was presented in the bicentenary exhibitions mounted by each group. One exhibition had artificial mountains twenty feet high constructed of bamboo and burlap around which were placed scenes of events from his life. Some of his clothing and the utensils used by him were brought out from the temples where they are ordinarily kept and placed on display. The other exhibition consisted of thirty-six tableaux depicting the life of Sahajanand Swami. Spectators walked by scenes of Sahajanand prohibiting widow suicide, infanticide, and animal sacrifice. In other scenes he was shown teaching the scholars in Varanasi and meeting with Sir John Malcolm. Since a charge of one rupee, then about twelve US cents, was made to see this exhibition, an exact record of attendance exists. Approximately 80,000 persons could go through the exhibition in one day; on the last days of the festival it remained open twenty-four hours a day. During the festival 1.5 million persons paid to see the exhibition. The tableaux were arranged so that the viewer was transported back into the career of the founder. Large floats drawn in processions from the center of the city to the large parks on the outskirts carried similar tableaux. The elaborate exhibition at Akshardham in Gandhinagar employs modern display technology to present moving and talking life-like images that portray Sahajanand speaking to his followers and his sadhu companions singing sacred songs. One sadhu explained the development of these large exhibitions in this way: "People come to the temples for darshan to develop their spirituality; they come to the exhibitions for pradarshan [to see an exhibition] in order to gain understanding."

Large halls seating thousands of people are constructed for the festivals. The halls were explicitly for verbal and ritual communication, but the physical layout incorporated aspects of communication. One example is the communication of status differentiation. An image of Swaminarayan presides over the proceedings. On each platform is a decorated couch (gadi) for the religious leader of the group, for Acharya Tejendraprasad Pande or for Pramukh Swami. Senior ascetics occupy places on the platform beside and somewhat lower than the seat of honor. The other ascetics have reserved places to the right and facing the stage. They are separated from the laymen and are facing in a direction that does not require them to observe the women. Seating for the women is in an area removed from both the ascetics and the laymen. Thus, status and rules for conduct are communicated and reinforced through the organization of physical space. The rules forbid ascetics to look at or touch women, and they prohibit the intermingling of the sexes in meetings and worship. The physical partitions in the temples and in the meeting halls are examples of the rule of the separation of the sexes "writ in stone," and collectively they are as effective in transmitting this part of the tradition as the rule written in a book. Thus, the millions of people who walk around the festival grounds, temples, and religious theme parks are the recipients of very elaborate messages about the Swaminarayan religion.

COMMUNICATION BY STANDARDIZED WAYS OF ACTING

Customary ways of acting in rituals and gestures transmit religious and other types of cultural information. Most of what humans do, from eating to worship, is governed by the traditional ways of acting. Some traditional ways of acting may be simply utilitarian, but most form highly complex messages. Edmund Leach suggests a useful distinction between the technical and communicative aspects of customary behavior (1968: 523). He argues that most customary human actions have technical aspects which do something and aesthetic, communicative aspects which say something. Ritual and gesture can be defined as the communicative aspects of customary behavior, and are not, therefore, distinct classes of behavior. Religious ritual and gesture in the Swaminarayan fellowship are means of communication. The language of acts and gestures by which much information is communicated is almost as complex as the language of words. The interpretation of ritual and gesture is the attempt to discover the grammar and syntax of a type of language. Just as verbal language is the gift of the group to the individual, so the range of customary behavior and the structure of non-verbal communication embodied in it is also the property of and a gift from the group – in this case from the Swaminarayan satsang.

Customary personal dress and decoration communicate information about status and commitment. Incongruous dress is socially offensive. The dress of the ascetics as they move around the mega-festivals is congruous with other elements of cultural transmission. The dress marks them as men who have renounced the world. The way in which it covers the body communicates standards of modesty. The lack of pockets and decorative stitching indicates that the ascetics have renounced worldly goods and keep the vow of poverty. Those who know the language can distinguish by the dress to which branch of the religion the ascetics belong. Moreover, the color of the garment, whether white or saffron, indicates status within the community and perhaps caste background. Similarly, a lay devotee is distinguished from other followers of Krishna by the double strand of *tulsi* beads around his neck and the tilak mark on the forehead made of yellow sandal paste and red kumkum, each of which has a symbolic meaning (*Shikshapatri*, 41–4). Thus, a person dressed or decorated in the distinctive manner of the sect is a living witness communicating thereby information about himself and the religion.

Two rituals of rites of passage were performed as parts of the bicentenary celebrations. Each was replete with gestures which communicated information about the new status gained through the ceremony. The initiation into the ascetic status (bhagavati diksha) was performed for 207 young men. Through the rituals of shaving, bathing, and receiving new clothing their new status was affirmed. Each was given new clothing, either white or saffron depending on status, a new necklace (*kanti*), and a turban, and finally Pramukh Swami whispered to each the mantra and the new name. Thereafter, each young man took up new study and work that is appropriate to his new status as a sadhu. He received the discipline of a new set of rules. A part of the message of the distinctive dress of the sadhu is the plea to others to help him maintain the discipline he has undertaken. As a part of the initiation ceremony a dramatic statement was made when Pramukh Swami gave saffron clothing to several men who were from lower castes and who had previously been in the status of permanent bhagats. No advance notice of his intention to perform this act had been given, and not a word was spoken to explain what was happening, but the moment was electric because the large audience understood that a dramatic announcement about caste status and relations was being made through ritual. This message about caste relations within this branch of the Swaminarayan religion was all the more dramatic because the ceremony coincided with the serious caste riots in Gujarat which threatened to delay the opening of the festival. The initiation of sadhus became a regular feature of festivals in the 1990s, especially of those held on Pramukh Swami's birthday.

Koshalendraprasad Pande was seven years old when he received the sacred thread of a Brahmin in a ceremony conducted in the courtyard of the haveli in the old temple at Ahmedabad as part of the bicentenary celebration in 1981. The ritual was the same as the thread ceremony for any Brahmin boy, but because of his status in the religion the event had special significance. The boy was changed from a child to a youth and was ritually transformed into a student. His head was shaved and he was bathed. His new clothing was that of a wandering student. Much of the symbolism reflected his entrance into the study of the sacred texts. The fiction was that he would engage in a period of wandering to learn from the wise men in the temples and ashrams. He was given a staff for the journey and sacred books for study. His father opened the sacred texts to him by giving him the mantra. At the Akshar Purushottam park, following the initiation of the ascetics, Pramukh Swami gave the sacred thread to approximately twenty-five Brahmin boys. What made Koshalendraprasad's thread ceremony different was his position in the religion; he will take his father's place. The ceremony in the midst of the bicentenary celebration reinforced his position and that of the acharya's family. Hundreds passed through the courtyard to view a portion of the ritual; closed-circuit color television was set up to permit more people to see; video tapes and films were made to be shown to devotees in other locations. The two sons of the acharya's younger brother also received the thread in the same ceremony. The brother's son would, of course, be a candidate to succeed the acharya if Koshalendraprasad were to be unavailable. Neither the thread ceremony nor the initiation of the ascetics was a necessary part of the celebrations of the birth of the founder, but the significance of each was heightened as a part of the festival.

The climax of the bicentenary on 12 April 1981 was the ritual at the hour of Sahajanand's birth at 10.10 p.m., which corresponds to the lunar reckoning of the birth on 3 April 1781. The ritual was a more elaborate form of the birth ritual performed annually in all the temples. The story was told in words, songs, and actions or gestures as in Christian Christmas pageants. A small image was placed in the cradle to be rocked by devotees with representations of his parents looking on. The waving of lights (arti) was performed by the leader with a candelabrum of 200 lights and by tens of thousands of people with individual lights. Folk dances of rejoicing were performed by some of the ascetics. Over 110,000 people participated in the event at one of the parks. These and thousands of other common acts make up the intricate gesture and ritual language of the religion.

The non-verbal communication of customary behavior is often accompanied by speech which reinforces the meaning of the action, as when a person says "No" and shakes his or her head. There is an immediate confusion when a different meaning is transmitted by an action from that conveyed by the accompanying speech. The Indian head gesture of affirmation resembles the Western gesture of negation. The foreigner is immediately confused when confronted by an affirmative word and a seemingly negative gesture. In normal intercourse the non-verbal communication of a customary action says the same thing as the accompanying speech. Words and actions are joined in programs of the Swaminarayan temples and were extended to larger groups in the bicentenary festival. One is reminded of the ancient Greek definition of myth as things said over things done. Myth and ritual is one context in which the unity of things said and the things done is expressed. The two combine to transmit one message.

COMMUNICATION BY LANGUAGE

The third and most obvious type of traditional material is that transmitted in language, either spoken or written. As Victor Turner suggests, all human acts and institutions are enveloped in webs of interpretive words (1980: 147). This material includes everything from long philosophical treatises of the *Vachanamritam* to the short "Jai Swaminarayan" which is the customary greeting of members, from the ancient *Vedas* chanted by the Brahmins to modern devotional songs sung in the style of film music and sold on cassette tapes or CD-ROMs. The material can take a wide range of forms – songs, narratives of varying length, proverbs, poems, legal injunctions, commentaries, even genealogies. Most of the traditions of the Swaminarayan religion are now in written form, and many were written down during the career of the founder. The contemporary focus on writing should not blind us, however, to the fact that even in modern, literate societies much of what one learns, especially about religion, comes in oral form rather than in books. In the Swaminarayan religion, as in Hinduism in general, oral transmission and written transmission go together – guru and scripture – and one is a check on the other.

Sahajanand Swami accepted as fundamental sacred scriptures eight texts from the amorphous canon of Vaishnava Hinduism. He urged his followers to study these and to use them as guides for devotion and discipline. His canon was: (1) the four *Vedas*; (2) the *Vedanta Sutras* of Vyasa; (3) the *Bhagavata Purana*; (4) the thousand names of Vishnu in the *Mahabharata*; (5)

Table 6. *Scripture of Swaminarayan Hinduism*

Canon accepted by Sahajanand	Works attributed to Sahajanand's inspiration	Other important works
Four *Vedas*	*Shikshapatri*	Nishkulananda Kaavya (*Yama Danda*)
Vedanta Sutras of Vyasa	*Vachanamritam*	*Bhakta Chintamani*
Yajnavalkya Smriti	*Satsangijivan*	*Shri Hari Lilamrit*
Bhagavata Purana	*Lekh*	*Swamini Vato*
Bhagavad Gita		
Skanda Purana (Portions)		
Vidurniti		
Mahabharata (1,000 names)		

the *Bhagavad Gita*, a copy of which he is said to have carried on his journeys; (6) the *Vidurniti*; (7) the Shri Vasudev Mahatmya from the Vishnu Khanda of the *Skanda Purana*; and (8) the *Yajnavalkya Smriti* (*Vachanamritam*, Vadtal 18 and *Shikshapatri*, 93–102). These works provide basic teaching about the three paths to spiritual development and release commonly followed in Hinduism. The tenth canto of the *Bhagavata Purana* gives the essentials of the devotional path (bhakti). *Yajnavalkya* presents a core of teachings about the path of discipline (dharma), and Swaminarayan instructed his followers to follow the prescriptions of this work if they had any questions about discipline. The commentaries of Ramanuja on the *Bhagavata Purana* and the *Bhagavad Gita* contain the basic philosophical wisdom (*jnana*) which the Swaminarayan religion appropriated from the Hindu past. Adherents claim that they follow the philosophical teachings of Ramanuja as modified by Sahajanand. Devotees are encouraged to study these texts, and sadhus give lectures on them in the temples.

These ancient texts are supplemented by works written during the career of Swaminarayan, much as the Christian writings supplement but do not replace the ancient Jewish scriptures. The most important texts, four in number, were written during the last ten years of his life (1819–29), either by him or by others taking their inspiration from him. They contain the primary theology, rules, hagiography, and administrative regulations of the religion. See table 6.

The *SHIKSHAPATRI* is a Sanskrit work of 212 verses containing regulations to be observed by various categories of devotees. It is the most accessible of the religious texts because of its size, scope, and applicability. Sahajanand Swami wrote the work in AD 1826 while he was staying at Vadtal. Visitors to the temple are shown the room where he is said to have written the work, and a text is preserved in the temple treasury. A copy in the Indian Institute Library of the Bodleian at Oxford is visited and treated as a relic because of its close connection with Sahajanand (Williams 1981: 114–22). The first Western edition and English translation were made in 1882 by Professor Monier-Williams, Boden Professor of Sanskrit at Oxford and founder of the Indian Institute Library (Monier-Williams 1882a: 733–72). Some of the prescriptions in the text are incumbent upon all followers; others are directed at particular classes: the acharyas, the acharyas' wives, women, Brahmins, widows, and ascetics of different ranks. The rules deal with both ethical and ritual behavior. Portions of the text are chanted every day by devout followers. Swaminarayan commanded that it be read daily: "The *Shikshapatri* which has been written by me should be read daily by all ascetics and householders, male and female, who have taken refuge in me. Those who cannot read should hear it from someone. If that is not possible, they should offer worship to it as prescribed in the *Shikshapatri*" (*Vachanamritam*, Gadhada III, 1). A copy is used in the morning devotions of the ascetics and devout laymen.

It was a central focus at mega-festivals. Many devotees take special vows to read the text a specified number of times or to memorize it for the occasion. Inexpensive editions in several languages are sold for a few pennies each at the bookstalls during the festival. Many of the lecturers in the meeting halls of the parks read and expound upon the *Shikshapatri*. It is said to contain the essential regulations for conduct for those who would follow the spiritual path.

The *VACHANAMRITAM* has secular as well as religious importance because it stands as the first major systematic prose work in Gujarati. It is a collection of philosophical sermons given by Swaminarayan in answer to questions raised by his disciples assembled at various places – Gadhada, Sarangpur, Kariyani, Loya, Panchala, Vadtal, and Ahmedabad. The title for each section of the work is the name of the town where the discourses in the section were given. The basic philosophy of modified non-dualism was expounded by Ramanuja in the traditional form of commentary on sacred texts; Sahajanand changed the pattern by giving the basic philosophy in the new form of answers to questions. The text is written in

Gujarati, and the sermons are ordered by place and chronological order, the first dated 21 November 1819 and the last 25 July 1829. Devotees assume that at this period in his career a secretary was taking notes during these sessions. In the authorized version of the Vadtal diocese, accepted also by the Akshar Purushottam Sanstha, there are 262 sermons compiled and edited by four of his close companions – Gopalananda, Muktananda, Shukananda, and Nityananda. The recension of Ahmedabad, made by Acharya Ayodhyaprasad, has eleven additional sermons which deal with Nar-Narayana, five delivered at Ahmedabad, one at Ashlali, and five at Jetpur. A fifth editor, Brahmananda, is mentioned. All sections have a standard format. The date, location, and a description of the apparel worn by Swaminarayan are given. He invites questions from those gathered around or asks a question himself to be discussed. Then follows the answer to the question or questions asked. Today his answers provide the texts for the regular discourses given in the temples and for the philosophical and theological work of the scholars of the sect (Mukundcharandas 1999).

The *SATSANGIJIVAN* is a long Sanskrit work in five volumes written in the style of the *Bhagavata Purana*. The 17,627 verses, written by Shatananda Muni, constitute a *summa* or compendium of all the teachings, history, and legends from the life of Sahajanand Swami. As in other works in the puranic style, there are narratives from the career of the divine figure, but these are interspersed with other types of material – philosophical discourses, legal material, and liturgical material. The first volume begins in prehistory when the mythical wise men receive the curse that they must be born in the world and then are made the promise that god will take human birth with them. The stories of the parents, the birth of Sahajanand, his activities as a child, his travels as a mendicant, and his leadership in the ashram of Ramananda Swami are then presented. This volume contains a section (chapters 32–6) on the duties of women which is given a separate title, the Shri Hari Gita or Narayan Gita.

Volume II contains a record of the travels of Swaminarayan as he gathered disciples throughout Saurashtra, Kutch, and Gujarat. Sections of teachings follow (chapters 11–15) in which he describes the five evil attachments of men and gives illustrations from the ancient texts of how the heroes of the past overcame these evils. He also describes the path of devotion. In volume III are descriptions of the festivals that are to be celebrated with a statement of the significance of each. A theological section (chapter 29) contains a description of the human form of god and the statement of the doctrine of the manifestation of god. Volume IV records the debate between Sahajanand and the scholars at Baroda who argued that his new teachings were not faithful to the *Vedas*. He established, at least to his followers' satisfaction, that the Swaminarayan religion is Vedic in character. An important section (chapter 40) recounts the appointment of the first two acharyas and lists their duties together with descriptions of the initiation ritual and other rituals to be performed by the acharyas.

Volume V is in the form of a law book (dharmashastra) and duplicates some of the injunctions found in the *Shikshapatri*. The duties of men from the four castes, along with those of women, married and widowed, are given. There are detailed regulations about purity, for example, during the menstrual period. This section on women (chapters 30–7) was edited by Muktanand Swami as a separate Gujarati document called the *Sati Gita* (trans. Mallison 1973). It is often chanted by female devotees and is thought to contain the description of the perfect female devotion. This fifth volume also contains a section (chapters 56–62) on yoga. Two texts taken from the *Satsangijivan* are especially important to the sadhus. The *Dharmamrit* contains rules for the ascetics to help them overcome the five evils of greed, lust, taste, attachment to family, and ego. The *Nishkam-shuddhi* gives the rules for the appropriate penance, usually some form of fast, if the ascetic violates the regulations. The ascetics are urged to study five verses from each of these documents each day. As the longest of the primary texts of the Swaminarayan religion, the *Satsangijivan* contains the greatest diversity of material; there is something in it for everyone, and it is widely used.

The shortest and most narrowly focused of the sacred texts is *THE LEKH*. It was written by Sahajanand Swami in 1827 at Gadhada and establishes the apportionment of the territory to the two dioceses of Ahmedabad and Vadtal. It contains the regulations about the donation of tithes and offerings to the two temples and some instructions about the succession of the acharyas. The document was accepted by the Bombay High Court as the authoritative document regarding the apportionment of the two dioceses, so it has legal standing. *The Lekh* is highly regarded in the Ahmedabad and Vadtal diocese, but members of the Akshar Purushottam Sanstha understandably do not give it much importance. It was not meant to be sacred scripture, they say, but only an administrative document. They do not, however, question its authenticity.

The authority for each of these primary works is traced back to Sahajanand Swami himself. Many secondary works exist that were produced by his close companions, some during his lifetime and the rest in the decades following his death. It is sufficient to give examples of the diversity of material produced by his companions, and no attempt is made here to give a complete catalogue of the material. The first work produced in the Swaminarayan movement is the *YAMA DANDA*, written by Nishkulananda Swami in AD 1804. It is a treatise in 1,100 verses on life, death, and salvation. The first half deals with the sorrows of worldly life separated from god, and the second half extols the joys of salvation. The work of Swaminarayan is praised, and the last chapter is a song of thanksgiving. The document is important for the history of doctrine in the religion because it gives the first evidence of the revering of Sahajanand Swami as a manifestation of god. Nishkulananda is also the author of one of several biographies of Swaminarayan. The *BHAKTA CHINTAMANI* has 8,527 verses in 164 chapters. The first two-thirds of the work contains details of the life of Swaminarayan given in chronological order. The last third has sections of praise of his divinity, names and descriptions of his followers, both ascetics and householders, accounts of marvelous deeds, and finally a description of his heavenly abode. The *SHRI HARI LILAMRIT* is a longer biography. In addition, theological works by prominent ascetics are preserved and read in the religious gatherings. The commentaries by Gopalananda are often read in Ahmedabad and Vadtal temples; the collected talks of Gunatitanand Swami, called *SWAMINI VATO*, are preserved and studied with special attention in the Akshar Purushottam Sanstha.

Some of the sadhus of the sect composed poetry during the early decades of the nineteenth century and had a profound influence on the Gujarati literature of the period (Munshi 1935: 216f. and Toothi 1935: 265–9). These poets composed songs about Krishna and Swaminarayan and about the devotion and love appropriate for a devotee (H. Dave 1981: 31–6). Muktananda (1758–1830) and Nishkulananda (1766–1848) are important for their poetry as well as for their works mentioned above. Brahmananda (1772–1832) wrote almost a thousand poems in which he extolled the ethical and moral life with the help of simple examples from contemporary life and illustrations from the cultural history of India. He was also the architect who was charged with building the temples at Vadtal and Muli, characterized by the elevation of the shrine on an upper floor. Premananda (c. 1784–1855) was a poet of high order from the Gandharva (minstrel) caste, and he played and sang with great ability. The most popular, and least sectarian, of the poets was Devananda (1830–54). He used the language of the simple agricultural folk, and most of his poems were set to simple native tunes. Traveling minstrels sang his warnings against worldliness, his praise of devotion, and his songs of hope. This body of poetry composed between 1800 and 1850 represents the last flowering of the medieval devotional poetry before the beginning of the modern period in Gujarati literature under Western influence. These devotional songs are significant in the history of Gujarati literature, but they also have a contemporary relevance. They are still chanted and sung in the religious meetings, and contemporary Swaminarayan writers and musicians try to imitate their style.

Material from the sacred literature mentioned above provides the verbal content for most of the rituals and programs in the temples. The daily schedule of the larger temples calls for a religious discourse on a sacred text to follow each of the five rituals of waving of the lights (arti) in the shrine. One of the ascetics usually gives a lecture in the meeting hall. When the ascetics go on preaching tours to the villages, they hold public meetings in which the sacred scriptures are read and explained. The ascetics in the temples of the Ahmedabad and Vadtal dioceses have groups of followers who come to the temples especially to hear their guru interpret the religious texts. Some laymen known for their piety and learning give regular lectures and attract groups of followers. The Akshar Purushottam Sanstha distributes to the temples and centers where there are no ascetics an instruction sheet for each of the weekly meetings of the fellowship in which the readings from the *Vachanamritam* and *Swamini Vato* are designated. Thus, a lectionary is provided so that followers in Gujarat and abroad study the same texts. A layman then gives a lecture on the text. One of the problems faced by the group is that many of the laymen do not have sufficient knowledge of the theology of the religion to give correct interpretations. Confusion and division result. A series of publications and a seven-year examination course for laymen have been prepared as a modern response to the problem. The provision of training for the lay leaders is difficult, and especially so outside of Gujarat. That is one reason Pramukh Swami and Acharya Tejendraprasad decided in the 1990s to assign sadhus to live in temples abroad. Nevertheless, the stories, lectures, and songs by laymen provide the basis of most of what goes on in the fellowship; the "things said" accompany the "things done."

The mega-festivals provide showcases for the literature. The best singers, lecturers, story-tellers, and dramatists are gathered and the programs are examples for followers of the many ways this material can be transmitted. At the bicentenary festival, Pujya Dongre, a popular story-teller, was invited to give a recitation of the stories of Krishna from the *Bhagavata Purana* in a parayana. Morning and evening he recited before some 50,000 people in the meeting hall. Two honored Brahmin scholars were engaged to participate with him in the parayana. Other Brahmin specialists chanted the Vedic texts to accompany the sacrificial rituals, a special yajna for world peace, the yajna for the thread ceremony, and the yajna for the initiation ceremony. The leading ascetics recited and lectured on other texts – the *Satsangijivan*, the *Shikshapatri*, and the *Vachanamritam*. A remarkable aspect of the transmission of the tradition in the Swaminarayan religion is the role played by the ascetics. They are trained in public speaking and in the arts of communication, and they are very conscious of their role in the transmission of the tradition. They are preachers, and part of their daily activity is the participation in the discourses. One explained: "The *murtis* [images in the temples] do not speak aloud, so we have to talk for them." Some of the ascetics are like "living books" as they preserve and transmit the tradition.

One layman who had been in the meeting hall for several days listening to the lectures complained that the program was "words, words, words." But there was more. Dramas were performed which reenacted events from the career of Swaminarayan and the lives of his close disciples. The films, slide shows, and exhibitions transformed the literature into new genres. The devotional songs were performed in programs of devotional music (*kirtan aradhana*) by professional musicians and by well-trained ascetics. Those who came to listen as well as those who came to see received the messages which were being transmitted in the bicentenary celebration.

An anniversary is an appropriate time to reflect on the tension in the transmission of tradition between homeostasis and change. Both aspects are essential to the maintenance of the group. A religious community as an organism has a tendency to maintain and restore steady states or conditions, and the work of the religious specialists as they teach and reinforce correct belief and practice is one of the means by which the unity of the group and the continuity with what has gone before are maintained. Yet, as they apply the teachings of the past to the present experience of the devotees and interpret the teachings for modern social conditions, the possibility exists for development and evolutionary change. Each group edits its past in order to affirm its present, and thus the past as it is expressed in the group is always changing. A delicate balance of conservatism and change remains because tradition provides both a justification of current practice and an instrument of adaptation and change. The tradition is continually created and recreated in new social situations and is held together by the slender thread of memory. The balance of continuity and change in the tradition is an expression of and consonant with the guru tradition of Hinduism in which the sacred tradition is transmitted by and studied with a religious specialist who has the authority to adapt the tradition to the needs of his disciple.

All the different branches of the Swaminarayan religion accept a common core of the tradition, but they emphasize different elements and use some different religious texts. Thus, they have different canons of sacred scripture. Ahmedabad and Vadtal value *The Lekh*; the Akshar Purushottam Sanstha emphasizes the *Swamini Vato*, which contains the sayings of Gunatitanand. The former emphasize those parts of the *Shikshapatri* which confirm the rights of the acharya; the latter emphasizes those which deal with the moral and ethical requirements for ascetics. The tradition is edited; it also grows. Stories and sayings from persons taken to be saints are used in the temples. Many of the stories recount marvelous deeds and miraculous escapes from evil or illness. Each person seems to have his own personal collection of stories and the tradition grows apace because there is a reluctance in Hinduism to impose the strictures of canonization; there is no strict separation of canonical and non-canonical as in Western tradition. Nevertheless, some leaders see the need to impose some constraints on the growth in the tradition, especially in its more "bizarre" aspects, if only so that Western-educated young people, both in India and abroad, will have some help in distinguishing between what is essential in the tradition and what is dispensable.

Traditioning in the religion has moved fully into the use of techniques of modern communication. Communication in Sahajanand's time was primarily through face-to-face conversation and through participation in ritual and use of gesture. Hand-copied manuscripts and letters were used, but mainly as aids to memory and as temporary substitutes for direct personal contact. Typefaces for printing Gujarati script became available at about the time of the growth of the new religion. The parallel with the spread of printing in the vernacular languages and the Lutheran reform in Europe is striking. The first Gujarati press was established in Bombay (now called Mumbai) in 1812. By 1832 there were nine presses in Bombay and one in Surat. Two presses were established in Ahmedabad in 1845 and the first newspaper was published in Ahmedabad in 1849 (Desai 1978: 281–4). The availability of the vernacular press gave impetus to the development of Gujarati literature and to the distribution of the literature of the Swaminarayan religion.

The bookstalls in the temples and at the mega-festivals are full of religious literature produced to propagate the teachings of the religion. The sacred texts have been prepared in cheap Gujarati editions and in translations into English, Hindi, and other languages. Several editions and translations of the *Shikshapatri* were published as a part of the bicentenary celebrations, as were collections of scholarly articles, devotional songs, and a three-volume biography of Sahajanand Swami. Small books in Gujarati and English, something like Sunday School manuals, have been published to help young people prepare for a series of extramural examinations administered by the Akshar Purushottam Sanstha. Weekly and monthly journals are prepared and mailed to the homes of members and to the centers. Leaders of the women's movement edit a quarterly magazine, *Premvati*, which is mailed to members of the women's organization. It is the oldest publication of the Akshar Purushottam Sanstha, begun in 1973. A concerted effort has been made to broadcast the message through religious publications. Moreover, during the bicentenary celebration a committee on press and publicity attracted the attention of the secular press, and the event received wide coverage in the popular magazines and newspapers of Gujarat.

Other forms of mass media are employed. Video tapes and tape cassettes recording some of the rituals, lectures, and devotional songs are made and sold. In a jarring mixture of the ancient and modern, some of the Vedic rituals are reproduced on closed circuit television to permit a larger audience to observe them. Mobile book vans visit festivals and temple dedications to distribute printed materials, ritual objects, videos, and CD-ROMs. Sadhus oversee sophisticated sound and film studios and computer centers to prepare and distribute materials in the most up-to-date formats. Poster and calendar art, as old as Sahajanand himself, but now produced in new forms, is in evidence at festivals and on the bookstalls. Just as the loudspeakers amplify the voices of the lecturers and musicians so that they can be heard throughout the festival sites, so the other forms of modern media technology are used to expand significantly the scope and range of the transmission of the tradition, with all of the potential and the many problems that result.

The end of the century saw the development of new technologies that hold some promise of breaking the ties to time and place in the transmission of traditions. Computer-assisted transmission of information over the Internet and on CD-ROMs brings the festivals into halls and homes everywhere and at any time. Earlier transmission in writing translated music, words, gestures, and architecture into words in sacred scriptures and trusted that in the hermeneutics involved in reading those elements would be imagined. Transmission of the images in digital form preserves the aural and visual experience. The pran pratistha of the temple at Rajkot in 1999 was transmitted around the world in real time over the Internet. Information and scenes from the large Swaminarayan temple in London are available. A CD-ROM attempts to reproduce for viewers an experience of being on the grounds of Akshardham and the information contained in its large, modern exhibitions. One of the early Internet sites contained beautiful pictures of the images in a popular Swaminarayan temple, but it contained the warning that the images could not be used for darshan in exactly the same way as images in the temple. Virtual images do not possess the powerful presence of god that was instilled in dedication; hence, they do not give darshan. That is an interesting theological distinction. Each of the Swaminarayan subgroups maintains a site on the Internet to communicate its messages. No one knows in what new ways religious traditions will be transmitted in the new century.

There is, of course, a fundamental difference between the transmission of tradition in oral form and that in the mass-media form. A sadhu said that communicating through the mass media speaks to the head, but communicating personally in oral form speaks to the heart. The intrinsic nature of oral communication has a considerable effect upon both the content and transmission of religious tradition. The act of imparting it is invested with meaning for the two parties, teller and recipient (guru and disciple), unlike the imparting of knowledge by written or mass communication to people unknown to the communicator. A directness of relationship exists in oral communication so that the tradition is an integral part of the social relationships of the hearers. Oral transmission is particularly suited to the process of adjusting the tradition to maintain the stability of the group. The past is true because only that which is true to the present circumstance is remembered and received. The past is viewed as an integral whole, a seamless robe. The traditional Hindu view is that religious teaching ought to be imparted by the guru to the pupil only after various requirements are met. Truth, it is believed, requires an authentic mediator, a qualified student, and the correct social situation in which it can be directly communicated. Nevertheless, modern communication is increasingly unmediated in ways that threaten the authority of teachers and gurus.

Claude Lévi-Strauss laments the fact that people are no longer linked to their past by an oral tradition which implies a direct contact with storytellers, priests, wise men, or elders. Now the links are the indirect intermediaries of written documents or media which extend people's contacts but which are, in his view, somewhat inauthentic (1963: 366). Along with the leaders of other Vaishnava devotional sects, the leaders of the Swaminarayan religion have taken the risk of making the religious teachings available indiscriminately to the masses through the translation of the sacred texts and through the use of modern mass-media technology (Carman 1981: 204–9). They maintain, however, that relationship with an appropriate religious teacher is essential to spiritual progress. The goal, one assumes, is that those reached through the mass media will be attracted to such a teacher.

All available means of communication, ancient and modern, are combined to broadcast the message. More is known about the religion by the people in Gujarat and abroad as a result of the publicity surrounding the mega-festivals, and the curiosity of many people has been aroused. Although the means used to transmit messages about the religion at mega-festivals are more concentrated in time and space, the same techniques are used in the temples and centers throughout Gujarat and abroad. One assumes that the skills honed in preparation for the celebrations will continue to be used in the future to dedicate new temples and to open new exhibitions like Akshardham.

During the celebration of Sahajanand's birth in the Ahmedabad temple, Tejendraprasad Pande took the sacred thread of the Brahmin, placed it over his son's shoulder, and whispered the sacred mantra in his ear, a quintessential union of physical symbol, ritual act, and sacred word. Within the following few days the boy was honored in the three main temples of the diocese at Ahmedabad, Muli, and Bhuj because, if all goes well, he will some day take his place in the line of acharyas. So, from the time of Sahajanand, the tradition has been handed down from generation to generation by physical symbol, by the communicative aspects of customary behavior in ritual and gesture, and by written and spoken words. When the transmission is effective the tradition reinforces the belief of all members and incorporates new members both young and old into the world-view of the sect. Members can then speak the same religious language, have the same ideals, know what is right, despise the same evils, and worship the same gods. This constitutes the group-building and world-building that are central to a living religious community. All three forms of transmission of tradition continue to be used to preserve the heritage as fathers pass on the sacred thread to new generations.

CHAPTER SEVEN

Transnational growth of Swaminarayan Hinduism

A Swaminarayan satsangi walked across the grounds of a festival in Ahmedabad, reached out his hand, and said in a broad Texas drawl, "Hello, I'm from Dallas, Texas." In 1981 he was leader of a fledgling immigrants' group in Dallas and had returned to Gujarat to visit temples, sadhus, relatives, and the bicentenary festival of the birth of Swaminarayan. Meeting him and others who traveled from East Africa, England, and the United States was a surprising introduction to the transnational reality of Swaminarayan Hinduism that developed rapidly in the last quarter of the twentieth century. Visual symbols of the transnational reality are the pictorial images of deities and saints originally sent from India to be installed in the Swaminarayan temple in Kampala, Uganda that were saved from destruction during the expulsion and then donated and installed in the temple in London. The images from the temple in Jinja were sent to the New York temple and are now installed in a new temple in Sydney, Australia – a mobility of deities that accompanies Indian emigration. The peoples of India have long been migrants seeking wealth, wisdom, and adventure abroad, and Gujaratis have been prominent among them. Dramatic changes in the world economy, politics, and technology create new patterns of emigration and new networks of relationship between migrants that characterize Swaminarayan Hindus in the continuing emigration of people of several religions and ethnic groups from India.

Such emigrations are best viewed as transnational movements – not as a generalized globalization – because related immigrants are found in several distinct locations where economic, political, and even religious forces have created space for particular types of immigrants. They participate in chain migrations that follow established networks to specific locations. Since the end of the Second World War emigrants have made their way in large numbers from developing countries into wealthy countries from which they had previously been systematically excluded.

"Transnational" refers to a new pattern of emigration made possible by modern mobility and rapid communication created by new technologies and to the multi-stranded social relations that lead migrants to take actions, make decisions, and feel concerns within a set of social networks that connect them to two or more societies simultaneously. The process of transnational emigration envelops locations and elements of older emigration and transforms the networks that define ethnic and religious identities in the several locations (Schiller, Basch, and Blanc-Szanton 1992: 1–24). Migrants draw upon and create fluid and multiple identities grounded in a similar past in India and their related experiences in several contemporary societies. In this transnational context, religions of the Indian subcontinent have become world religions in ways that call into question rubrics of analyses developed in relation to earlier immigrant groups.

Gujaratis, including Swaminarayan Hindus, are prominent among the emigrants from India to several countries, and they maintain close social and religious networks spanning several nations and cultural contexts. The three most important strands creating the networks necessary for transnational emigration and intercourse are economic opportunity, family, and religion. Religion anchors identity in a transcendent reality and hence is a powerful element in shaping personal and group identity among immigrants and in strengthening social ties that cross national and political boundaries. Swaminarayan Hindus have been particularly adept in moving successfully between several countries and in establishing the infrastructure and emotional ties that both preserve their identity and gradually transform aspects of Swaminarayan Hinduism, which has become in the process a transnational world religion.

New immigrants regularly affirm that they are more religious in their new countries of residence than they were prior to emigration. However, the social function of religion, and specifically of the Swaminarayan religion, is different among an immigrant community from its function at home in Gujarat. It is the religion of a small regional, ethnic minority group. For example, in foreign countries the temple or the gathering place for the Sunday meetings of the Swaminarayan followers may be the only place where Gujaratis gather in a dominant social position. Meetings where Gujarati language, food, music, and rituals are used form the first bulwark outside the home against the considerable pressures of the host society and culture. To provide this bulwark is the latent function of the religion as viewed by an outside observer. Satsangis invariably describe the manifest function as the same as in the Indian setting. The goal is to spread the teachings of Swaminarayan and to lead the followers along the spiritual path to salvation. The manifest function is obvious; the latent function is equally important, though any attempt to universalize the religion may cause the two to be in some tension. Nevertheless, even members recognize that Swaminarayan spiritual goals are more difficult to achieve in an alien environment.

The transnational character of Swaminarayan Hinduism affects institutions in India at the same time it expands and develops abroad. Networks that extend like satellite base stations across the globe facilitate multiple strands of communication – no longer just two-way – that preserve and strengthen the various branches of the religion. The network supports a constant movement of leaders, marriage partners, money, literature, and ideas. Every summer acharyas, sadhus, and other religious specialists tour several countries to instruct and encourage followers and, in the process, learn about other cultures and customs. Large sums of money are transmitted across these networks to support religious activities in India and in other countries, especially the building of temples, schools, medical clinics, and other social welfare projects. One of the largest sources of foreign exchange for India is remittances from nonresident Indians, and a portion of those remittances is donations to support religious activities.

The three settings where large communities of Gujaratis reside and where the Swaminarayan religion is firmly established are in East Africa (Kenya, Uganda, and Tanzania), Britain, and the United States.[1] These provide the loci for the study of the transnational development of Swaminarayan Hinduism among overseas Gujaratis, of the function of this religious affiliation in the preservation of cultural and ethnic identity, and of the problems and potential inherent in the growth of the movement in these three locations. Differences in the context and stage of development require that the community in each setting be viewed separately.

The Indian communities in East Africa, Britain, and the United States have resulted from different sets of push/pull forces. Any pattern of emigration can be analyzed according to the forces in the home area or

---

[1] A large number of Gujaratis from the area of Kutch are engaged in the construction trades in the Gulf States of Oman and the United Arab Emirates. They maintain close contacts with Kutch because their wives and families are not allowed to live with them. Many of them are devotees of Swaminarayan, but official and unofficial restrictions govern their religious activities, which take place primarily privately in homes. The Acharya of Ahmedabad and other religious leaders visit regularly. The donations of these Kutchis are returned to the temple in Bhuj or to their home villages, to which they return after temporary appointments in the Gulf States.

society which caused persons to leave their native place to seek education or livelihood elsewhere. The most obvious of these are natural disasters such as famine or plague, political pressures and wars, overpopulation, and underemployment. These are common push factors which have led to emigration out of Gujarat. Complementing these are the pull factors in the host countries – the opportunities for jobs, education, political and economic freedom. The push-pull factors have been different in the three sister communities.

Major emigrations from Gujarat to East Africa took place in the first half of this century, and the Indian community and the Swaminarayan religion became well established. The great exodus came following the granting of independence to the East African countries. The immigration to Britain originating from East Africa and India began to be significant after the Second World War and was greatly expanded by the flood of immigrants in the late 1960s and early 1970s. Significant growth in the numbers of Indian immigrants to the United States took place in the 1970s and continued for the rest of the century. A few Indian graduate students elected to remain in the United States prior to 1965, but they were a tiny and inconspicuous minority. The major immigration as part of what has been termed "the new ethnics" took place following the enactment of the new Immigration Act of 1965.

Because the communities result from different waves of emigration, the three differ significantly in size, age, social standing, level of institutional organization, and manner of adaptation to the host society. In East Africa the Indian community and the Swaminarayan religion grew strong and wealthy under the protection of the British colonial power in close contact with home, which was under the same rule. The experience in independent Africa in the latter part of the century has been chaotic. The community that remains has to preserve itself as best it can under constantly changing political and cultural structures. The community in Britain is primarily the result of the resettlement of refugees from East Africa, many of whom entered Britain with little more than the clothes on their backs. They have been the beneficiaries of the laudable resettlement efforts of the British and of their own industry in a free community. At the same time they are often victims of racial prejudice and discrimination from those who see the Indian community as part of a threat to the preservation of the British way of life. The Indian community in the United States is a relatively new ingredient in the melting pot, but they have arrived at a time of new emphasis on ethnicity and on the role of the new ethnics in American society. Indians constitute a rapidly growing, young, well-educated, and increasingly prosperous group that has just begun to establish itself and its ethnic identity in a new place. The result is the establishment of new organizations and institutions, with the accompanying infrastructures and buildings, usually centered on Indian regional or linguistic identity.

A large percentage of the Indian immigrants in all three locations are Gujaratis, and among Gujarati immigrants in all three places the largest and fastest-growing religious group is Swaminarayan Hinduism. For those who are members and for those who participate in their large gatherings and festivals, the Swaminarayan fellowship provides the primary social group outside the family which relates them to their Gujarati heritage and which attempts to transmit that heritage to the next generation. Clearly that task is somewhat different in each cultural setting and for each subsequent generation. The development and function of the Swaminarayan religion among the Gujarati communities in East Africa, Britain, and the United States provide three case studies of the role of religion in immigrant groups.

"Wherever a Gujarati resides, there forever is Gujarat" is a familiar saying from the Gujarati poet Ardeshar Khabardar. It touches the nerve of Gujarati pride and the loyalty to language, customs, culture, and ethnic identity among Gujaratis who reside outside India. Others have added "Wherever a Gujarati resides, soon a Swaminarayan temple appears" as a witness to the mobility and adaptability of the religion (see plate 16). Swaminarayan Hinduism is a major element presenting Gujarati identity and ideals against forces which would erode them. At the same time it is an important element of the transnational network that transforms the experience of emigration and channels its impact in India and abroad.

EAST AFRICA

The Indian community in East Africa predated the modern experience of transnationalism, but has been enveloped by it so that the networks are no longer between just India and East Africa, but extend through family, economic, media, and religious ties to many other countries. For centuries prior to the modern era Indian traders had traveled from the western coast of India, primarily from Gujarat and Kutch, to East Africa in search of trade and wealth. Intercourse and communication were regular as they moved in sailing ships and dhows with the prevailing seasonal winds between Gujarat and Africa.

16 Pramukh Swami reviewing architect's drawings for temple

The immigrants who arrived after 1895 came for different reasons and exhibited different patterns of settlement. A major factor for these later immigrants was the construction of the Ugandan Railway, which opened up the interior for employment, residence, and trade. Many men went from Kutch to East Africa on the steamer that plied from Bhuj to Mombasa to work as poorly paid construction workers. Others followed during the first half of the century to take up positions in the government service and commerce.

P. M. Bhatt presents a study of the push-pull factors which led to the emigration to East Africa (1976). First, the vagaries of nature made residence in Gujarat at times difficult and dangerous, just as they had during the time of Swaminarayan. Famines were frequent, and between

1899 and 1900 the whole of Gujarat suffered a severe famine due to the failure of the monsoon. Even fertile Kaira district was affected. An outbreak of the plague which lasted from 1899 to 1902 nearly wiped out the population of many villages. Another outbreak of the plague came in 1916–18, followed by the influenza epidemic of 1918–19. Many persons walked to the coast to escape the suffering and hardships by sailing to East Africa. Second, poor economic conditions became a prominent factor later in the century. Third, the establishment and consolidation of British rule in India resulted in the flooding of Indian markets with cheap machine-made goods from the industries of Britain which created severe dislocation among artisans. Fourth, the adventure of travel, the challenge of new opportunities, and the desire to escape certain social pressures and familial obligations caused many young men to migrate to East Africa.

The situation there became increasingly more attractive, and several factors encouraged immigration. First, the political atmosphere in East Africa was relatively favorable for British Indian citizens, who were granted security and freedom of enterprise. In the last decade of the nineteenth century and the early years of the twentieth, imperial policy encouraged economic development through Indian immigration. Second, the demand for skilled workers and government servants along with the opportunities for trade attracted many workers. According to census reports in 1948 92 percent of all the carpenters, masons, and builders in Kenya were Indian (Bhatt 1976: 67). Third, the proximity of East Africa to Gujarat and the ease of communication enabled the immigrants to maintain caste and kinship ties, which both aided them in establishing themselves in Africa and facilitated return to India for visits or retirement.

The construction of the railway was of great significance for urban development and industrial growth in East Africa. The presence of the railway also influenced the growth and location of the Gujarati population there and the subsequent development of Swaminarayan Hinduism. Nairobi, Mombasa, Nakuru, and Kisumu, the four largest cities of Kenya, are on the Uganda Railway. Of the four, only Mombasa existed before 1896. Nairobi is wholly a product of the railway. Kampala, Jinja, and Tororo are railway centers (Naseem 1975: 174). Many Gujaratis came to serve in the railway as clerks, stationmasters and guards. Because of the predominance of Gujaratis in the railway service, it was called "the Patel Railway." Traders followed the railroad and soon large and prosperous Indian communities developed in the administrative and bazaar centers

along the route. Indian construction workers, mainly from Bhuj, were
engaged in the construction which accompanied the growth of trade and
industry. The Gujaratis, including the Kutchis, were the largest Indian
group, representing 80 percent or more of all Asians. Roughly three-
quarters of the Gujaratis were Hindus, and the rest were Muslims, pre-
dominantly Ismailis (Tinker 1977: 120).

In the first quarter of this century members of Swaminarayan
Hinduism, widely scattered in East Africa, continued their religious
activity privately at home and met with other members only during visits
back to India. There they visited the home temples and met with ascetics who were not permitted to reside outside India. The workers from
Kutch formed especially strong attachments to the temple and ascetics
at Bhuj. Those attachments were strengthened by Dharmajivandas
Swami, a mahant of the Bhuj temple, who had lived and worked in East
Africa as a young man. He went to East Africa in 1925 to work in a food
shop and stayed there for three years. A devout young man, he returned
to Bhuj to take initiation as an ascetic in 1929 or 1930. He became the
major force behind the organization of the Kutchis and the establishment of the Swaminarayan fellowship of Kutchis in East Africa. He
wrote letters to encourage Karsan Gopal, a building contractor, and
Lalji Makanji, the owner of food shops in Nairobi and farms in Dar es
Salaam, to create organizations there. Dharmajivandas became mahant
in Bhuj in 1953, a position he held for twenty-two years. The Kutchis
have remained loyal to the temple in Bhuj and to the acharya of
Ahmedabad.

Another line of development, now associated with the growth of the
Akshar Purushottam Sanstha, comes from the work of Harmanbhai
Makandas Patel, an assistant stationmaster on "the Patel Railway." He
was from the Vadtal diocese, but his work in spreading the religion was
inspired by his association with Shastri Maharaj. Beginning in 1932, after
a visit to India, Harmanbhai Patel initiated conversations with his fellow
workers in Mombasa to encourage them to follow the dictates and rituals
of their religion. Tribhovandas M. Patel joined with him to establish
contacts with the followers of Swaminarayan in Mombasa and other
towns of Kenya. Harmanbhai Patel continued his religious activity after
he was transferred to Kibwesi. Maganbhai Patel, his superior as stationmaster there, was not a religious or devout person, but Harmanbhai was
successful in convincing him to become a devotee. These two railway
officials became leaders and organizers in East Africa, with Maganbhai
Patel gradually becoming the more prominent. Pictures and statues of

these two are displayed in the Akshar Purushottam temples in East Africa and in some temples in Britain and India to honor their contribution to the spread of the religion.

Generally religions spread along the major lines of travel and communication. If in India the main temples and centers are located in places marked by the footprints of Swaminarayan, the temples and centers in East Africa developed along the railway in conjunction with the growth in trade and commerce among Indian immigrants. An important point was reached in 1932 at Kibwezi when Harmanbhai Patel and Maganbhai Patel decided to have regular Sunday evening meetings for Hindus similar to meetings held by Christians, Ismailis and Sikhs. At about the same time Kutchis began to meet in caste and religious groups. At first weekly, and then daily prayers were held in Harmanbhai Patel's house, and the number of worshipers and members increased. After a few months Maganbhai Patel was transferred to Makindu, and Harmanbhai Patel was moved to Mackinnon Road Station, both on the line between Mombasa and Nairobi. Other followers moved to other centers of government service or of trade and commerce. The first general meeting was held in Makindu in August, 1933, and it was followed by annual meetings in Simba, Mombasa, and Nairobi.

Some prominent leaders of the organization in East Africa and in Britain remember those early days. They speak of the small numbers, the relative poverty of the members, the poor roads, and the difficulties in building the institution. Some of these leaders were converted from other Hindu traditions, in part because the satsang provided for fellowship with other Kutchis and Gujaratis. The railways and some other governmental institutions were inter-territorial under British administration, and persons were transferred and workers migrated across Kenya, Uganda, and Tanzania. Maganbhai Patel was transferred to Jinja on Lake Victoria about fifty miles from Kampala and then to Tororo near the Kenyan border. As other members were transferred, centers were established in the growing towns of all three territories.

Communication between East Africa and India was frequent. Lay leaders traveled to India to visit their families and home villages, and also to make pilgrimages to temples, where they conversed with their preceptors (gurus) among the leading ascetics. Mention has been made of Dharmajivandas Swami, the mahant of Bhuj, who encouraged the Kutchis to build a temple in Nairobi. Both Maganbhai Patel and Harmanbhai Patel are reported to have spent time with Shastri Maharaj, who is credited by followers of the Akshar Purushottam Sanstha with inspiring the growth of Swaminarayan Hinduism in Africa. Growth was encouraged by Sadhu Nirgundas Swami, who supported the followers in East Africa in the early days by sending them long letters. He had been the mahant of the Swaminarayan temple in Bombay associated with the Vadtal diocese. Over a span of several years he wrote long letters which were circulated among the followers at various centers, much as one imagines Paul's letters circulating among Christians in the Roman empire. Nirgundas' correspondence had a profound effect on the development of leadership and the growth of the religion.

The first temple on the continent was the East Africa Swaminarayan Temple in Nairobi, built in 1945. The pictorial images were consecrated in India and then were shipped to Nairobi. This temple is associated with the Ahmedabad diocese, and in 1957 Tejendraprasad visited the temple for his father and installed the images in the women's shrine. When it was first built, however, the divisions in evidence in India had not become pronounced in East Africa, and followers of the various branches joined together in building and worshiping in the temple. The largest and most prominent group at this time was the one, primarily of Kutchis, loyal to the temple at Bhuj and to the acharya in Ahmedabad.

After 1950 the groups began to divide from one another and to establish separate temples. Muktajivandas traveled to Nairobi after he separated from the Ahmedabad diocese, stayed in the newly built temple, and gathered a few families who still remain loyal to the Maninagar group. In 1950 Shastri Maharaj instructed his followers in East Africa to hold separate meetings, and in 1952 the constitution for a separate Akshar Purushottam Swaminarayan Sanstha was adopted at a large gathering at Mbale in Uganda.

Although Shastri Maharaj never visited East Africa, the tradition is that it was he who determined that the first temple of the Akshar Purushottam Sanstha would be built in Mombasa and the second at Kampala at the other end of the railway line. Then temples were to be built in other towns along the way. His wishes were acted on, and a temple was consecrated in Mombasa by Yogiji Maharaj during an extended visit to East Africa in 1955. This first visit by any ascetic of the Akshar Purushottam Satsang spurred the growth of the satsang, and in the next decade and a half several temples were constructed. Temples in Kampala, Tororo, and Jinja were consecrated by Yogiji Maharaj during his second visit to East Africa in 1960. The Akshar Purushottam

Temple in Kampala was the most spacious and imposing among all the temples in East Africa, and it was built in the style of the temples of India. In 1963 a temple was built in Gulu on the northwest spur of the Uganda Railway. The consecration ceremony was not performed by an ascetic or an acharya; rather, A. P. Patel was delegated by Yogiji Maharaj to install the images. Temples were eventually built in Tanzania at Dar es Salaam and Mwanza. Another temple area was set apart in a residential compound in Kisumu. Thus, the Akshar Purushottam group had four temples in Uganda at Kampala, Jinja, Tororo, and Gulu; three in Kenya at Mombasa, Nairobi, and Kisumu; and two in Tanzania at Dar es Salaam and Mwanza. Other worship centers, some in private homes, were established for regular meetings in other towns.

The larger group loyal to Bhuj and the Ahmedabad acharya developed their own temples and centers. A second temple in Nairobi, the Shree Kutch Satsang Swaminarayan Temple, was built in 1954. Karsan Gopal was president of this temple. Lalji Makanji had moved to Tanzania and was instrumental in the building of the Tanzanian Swaminarayan Temple in Dar es Salaam in 1958. The Shree Kutch Satsang Swaminarayan Temple in Mombasa was dedicated in February 1960. This large, well-appointed temple has become one of the tourist sights of Mombasa and is about a hundred yards from the Akshar Purushottam Temple on the same street. As the name implies, the temple serves primarily followers from the area of Kutch, many of whom are in the construction business. Inside the main building of the Kutchi temple are two large shrine rooms. The one on the ground floor is for women, and the one on the upper floor is for men. The images in the form of large pictures are situated at the end of each room. The central picture is of Swaminarayan. The picture on the left is of Swaminarayan with Krishna and Radha; the one on the right is of Nar and Narayana. Women do not have a separate shrine room in the Akshar Purushottam temple up the street, but there is a separate section of the main shrine room designated for them. The images there are the same as those in the Akshar Purushottam temples in India. Pictures of Swaminarayan and Gunatitanand are in the center. On the right are those of Krishna and Radha with Lakshmi Narayana above pictures of Shastri Maharaj and his successors. On the left are pictures of Nar Narayana, of Acharyas Raghuvira and Ayodhyaprasad with the four sadhus who compiled the *Vachanamritam*. The two groups go their separate ways in Mombasa and throughout East Africa, and there seems to be little cooperation or conflict.

Temple building is a sign of the growth in numbers and the increased prosperity of the Gujarati immigrants. The two decades between 1950 and 1969 were a heady period of success for the Gujaratis of East Africa. The Swaminarayan followers and the satsang as an institution enjoyed the results of this growth and prosperity. Michael Lyon has observed that the Gujaratis acquired a new role in the colonial economics of East Africa, and ultimately a tragic one. They became a privileged racial estate under British protection (Lyon 1973: 8f.). The Indian population in Kenya increased from 43,625 in 1931 to 176,613 in 1962. In Tanzania the growth was from 46,254 in 1948 to 88,700 in 1962. More than 80 percent were Gujaratis. The Indian population of Uganda totaled only 74,308 in 1969, but though smaller than that of Kenya or Tanzania, it had grown rapidly from 3,518 since 1948 (Tinker 1977: 119–20, 151). Gujaratis were primarily urban and employed in the civil service, the professions or trade and industry, and as a community they had reached a level of significant prosperity. The Indian population in Nairobi increased between 1931 and 1969 from 13,582 to 139,037, and in Mombasa from 11,847 to 39,049 (P. M. Bhatt 1976: 72). At their peak, the Indians formed no more than 2 percent of the population of Kenya, but they were one-third of the population of Nairobi (Tinker 1977: 121). For a time, the Gujarati community as part of the Indian population had a relatively secure social position between the British and the Africans.

The tripartite colonial system was based on a separation of the Europeans, Asians, and Africans which led to the establishment of separate schools, hospitals, and recreation and other facilities for each community. Social interactions between the various races were minimized. Each racial group was governed by its own set of communal laws. The policy of separate development of different communities gave each community some measure of freedom to pursue its own culture, language, and religious beliefs and activities. The policy reinforced Gujarati regionalism and ethnic self-awareness, and one of the results was that religion functioned as one of many aspects of cultural identity. Migrants transplanted Indian culture and values by forming themselves into voluntarily exclusive communities and retaining contacts with India wherever conditions and means of communication permitted. East African Gujaratis continued to return home to negotiate marriages in one of the preferred villages of the marriage circle according to the rules of caste, within the caste and outside one's ancestral village. Although many elements of caste differentiation were not observed in East Africa, such as commensal rules or the wearing of the sacred thread by Brahmins, caste regulations were a part of their associations with family and village society back in India. Until just prior to the Second World War, the common practice was for the men to return home for marriage and to send the children to Gujarat for their education. Even after families moved to East Africa, the sons were regularly sent to India for their education. This practice changed during the war because of the hazards of and restrictions on travel, and marriages were increasingly contracted among Gujaratis born in East Africa. It became a practice to educate the children in the schools in East Africa, at least through secondary level.

The tripartite colonial school system separated the three races. Indian schools were for Indian children and were managed by Indians. Gujarati was used both in the homes and the schools, though some instruction was in English. Gujaratis emphasized education, and sought opportunities for their children. The largest secondary school in East Africa just prior to Independence was the Mahatma Gandhi School in Nairobi, and when university education started in Kenya in 1956, of the 157 students first admitted, 6 were European, 57 were African, and 94 were Indian (Tinker 1977: 121). Part of the tragedy of the history of Gujaratis in East Africa is that the first generation of those born and educated there was the generation forced out after Independence.

Significant differences developed between the generations of Indians in East Africa. Members of the older generation had typically been born and educated in India and were married to women who had come to East Africa after marriage. Many of them expected and looked forward to retirement at home in their native villages after they handed over their businesses or positions to their sons according to the traditional Indian practice. They were most comfortable with the use of spoken and written Gujarati, though the men and some women could converse fluently in both English and Swahili. The primary social identity of the men and the exclusive social identity of the women was formed within the Gujarati community. The Swaminarayan temple or center was an important institution, though one among many, where the Gujarati language was spoken, Gujarati food eaten, Gujarati songs sung, and Gujarati culture and values were celebrated.

The religious institutions became instruments for the socialization of the younger generation as they grew up in East Africa. They were educated in the schools of East Africa, which normally followed the Western model of education and attempted to prepare their students to take the general Cambridge examinations. While students were relatively skillful in the spoken and written use of English, they had not advanced in Gujarati beyond the use of the language in home and temple. Moreover, over the years the form of Gujarati in East Africa diverged noticeably from that spoken in Gujarat. The Swaminarayan temple and its programs provided a point of contact with India and a cultural heritage that most of this generation had not seen and could only conceive by close analogy to the East African Gujarati community. Each of the Swaminarayan groups formed a youth organization associated with the temples to teach the language and religious values to the young people.

Swaminarayan Hinduism in East Africa formed a vital part of the Gujarati Indian culture. No attempt has been made to attract Europeans or Africans as members. The Gujarati language, rituals, and theology remain inaccessible. A few Africans visit the temples to request help from the deities, but they do not participate in rituals or become members.

Membership in Swaminarayan Hinduism grew faster than the Gujarati population in the period prior to Independence. As the community became larger and more prosperous, members founded temples and developed institutions to help preserve Gujarati culture and transmit it to the new generation. Each temple and center had its managing committee to plan its program, and the Akshar Purushottam Sanstha organized a central committee in Mombasa in 1952 to coordinate the activities of the fellowship all over East Africa. A strong and effective lay leadership developed which had standing within the total Gujarati community. When Yogiji Maharaj visited East Africa in 1970 and Acharya Tejendraprasad Pande visited the following year, African political leaders and thousands of Indian devotees gathered to welcome the religious leaders from India. Swaminarayan Hinduism was at its zenith in East Africa.

While at its height, the fellowship in East Africa returned significant contributions to the institution in India. Overseas Indians have always been important in the economy of parts of India because of the return of funds and foreign exchange to families, villages, and institutions at home. The major source of income for some villages, especially in the poorer areas of Kutch, is the foreign exchange sent home by husbands, fathers, or sons working abroad. Indian consulates abroad are well aware of the importance of this source of foreign exchange.

More important than the monetary contribution has been the contribution of sons and fathers to the Akshar Purushottam work in India. Yogiji Maharaj's three trips to East Africa could be viewed as scouting and recruiting trips to choose and attract young men to become ascetics. Many returned to India with him or joined him after they completed their schooling to "renounce the world" and take up the life of an ascetic. Several ascetics from East Africa occupy positions of considerable responsibility in the temples and programs in India. Indeed, the recruitment of Western-educated and English-speaking young men from East Africa has given the Akshar Purushottam Sanstha a well-trained corps of sadhus equipped to establish contact with devotees in East Africa, Britain, and the United States. Young men who were friends and colleagues in satsang activities in East Africa in the 1950s and early 1960s and trained by C. T. Patel are prominent Swaminarayan leaders in Britain, Canada, and the United States. Their friendships are part of the network that binds together Swaminarayan Hinduism as a transnational movement. Moreover, many of the older generation have retired to India, and some of these householders have volunteered their full-time service to temples where they perform whatever tasks are assigned by the mahant or kothari of the temple. These persons, young and old, have proved to be a valuable resource.

Swaminarayan Hinduism prospered in East Africa as the population grew; it has suffered reverses with the decline of the Indian community following the independence of the East African countries. Between 1962 and 1964 all three territories, Kenya, Tanzania, and Uganda, became independent states, and the political status of Indians who had been citizens of India or of the British Commonwealth was changed. The constitutions of Kenya and Tanzania made provision for granting citizenship to those who had resided in the territories prior to Independence. Registration was required within two years, and dual citizenship was not allowed. British passport holders were permitted to remain, but only under the provisions of temporary work permits. Those born in the territories after Independence were automatically citizens. The easy entry of Indians to East Africa was no longer possible, so the flow of immigrants from India was effectively stopped.

More ominous from the perspective of the Indian community was the policy of "Africanization" undertaken by the new governments. The policy resulted in a difficult time for Indians, especially for those who for various reasons did not apply for citizenship in Kenya or Tanzania. The primary instrument of official discrimination was the Kenya Immigration Act of 1967, which took effect on 7 December 1967. The Act controlled not only entry into Kenya, but also the economic activities of all non-citizens by stipulating that priority must be given to citizens of Kenya in matters of employment. All existing residents' permits were withdrawn, and non-citizens had to acquire new permits to work in Kenya. Many Indians were thus driven out of their positions in government and commerce. According to the Kenyan government figures, a total of 15,000 British passport holders of Indian origin left Kenya during the three months from December 1967 to February 1968. The majority went to Britain (P. M. Bhatt 1976: 372).

Emigration was substantially increased because of the panic caused by the British Commonwealth Immigrants Act of 1968, which restricted the entry of East African Indians to Britain. Many left East Africa to gain entry before the proposed new law took effect. Afterward, there was continued pressure to increase the voucher quota to permit hard-pressed Indian residents in East Africa to enter Britain. Emigration became a rushing torrent when the worst fears of the Indians were confirmed in the forced exodus of Indians from Uganda. With degrading harshness Idi Amin forced all Indians to leave Uganda in 1972–3. They became "migranauts," as Mr. Praful Patel named them, dispossessed of their property and looking for new homes. Some took refuge in India and Canada; most went to Britain.

The last quarter of the twentieth century was a period of enormous economic and political change in the three East African countries, and Swaminarayan Hindus have experienced resulting ups and downs. Nowhere has the change been more dramatic than in Uganda. Only a few Asians stayed in Uganda after the expulsion, and all the Swaminarayan properties were confiscated by the government or occupied by others. The economic difficulties and security problems continued, so most gave up all hope of returning to Uganda. A change began when a new president, Lt. Gen. Yoweri Kaguta Museveni, a Protestant Christian, took power in Uganda, first as a military ruler in 1986 and then as an elected official in 1996. He encouraged Indians to return to assist with the rebuilding of the country and he started returning to Indians the properties that had been confiscated or stolen. He also reaffirmed the freedom of worship. In 1991 a Ugandan official attended the dedication of Akshardham in Gandhinagar and in a symbolic act returned the deed to the Swaminarayan temple property in Kampala. The next year all Swaminarayan schools and temples were returned.

A few businessmen went back to Uganda to take possession of their property and restart their companies, but most of them attracted staff from India to run the businesses so they could return to Britain. Hence, most of the Indian immigration to Uganda in the 1990s has been directly from India; the immigrants are primarily teachers, accountants, clerks, and managers from Gujarat. Most are young. In 1999 only one Akshar Purushottam Sanstha member was over fifty years of age. Estimates are that approximately 10,000 Indians were in Uganda in 1999, and some 4,500 of those in Kampala.[2]

At the same time as they rebuilt the Asian business infrastructure, they reestablished Swaminarayan activities. The temple in Kampala was reconsecrated and a national committee was appointed by Pramukh Swami in October 1991. Between 30 and 50 people visit the temple each day, approximately 150 attend the Sunday sabha meetings, and as many as 1,000 attend the major festivals. There is also a Sanatan Hindu Temple in Kampala, just opposite the Swaminarayan temple, and another in Jinja. The Swaminarayan leader travels from Kampala to Jinja and Iganga each fortnight for satsang activities involving approximately 150 people. Only six families live in Tororo, so even though they have possession of the temple, it is not functioning. They have not taken possession of the temple in Gulu because a school meets there, not a single Indian lives there, and it is in a very unsettled area near the Sudan border. Pramukh Swami visited Kampala during his tour of East Africa in 1999. The Kutchis are establishing a temple in a converted bungalow in Kampala where none existed prior to the expulsion. So, the reestablishment of Swaminarayan Hinduism continues apace in Uganda. In 1996 during a state visit to Britain, the President of Uganda met Pramukh Swami and a huge crowd of Gujaratis at the new Swaminarayan temple in London to mark the twenty-fifth anniversary of the expulsion of Asians from Uganda. A poignant moment for many of the exiles resettled in London!

The political situation has remained more stable in Kenya under the long presidency of D. T. Arap Moi, but economic difficulties, civil disturbances, and lack of security have caused many families to emigrate, primarily to Britain. Over half of the Swaminarayan followers who were active in 1970 had left by the early 1980s. During the 1990s the number of Indians in Kenya stabilized; young people continued to leave Kenya for education in Britain or the United States, but it has been easier for other young people to enter Kenya from India (albeit somewhat more difficult in the late 1990s because of a financial crisis). Indian families in East Africa now seek marriage partners primarily in Britain rather than

---

[2] Information and statistics about Indians and Swaminarayan followers in East Africa were gathered from the Acharya of Ahmedabad, several sadhus, and leaders from East Africa visiting India and London in January and March 1999. Some discrepancies regarding statistics emerged; what are given here represent a compilation from several sources.

in India in order to establish familial networks in the West. Hence, East Africa is again a way-station for families in the transnational network reaching from India to East Africa to Britain and/or North America. A Swaminarayan leader in Nairobi remarked, "There is always an exchange with some people leaving for the UK and USA and new ones coming from India for management positions in Asian companies."

In spite of financial difficulties and the possibility of political instability, both the old school and the Akshar Purushottam Sanstha have constructed new temples in Nairobi that were dedicated in 1999 (even though both already had functioning temples there). Pramukh Swami assigned several sadhus to reside in the Nairobi temple and visit the Indian community to build up the satsang in East Africa. New temples are also under construction in Eldoret and Nakuru. Estimates of the number of Akshar Purushottam Sanstha families in Kenya in 1999 were: Nairobi 130; Mombasa 50; Eldoret 50; Nakuru 50; Kisumu 60; and Kakamega 20. Families loyal to Bhuj and Ahmedabad were approximately twice those numbers. The Swaminarayan Gadi claimed approximately 1,000 satsangis in East Africa.

The situation in Tanzania is similar to that in Kenya; the Indian community hangs on and the Swaminarayan groups maintain temples and meetings for an Indian community greatly reduced in size and wealth from the pre-Independence days. The Akshar Purushottam Sanstha has centers in Dar es Salaam (75 families), Malindi (20 families), Munza (85 families), and Arusha (18 families). For many years following Independence, the border between Kenya and Tanzania was closed, so it was virtually impossible to coordinate activities, but that changed in the late 1990s.

The Presidents of Kenya, Tanzania, and Uganda met in 1998 in Arusha, on the border of Kenya and Tanzania, to establish greater East African cooperation. While they could never recreate the old East African Union, greater cooperation has led to more open borders, an East African Identification Card that permits free travel, and initiatives to solve the currency problems of the three countries. Relations are certainly better, which makes travel to festivals and the coordination of Swaminarayan activities in East Africa much easier. Pramukh Swami appointed a national board of trustees in each country and an East African Board of Trustees under the chairmanship of Mahendra (Barrister) Patel, a long-time leader in Nairobi. Local trustees administer the individual old-school temples. Swaminarayan Hinduism in East Africa is at about the same place in development that it was in the post-

Second World War years, and now as then, its future depends on the political, economic, and cultural winds blowing across Africa.[3]

BRITAIN

The Shri Swaminarayan Hindu Temple and Haveli in Neasden in North London is the most visible and remarkable monument recording the impact of Indian emigration from East Africa to Britain. Swaminarayan growth and development in Britain can be traced from meetings in homes, to regular weekly meetings in a small, dilapidated converted chapel in Islington, to larger gatherings in a converted warehouse in Neasden, to the major temple complex and school in Neasden that have attracted over 600,000 visitors each year since the opening in 1995. The temple is an impressive statement that the Indian immigrants are permanent residents in Britain and are prepared to make their contributions to national cultural and religious life. The beautiful temple complex, which was named one of the seventy wonders of the modern world in a book published by the Reader's Digest Association (1998), represents a stark contrast to the lack of resources of the early immigrants.

Immigration directly from India developed following the Second World War. In 1945 there were only about 7,000 Asian residents, but the next fifteen years saw a dramatic increase. Economic expansion and the shortage of unskilled laborers attracted immigrant workers from many parts of the Commonwealth. Travel and immigration were easy; until 1962 all citizens of the Commonwealth were admitted, and even after 1962 work vouchers were still issued for various types of laborers. The benefits of the welfare programs instituted after the war made settlement relatively easy and risk free. Still, compared to the later influx, the immigration of the 1950s was on a minor scale; there were about 47,500 settlers from India – 30,500 males and 17,000 females (Tinker 1977: 167). More workers, mainly unskilled, came from India in the 1960s. They took jobs others did not want to do in the prospering economy. Throughout the period students came to British universities from India and East Africa and stayed on after the completion of their studies.

The large influx of Indians from East Africa, the majority of whom were Gujaratis, came in two successive waves. The first came in the

---

[3] Small, shrinking communities of Indians and Swaminarayan followers are located in Central Africa, and sadhus visit those families on their African tours. The main African center of growth outside of East Africa is South Africa. A temple and several meeting places are located in Johannesburg, and both Durban and Lancier have smaller hari mandirs.

mid-to-late 1960s, spurred by the independence of East African countries and the Africanization programs and uncertainties which followed. Approximately 62,500 Indians left Kenya for Britain in the
period between 1963 and 1968 (Steel 1969: 252). On 28 February 1968
the British Home Secretary announced that under the Commonwealth
Immigrants Act Britain would issue 1,500 vouchers annually to Kenyan
Asians. The panic in East Africa mentioned above caused large
numbers of Indians to attempt to reach Britain. To alleviate hardship,
the British government increased the voucher quota from 1,500 to
3,000 in June 1971. Many of the unskilled workers returned from East
Africa to India, and some of the best educated and most prosperous
migrated to Britain (P. M. Bhatt 1976: 373, 389).

All plans for the orderly emigration of East African Indians were
knocked into a cocked hat by the actions of Idi Amin in Uganda. After
a period of harassment in 1972–3, all Indians were forced to leave
Uganda. While most eventually found refuge in Britain, very few were
able to get their valuables or financial resources out of Uganda.
Through a major British resettlement effort, they were able to establish
themselves in the urban centers of England and Wales. The poignancy
of the situation is highlighted by Lyon's comment: "So the refugees from
empires only just dead find temporary shelter in a shell at the heart of
an empire destroyed half a century ago by nations struggling to become
independent states" (1973: 8f.). Some tension existed within the Indian
community between the "Africans," who migrated from East Africa in
the 1970s, and the "Indians," many of whom came directly from India
earlier. The community has grown in numbers and in prosperity since
the arrival of the "Africans," who are now more numerous and have
taken the lead in the creation of Indian organizations and institutions
and are effective participants in the transnational networks that sustain
the Indian community and Swaminarayan Hinduism.

The earlier immigrants were too few in number, too scattered, too
poor, and too involved in gaining a foothold to engage in elaborate
institution building. After the East African Gujaratis came and established themselves, the community was able to form organizations and
build temples. The Indian community has become increasingly affluent.
One leader of a temple recalled that in 1970, when Swaminarayan
sadhus first visited Britain, the membership was small and only three
cars were owned by satsangis with the result that there was difficulty
arranging for transportation for the visitors. Twelve years later they
moved into a new temple complex, in part because the old church build-

ing in Islington converted into a temple could not contain the crowds and because the neighbors were inconvenienced by the traffic jam and parking problems created in the area when meetings were held. The immigrants brought with them the organizational abilities developed in running the temples and centers in East Africa. An official of a temple in London remarked in 1980, "We inherited five presidents, ten vice-presidents, and one hundred committee members from the temples in East Africa." They provided the leadership necessary for organization and rapid growth. There are hundreds of Hindu religious groups in Britain, but Swaminarayan Hinduism is at present the largest and the fastest growing.

The divisions within Swaminarayan Hinduism in India and East Africa were sufficiently clear and fixed by the time of the major migration to Britain for institutions and temples to have been built separately by each group. Transnational networks developing among followers of branches of Swaminarayan Hinduism are primary and more formative than relations with other Hindu or Swaminarayan groups in Britain. A dinner with special guests in the Swaminarayan temple in Neasden is a transnational gathering likely to include leaders from the British Midlands, Nairobi, Kampala, Mumbai, Rajkot, Chicago, and Edison, New Jersey. Moreover, the chances are good that the people share school ties, family relations, common memories of travel with Yogiji Maharaj or other sadhus, and common participation in Swaminarayan festivals in several countries.

Each Swaminarayan group has a slightly different history and strategy of adaptation in Britain. Followers of Muktajivandas Swami were the first Swaminarayan followers to establish regular meetings and a temple in Britain. In the early 1960s a group of Leva Kanbi Patels, originally from twenty-four villages near Bhuj in Kutch, emigrated from East Africa. At the urging of Muktajivandas, they started meeting in 1964 in a single room and in 1966 purchased a house in Hendon in Northwest London and converted it into a temple for the Swaminarayan Siddhanta Sijivan Mandal. Muktajivandas visited London in 1970 and participated in a formal religious procession from Hyde Park corner to Trafalgar Square led by a Scottish pipe band, which was a mark of prestige during the British Raj in India. The next year they dedicated a larger hall in Hendon as their temple. Rohit Barot estimated the membership in 1972 as 500 (1973: 34–7). Increased emigration of Kutchis from East Africa led to rapid growth. Whereas the Swaminarayan Gadi in India attracts followers from other parts of Gujarat as well as Kutch, over 95 percent in Britain are Kutchis. The older generation are primarily in the construction industry, a carry-over from their businesses in East Africa, but the younger generation are university graduates in the professions.

Having outgrown the temple in Hendon, they bought a large church building in Golders Green in 1981 and converted it into a temple, where approximately 1,000 people gather for sabhas. A smaller temple is located in Bolton and serves the Midlands. The group has not grown as rapidly as other Swaminarayan groups, perhaps because, they claim, they follow Swaminarayan's regulations strictly or because they follow in Britain a relatively narrow ethnic strategy of adaptation that emphasizes Kutchi aspects of culture and devotion which is attractive primarily to Kutchis. They have a full range of language and religion classes for young people. An interesting development that transcends a focus on ethnicity is that the temple sponsors a Shree Muktajeevan pipe band established in 1972 and made up of forty young men of the temple who have performed at major festivals and processions in Britain, Kenya, France, and India.

Muktajivandas Swami died during a visit to Britain at Bolton on 28 August 1979. Each year the followers make a pilgrimage to the Lake District as a memorial to Muktajivandas because he gave his final discourse there and the final photograph was taken of him with his successor, Purushottampriyadas Swami. Purushottampriyadas visited the satsangis in Britain annually until his cardiac surgery in 1998.

The Akshar Purushottam Sanstha was the fastest-growing Hindu group in Britain during the last quarter of the twentieth century. A few graduate students and early immigrants began to meet in the 1960s, and Yogiji Maharaj visited London in 1970 to install the deities in pictorial form in a temple in a small renovated burned-out church building in Islington. Many more Gujaratis moved from East Africa to England in the late 1960s and the 1970s. Praful Patel, the president of Akshar Purushottam Sanstha, was the only Asian on the Ugandan Resettlement Board. Several young men from Britain offered themselves for initiation as sadhus in 1981 during the bicentenary celebrations of Swaminarayan's birth at Ahmedabad. Some of them have now returned as sadhus to reside in the new temple in Neasden and oversee satsang activities.

Rapid growth in Britain by the early 1980s enabled them to purchase for £310,000 a warehouse complex in Neasden in North London that they converted into a temple large enough for 3,000 people. Pramukh Swami returned to London with a group of sadhus in April 1982 to open the remodeled facilities. The roots of the majority of the devotees in East

17 Carved dome of Swaminarayan temple in Neasden, London

Africa were symbolized by the fact that the images which had been in the temple in Kampala were enshrined in the temple. The second largest concentration of Gujarati immigrants is in Leicester, where a union hall was purchased in 1977 and converted into a temple. A large plot of land was acquired in 1999 for the construction of a new temple in the Leicester suburb of Hamilton planned to be "a small version of the Neasden temple."

A major impetus to recent growth was the successful month-long mega-festival held in the grounds of Alexandra Palace in London in the summer of 1985 to celebrate the bicentenary of the birth of Gunatitanand Swami. It was a huge public relations coup because the festival attracted media attention and many visitors, both Indians and others. It put Swaminarayan Hinduism on the cultural and religious map of Britain, established Swaminarayan Hindus' premier position among Indian immigrants, and gave the group confidence to undertake even larger projects. The leadership and organizational structure put into place to run the festival then facilitated additional growth so that ten years later they were able to construct the first and largest temple outside of India built in traditional Indian architectural style (see plate 17).

The temple has over 26,000 intricately carved pieces of Italian Carrara marble and Bulgarian limestone that were shipped to India to be carved by more than 1,500 traditional craftsmen and then shipped back to London for the construction. The basement contains a permanent exhibition on "Understanding Hinduism." The attached cultural center is called a "haveli" because the large foyer has Burmese teak and English oak carved by craftsmen in India to resemble the courtyards of traditional Gujarati houses. It contains a large prayer hall, residence for sadhus, kitchen and dining areas, a gymnasium, and offices. The total cost in addition to volunteer labor is estimated at sixteen million British pounds. The temple is a major place of worship for Hindus who are not satsangis; in 1999 over 13,500 Shivites visited the temple on Shivaratri for special rites and puja. The temple complex has become a major tourist attraction as well as serving as the administrative center for the Akshar Purushottam Sanstha in Britain and Europe. In the first three years following the opening in August 1995, over 55,500 school children from 1,123 schools made scheduled visits to the temple to learn about Hinduism, and each year sees an increase in numbers.

A school building across the street was purchased and converted into the Swaminarayan Hindu School in 1992. It serves 450 students in the National Curriculum up to their A-level examinations and won awards in 1998 for the success of its sixteen-year-olds in their GCSE exams, in which they ranked first in Brent and very high nationally. The school days are lengthened to accommodate special classes in religious education, Gujarati, and the arts. Approximately 20 percent of the students are Swaminarayan Hindus, 15 percent are Jains, and the rest are from other Hindu families. The school building is used on Sundays for Gujarati classes for 500 children from eight to fifteen years old.

It had not been the practice of the sadhus to reside permanently outside of India until Pramukh Swami appointed Atmaswarupdas Swami as mahant of the London temple in 1995 and placed other sadhus in the temple to assist. It is now the custom for sadhus to live and tour constantly in East Africa, Britain, and North America. Fifteen sadhus reside in the Neasden temple – nine of whom grew up in Britain, one in East Africa, one in the United States, and four in India, which illustrates the transnational character of the movement. They are responsible for a wide range of activities that illustrate both the organizational structure of most temples and the assignments of sadhus: Atmaswarupdas Swami is mahant and exercises general oversight, two are pujaris and conduct the rituals in the temple shrines, one oversees the kitchen that serves over 100 people daily and over 3,500 at the major monthly gathering, four oversee the program of activities for various age groups (children from 8 to 15 years, teenagers from 15 to 23 years, youths from 23 to 45 years, and seniors above 45 years), two travel constantly to visit other centers in Britain and Europe, one oversees the information and technology department, one coordinates the work of volunteers who maintain the building and services, and three travel with other sadhus. Approximately 50 volunteers come to the temple each day to give service in addition to 18 employed staff, and 25 young men from India volunteer for three-year service contracts to assist with the temple, for which they receive money for travel, a small stipend, room and board. It is a major undertaking.

The old warehouse building nearby that had been used as a temple is now converted into a surprisingly successful food service enterprise that grew out of efforts to raise funds to build the new temple. Volunteers run Saya Enterprises, which is one of the largest catering firms in Europe. They prepare and serve vegetarian Gujarati meals at functions through-out London and beyond, and they run grocery stores that provide foods and spices used by the Asian community. Saya Enterprises had several independent branches in 1999 located in London, Los Angeles, Chicago, Houston, Edison, N.J., Leicester, Nairobi, and Atlanta. Volunteer work both for the satsang and for the larger community is a hallmark of the organization, and the contributions and donations raised by Saya Enterprises are an asset to the temple.

The work of the Akshar Purushottam Sanstha in Britain and Europe is centralized and administered from the London temple under a new Satsang Parsar national plan put into place in 1998. Pramukh Swami appoints the national board of trustees who work with Atmaswarupdas to plan activities. Twelve regions cover Britain and Europe (although there was no activity in Ireland or Scotland and only one small gather-ing in Wales in 1999), and a regional coordinator organizes each region. Six Akshar Purushottam Sanstha temples are located in London (2,477 active and devoted families), Leicester (120), Wellingborough (40), Birmingham (25), Preston (20), and Ashton-under-Lyne (74). Weekly area meetings are held in each of the ten active regions (fourteen in greater London) under the direction of a volunteer area coordinator, and sadhus travel from the London temple every evening to attend local meetings within driving distance. Some areas have large concentrations: Crawley (96 families), Luton (72), and Wickford (182). Regular training is provided for the volunteer coordinators, called "karyakars," and a *Sahajanand Newsletter* appeared in 1998 to instruct them in sanstha affairs.

Gujaratis and other Hindus are scattered throughout Europe, and the London temple reaches out to them by means of regular visits by sadhus and teams of volunteers. Pramukh Swami occasionally tours selected European cities, as do Tejendraprasad Pande and other Hindu leaders. A number of East African Indians were resettled in Sweden and Norway, and The Netherlands has a large number of Hindus with roots in Surinam. Lisbon (150 families) and Paris (100 families) have fairly large concentrations of Indian cloth merchants who import items from India to sell in the markets. They hold regular weekly Swaminarayan local meetings. Those in Lisbon have roots in the Portuguese colony at Diu in South Kathiawar and in South Gujarat near Surat. Indian immigrants in Europe are becoming part of the transnational network.

The largest and most influential temple associated with Bhuj and the Ahmedabad diocese is in Willesden in Northwest London. Kutchis immigrated from East Africa in large numbers in the early 1970s and began to have meetings in private homes. Acharya Tejendraprasad visited London for the first time in 1971, and at his urging and with the encouragement of Dharmajivandas, mahant of the Bhuj temple, they purchased an abandoned church building in Willesden in 1975. Acharya Tejendraprasad installed the images in October 1978. Approximately 3,000 families are associated with the Willesden temple and support a full program of worship, study, and service. The temple also runs a Gujarati school on Saturday and Sunday for 500 students. It is affiliated with the Ahmedabad diocese through the Bhuj temple and takes instructions from the mahant of that temple. Bhuj sadhus visit Willesden and the other temples in Britain every summer.

House prayer meetings were held during the 1970s in other towns, and satsangis purchased buildings and converted them into temples in Cardiff (a former synagogue purchased in 1979 and dedicated in 1982), Oldham, and Bolton. Other temples have been purchased in Forest Gate (1986), Leicester (1990), Woolwich (1998), Streatham (1995), and Brighton (1999). The Cardiff temple moved to a larger building, which was dedicated in September 1993. In 1978 Acharya Tejendraprasad Pande established the International Swaminarayan Satsang Organization as the international arm of the Ahmedabad diocese, which unites old-school temples and maintains a relationship with the older Kutchi temples established in association with the Bhuj temple. The Leicester temple serves as the headquarters of the organization in Britain. The International Swaminarayan Satsang Organization is transnational and is incorporated in several countries where Indian emigrants have established themselves, including the United States.

THE UNITED STATES

On Memorial Day weekend in 1971 ten Swaminarayan Hindus from Chicago joined about forty other newly arrived immigrants from India on the banks of the Mississippi River at Davenport, Iowa to immerse the ashes from the cremation of Yogiji Maharaj, who had died earlier that year in Gujarat. Leaders in India had decided that portions of the ashes would be sent to sanctify major rivers where Swaminarayan Hindus lived: the Ganges in India, Murchison Falls in East Africa, the Thames in London, and finally the Mississippi somewhere near Chicago. It was a symbol of the developing transnationalism of Swaminarayan Hinduism.

A few months before his death, Yogiji Maharaj was in London to install images in Akshar Purushottam Sanstha's first temple in England. He took the initiative of commissioning K. C. Patel, a young chemistry instructor at Brooklyn College, to organize Swaminarayan followers in the United States and appointed him founding president, a position he has held for three decades of remarkable growth. Yogiji Maharaj gave him the names of twenty-eight followers, mostly students, and sent four sadhus to tour the United States in August 1970. In Chicago, for example, the touring sadhus visited six Gujarati homes, and thereafter three families started meeting regularly every Sunday in their homes. Similar small gatherings were started in other cities at the same time.

Before Acharya Tejendraprasad Pande traveled to the United States for the first time in 1978, he had only two addresses of satsangis. During darshan at the Kalupur temple he made a vow that if he received gifts during his tour sufficient to cover the expenses of his travel party of seven sadhus and three satsangis, he would walk from Ahmedabad to Jetalpur each year. He was met in New York by five satsangis and visited a few homes, but was relatively inactive for several days, as he said, "enjoying the fresh air of New York." A dramatic change occurred when he decided to place an advertisement in an Indian newspaper, *India Abroad*. A large response to that advertisement contributed to the success of his tour. A follower drove him nearly 20,000 miles across country to visit Swaminarayan satsangis and other Gujarati families who requested his presence. The International Swaminarayan Satsang Organization was established on Sahajanand's birthday, and the acharya was able to announce the success of the trip and that he must fulfill his vow. Such were the modest beginnings of Swaminarayan Hinduism in the United States in the 1970s (see plate 18).

18 Tejendraprasad Pande and son Koshalendraprasad with sadhus in the
United States

The reason for the small beginnings is that very few Indians were in
the United States before dramatic changes in immigration laws in 1965.
Indians were excluded by a series of laws culminating in the Immigration
Act of 1924, which codified the "Asiatic Barred Zone," placed the first
permanent limitation on immigration, and established a "national
origins" quota system. From 1820 to 1960, a total of only 13,607 persons
emigrated from the Indian subcontinent, and an unrecorded number of
these departed (INS 1982: 2–4). The years between 1925 and 1965 were a
peculiar period of American history when there was a major lull in
immigration. Because of a variety of special circumstances during that
period, which included the passage of restrictive laws, the Great
Depression, and the Second World War, many fewer people immigrated
to the United States than before or since. The Immigration and
Nationality Act of 1965 was passed in the emotional aftermath of the
assassination of President John F. Kennedy and established a nondis-
criminatory quota for immigrants from every country. The changes were
primarily two: (1) in the countries of origin and (2) in education and professional status. Immigration from Europe and Canada fell sharply, while
migration from Asia and Mexico increased. Those arriving in the first

decade were part of the brain drain – physicians, engineers, scientists, nurses, and computer specialists needed in the growing American economy. Indians, Gujaratis, and Swaminarayan Hindus participated actively in this transnational movement and were among the best educated, most professionally advanced, and most successful of any immigrant group. After 1980, however, most immigrants entered under the family reunification provisions of the immigration law.

The number of Asian Indians (the official designation of people with ethnic roots in India) grew 125 percent in the 1980s from 361,544 to 815,474. The most important fact about the new immigration is that it continues unabated. Even though the number of immigrants changes year by year and new regulations revise the preference categories slightly, the door remains open, and new immigrants arrive every year to join established communities and religious groups and to transform them. Hinduism and its Swaminarayan form have become world religions in the modern period because of the transnational networks that unite these new immigrants with their religious brothers and sisters in several countries.

Nevertheless, the emigration pattern and profile of Swaminarayan Hindus in the United States are different from those in other countries. A profile from data on questionnaires completed by 224 people at Swaminarayan meetings in 1987 confirms that they are primarily Gujarati immigrants. Most are first-generation immigrants not born in the United States (83.5 percent), most of whom (84 percent) emigrated directly from India. A few emigrated from England (5.8 percent), Canada (1.8 percent) or Africa (4 percent). The native place in India is in Gujarat (88 percent), and a larger number (95.5 percent) indicated that Gujarati is their native language. The respondents occupy a high educational, professional and economic status. Exactly half indicate that they have at least one graduate degree. A surprising number (84.8 percent) report that they are more active in religious affairs in the United States than they were before emigration. The strategy of the formation of a Gujarati regional-linguistic group in the United States is successful in attracting the attention and allegiance of Gujaratis. In the 1990s a number from other Indian ethnic groups also were drawn to Swaminarayan Hinduism. Swaminarayan Hindus are relatively young, well-educated, professional, affluent people who have the skills and resources to administer and support their growing religious organizations.

The size and diversity of America create significant problems for a small immigrant organization. Members and potential members are

scattered across the country. In the early days of immigration, the networks available were small-scale and nascent – newspapers, caste associations, Gujarati associations, and Swaminarayan groups. A major problem
was what is called in mundane affairs "identifying the market." Another
challenge was sorting out primary loyalties and roots of identity, which is a
common experience of a growing immigrant community. Swaminarayan
Hindus have been remarkably successful in facing these challenges. The
regular tours in the 1970s and early 1980s by Acharya Tejendraprasad of
Ahmedabad (1978 and 1981), Acharya Ajendraprasad of Vadtal (1981),
and Pramukh Swami (1974, 1977, and 1980) have been very important in
identifying and reaching "the market" and for the initial formation and
growth of the sanstha. These three and other Swaminarayan leaders
toured the United States almost every year throughout the 1990s.

Indian immigrants have faced little in the way of discrimination, in
part because their numbers are relatively small, other citizens have a
generally positive view of India, and the early immigrants have become
prosperous and successful. They also entered at a time when ethnicity
was receiving a positive emphasis. They have been encouraged by the
circumstance in their desire to proclaim, "Hindu is beautiful," as a part
of the American mosaic. They have been at the forefront in developing
new transnational networks that are changing the meaning of ethnicity
and nationality. Still, as one leader suggests, "The tilak the Indian community wears on its collective forehead is in the shape of a question
mark" (Badhwar 1980:16).

Nowhere is this question mark larger or more troublesome than with
respect to the children of the second generation raised in the American
cauldron. Children of the second generation are moving through college
and into the professions, and the third generation is beginning to appear.
The young people speak English with American regional accents, and,
to the discomfiture of their parents and grandparents, imitate the attitudes and practices of their American peers. Some parents fear that they
have made a Mephistophelian pact under which, in exchange for *la dolce
vita* of the American society, they have agreed, forever, to surrender their
offspring to an alien culture (Badhwar: 16). The parents have the desire
to socialize their children in the morals, language, religion, and culture
of home, but it proves to be a difficult task for a small minority in an alien
society. Their frustration is the point of an article by a sympathetic
observer entitled "Indian parents and their American children" (Bharati
1979). A major catalyst for the development of religious and cultural
organizations is the need to provide identity for the descendants of

immigrants that will help to socialize the children, help to bridge the generation gap, and, in the process, authenticate the community and the parents as transmitters of a socially viable tradition. The development of Swaminarayan institutions and temples by Gujarati immigrants can be viewed as one instance of the attempt to preserve and transmit cultural and religious values within an immigrant community.

The president, K. C. Patel, attributes the rapid growth of the Akshar Purushottam Sanstha in the United States during the 1990s to the mega-festival held as the Cultural Festival of India on the campus of Middlesex County College in Edison, New Jersey in 1991. The month-long festival attracted media attention and served to instruct both Asian Indians and others about Indian culture and Swaminarayan Hinduism. More important than the occasion was the organization and preparation undertaken for the festival. The organizational structure was expanded and people were trained for volunteer activities that strengthened their religious knowledge and commitment: they engaged in numerous fund-raising activities; they embarked on a program to visit every Gujarati home in the country to show a video about plans for the festival and to invite people to attend; they organized the public relations activities leading up to the festival; they volunteered months of labor to prepare the site and construct temporary structures; and then they volunteered during the festival to run everything from the kitchens to the exhibition halls. They were led by sadhu specialists who came from India to organize the festival (because until the 1990s Swaminarayan sadhus were not permitted to live outside of India). Many followers developed close ties to the sadhus and a few young men decided to join them in renouncing the world. The results were a highly trained and committed volunteer force and a network of leadership that after the festival could be redirected to building up the programs in centers and temples across the country.

The first Swaminarayan temple in the United States was a small shrine installed in the basement of a house on Bowne Street in Flushing, New York, appropriately on a street named for a proponent of religious freedom and toleration in the early American colonies. The first building newly constructed as a temple is next door, where, in August 1977, Pramukh Swami installed the pictorial images from Jinja that followers saved from destruction during the expulsion from Uganda. The Flushing temple remains the administrative center even though other temples and centers have grown larger. By the end of the century the Akshar Purushottam Sanstha developed over 148 centers and 22 major temples in North America – including those at Flushing, New York (1977), Glen Ellyn, Illinois (1984), Whittier, California (1984), Houston, Texas (1988), Atlanta, Georgia (1988), Stow, Massachusetts (1990), Toronto, Canada (1990), Edison, New Jersey (1991), San Jose, California (1991), Orlando, Florida (1994), Dallas, Texas (old temple in 1988 and new temple in 1994), Cleveland, Ohio (1996), Charlotte, North Carolina (1996), and Washington, D.C. (1998). Ground was broken in 1998 for a major new temple and complex in Bartlett, Illinois that will be larger than the one in London, and there are plans for a cultural center in Edison, New Jersey that will be on the scale of Akshardham in Gandhinagar, India. (For a history of the Akshar Purushottam group in Chicago, see Williams 1994.) Now a group of seven sadhus, including four who grew up in the United States before going to India to be trained as sadhus, live in the American temples and travel to visit centers organized in five regions. They lead the volunteers in satsang activities, children and youth programs, and indirectly to oversee the women's work. New initiatives in Australia and New Zealand are administered from New York. A new temple was dedicated in Sydney in 1997, and the pictorial images originally from Uganda were sent from the United States. Land was acquired in 1998 for a temple in Oakland, New Zealand. Leaders travel from the United States to advise the growing satsang in Australasia.

The International Swaminarayan Satsang Organization has fewer temples and centers in the United States than the Akshar Purushottam Sanstha. The first images installed by Acharya Tejendraprasad Pande were dedicated on 25 May 1987 in a converted Christian Science Church building in Weehawken, New Jersey, just across the Hudson River from Manhattan. Other affiliated temples are in Lowell, Massachusetts (1990), Itasca, Illinois (1998), and Houston (2000). Satsangis purchased property in Norwalk, California in 1991 for a temple, but opposition and difficulties with zoning and building with their accompanying court cases delayed construction until 1999. Sadhus from the Ahmedabad diocese now obtain temporary visas that enable them to live for extended periods in these temples.

Several influential sadhus from the Ahmedabad and Vadtal diocese travel regularly to visit temples and raise money for religious and educational projects in India. Until his death, Dharmajivandas Swami traveled regularly to raise money for the Swaminarayan Gurukul, and others hoped to emulate his success. The constitution of the International Swaminarayan Satsang Organization now stipulates that any contributions given to the acharyas or sadhus during their tours will remain in the United States to support temples and programs. Moreover, the sadhus must have authorization from the acharya for their travels. Some divisions have been caused because some members give primary loyalty to one of the sadhus and to the educational or religious activities they sponsor in Gujarat.

Several temples have appeared that are independent, although associated with the acharyas of Ahmedabad and Vadtal, and identify their allegiance as the International Swaminarayan Satsang Mandal. The large temple in Wheeling, Illinois claims affiliation with both the International Swaminarayan Satsang Organization and the International Swaminarayan Satsang Mandal. There are also temples in Grand Prairie, Texas and Sunnyvale, California, and construction started in Somerset, New Jersey in September 1999. These four temples are more closely allied with the southern diocese of Vadtal and are named "Vadtal Dham" because a majority of the leaders are originally from that diocese. There are, in addition, nineteen centers where regular sabhas are held associated with the Vadtal and Ahmedabad dioceses.

It is valuable for even small Swaminarayan groups to have a presence in the United States. A temple or ashram provides a pilgrimage site for followers and a home base for sadhus and other religious leaders as they tour the United States. A following in America also lends prestige as well as financial support to the institutions in India. The Swaminarayan Gadi established an organization in the United States in 1987 during Purushottampriyadas Swami's first tour. A group of approximately 400 people meets in a rented hall in New Jersey and construction on a large temple costing $4.25 million began in the fall of 1999 in Seaucus, New Jersey. It is the first Swaminarayan Gadi temple in the United States. The Anoopam Mission USA was established in 1983, but it was not until 1993 that the group purchased buildings and land for a temple and ashram in the Pocono Mountains near Stroudsburg, Pennsylvania. Three sadhus live at the ashram and conduct their daily affairs and rituals according to the rules of the Mission. A national conference attracted 325 people in the summer of 1999. Their religious leader, Saheb, attended the conference and then toured the country.

Formal membership boundaries of Swaminarayan Hinduism are relatively flexible in the United States. Most members go through the simple ritual of initiation – 96 percent of the people responding to a 1990 survey taken at Swaminarayan temples considered themselves Swaminarayan satsangis – but no formal record of names and addresses

of those initiated is kept. Nor do all who go through the ceremony continue active participation in temple life. No "transfer of membership"
exists, and people come and go into and out of more active participation, depending on family situation, stage of life, job demands, and life
experiences. A religious group, even one which is growing rapidly, seems
relatively stable in structure from the outside, but inside people are
moving all the time, toward or away from active participation and in and
out of leadership positions.

Even though the formal boundaries are relatively loose, informal
boundaries are strong. Cultural boundaries are related to Gujarati
ethnicity. The ability to communicate in the Gujarati language and to
appreciate Gujarati culture makes one an insider, and lack of such
ability makes one an "outsider guest" regardless of one's religious
inclinations.

The earlier version of this book concluded this chapter with the statement, "The shape of the future of the Swaminarayan religion in the
United States is uncertain, but it provides an important example of the
establishment of a religion in a community of 'new ethnics' as it
attempts to adapt to a new social situation without losing its identity"
(Williams 1984: 200). A Swaminarayan leader in Chicago takes the word
"uncertain" as a challenge, referring to it at every meeting and asking,
"How are we doing?" The response has to be that they are doing very
well so far, moving from success to success. The satsang has grown in
numbers and institutional infrastructure in the interim and it has been
remarkably successful in training its children and youth and maintaining their loyalty and support.

India, East Africa, Britain, and the United States represent very
different cultural, economic, and political contexts, and the emigration
patterns of Swaminarayan Hindus from India to the other countries
spring from different push-pull factors and involve Swaminarayan Hindus
with different educational and professional backgrounds. Nevertheless,
the transnational network that sustains the emigration and unites
Swaminarayan Hindus living in several countries strengthens their identity and resolve. Modern communication, media, economy, and travel are
changing India at the same time that emigration is changing Indians
abroad. Even a brief residence in a temple in Ahmedabad, Mumbai,
Mombasa, London, or Dallas makes one a witness to a constant pattern
of communication and visitation that identifies Swaminarayan Hinduism
as a transnational form of Hinduism. Satsangis participate in the daily
activities of Pramukh Swami and Acharya Tejendraprasad by reading

regular reports from the Internet and seeing photographs of their tours on their computers. Prominent sadhus and religious leaders tour the United States every summer, and their followers travel to India and other countries on pilgrimages to visit holy shrines and people and to participate in international festivals. These illustrate only the tip of the iceberg of intricate relationships that cause Swaminarayan Hindus to experience a transnational existence in almost everything they do, especially in their religious devotion. One observer noted, "If America is not a melting pot, it is a kind of shredding machine which leaves nothing exactly as it was" (Tinker 1977: 195). A key to the future of Swaminarayan Hinduism will be the nature and strength of the transnational networks and leadership that are transforming religion in India and the experience of immigrants from India in many regions of the world.

Afterword

John Carman points out that the English word "tradition" is a noun and that both its religious and its cultural use frequently suggest a deposit from the past. That noun comes, however, from the Latin verb *tradere*, which means both "to give away" and "to transmit." Transmit literally means "send across." Hence, he suggests that we might paraphrase both "tradition" and "transmission" with two verbal nouns: "handing down" and "reaching across" (1992a: 8). Swaminarayan Hindus are engaged in the complex task of handing down the particular form of Hinduism that developed over the past two centuries from the life and teachings of Sahajanand Swami and of sending across networks that encompass a transnational community. Religion in its many forms – and Swaminarayan Hinduism in particular – functions to provide a transcendent basis for personal and group identity. Such transcendence is, potentially, a powerful force both in the conservative stabilizing of a social world and in the transformative challenge to elements of a received tradition, the latter because religious commitment permits an individual to stand within a tradition with the power to call into question all traditions, including ultimately aspects of itself. It provides ballast that enables satsangis in the midst of rapid changes in India and immigrants making new lives for themselves abroad to preserve their identities and to adapt to new surroundings. Transmission of a religious tradition is always both a celebration and a quest.

As a modern form of Gujarati Hinduism the Swaminarayan satsang is rooted in the cultural soil of Gujarat. The language of its ceremonies and meetings has been Gujarati, and the gesture language of all the rituals is that developed in the Vaishnava sects of that area. The Gujarati vegetarian cuisine eaten in the homes is prepared, sung about, offered to the deities, and received as sacred food in the temples. The religious universe that is created coheres with the traditional culture in what has been in the twentieth century an easy symbiosis that supports both.

Swaminarayan Hinduism has functioned to preserve ethnic and linguistic identity both in India and abroad. At the beginning of the twenty-first century the spread, wealth, and expansion of Swaminarayan Hinduism in urban areas of India and abroad where new generations of Gujaratis are separated from their Gujarati heritage and where Indians other than Gujaratis are attracted to this expression of Hinduism create tension between its ethnic roots and the challenge to hand down and reach across in the future. That is reflected in decisions to publish literature and to conduct meetings in the regional language Gujarati, in the national language Hindi, and in the international language English. It represents the major question of adaptation in the context of modern mobility and mass communication.

Hindus in India and abroad are engaged in processes of adaptation within five major trajectories. The negotiation of adaptive strategies is a long, involved affair in which the religious groups function differently in the sacralization of personal and group identity. These differences are due to elements of theology, peculiar group histories, and the social and political contexts in new settings. Differences among strategies are evident in the characteristics of religious leadership, creation of sacred spaces, observance of sacred times, and use of language and arts in the transmission of tradition. Five strategies of adaptation in evidence among Hindu groups are: individual, national, ecumenical, ethnic and hierarchical. (See Williams 1992b for elaboration of these strategies.) The individual strategy is valuable to emigrants in preserving religious identity through acts of private devotion and study. The national strategy involves emphasizing the all-India aspects of Hinduism and stressing the close association of national identity and Hindu culture. The ecumenical strategy of adaptation incorporates all Hindus under the banner of an inclusive definition of religion that transcends ethnic or sectarian identification, implying a homogeneity that does not exist in any religion. It emphasizes the all-India Hindu "great tradition," devotion to major deities, and some elements of the Sanskrit tradition. Deities from many regions and sectarian traditions are united under one roof in ecumenical Hindu temples. Ethnic strategies unite people from the regional-linguistic areas of India in religious groups where the ethnic identity is evident in dress, cuisine, iconography, music, dance, and rituals. The chief characteristic of organizations adopting a hierarchical strategy is loyalty to a living religious leader who provides a unity for the group beyond ethnic or national loyalties. The group preserves a specific tradition and set of rituals transmitted and authenticated by a hierarchy, and the current religious leaders are the living symbols of the hierarchy who attract personal loyalty and marshal resources for institutional development. These authoritative religious leaders are often the mediators between past and present, between parents and children, between the forms of Hinduism in India and their emerging counterparts abroad.

The strength of Swaminarayan Hinduism and its success in adapting in several rapidly changing social contexts result from a powerful combination of a Gujarati ethnic strategy and loyalty to clearly defined hierarchies – in one group to the acharyas as lineal descendants of Sahajanand's family and in the other to the sadhus who are honored as the abode of the divine. That combination has been very successful in helping emigrants and their children shape their religious and cultural identities in several heterogeneous contexts at the same time that it has been effective in reaching larger numbers of Gujaratis living through the modernization of society in Gujarat itself.

A parallel contemporary movement within Hinduism is often referred to as "the Hindutva movement" because it stresses pride in Hinduism and reclaims a dominant position for Hinduism in Indian cultural, religious, and political affairs. The Hindutva movement results from an equally strong combination of the national and ecumenical strategies of adaptation. This has been a potent mixture because of the union of religious commitments with political powers and emotions. The Vishwa Hindu Parishad is the organization most closely associated with the religious component of Hindutva, encouraging pride among Hindus and activities to reestablish Hinduism as a dominant religious force in Indian culture and affairs. The Bharatya Janata Party gained majority status in Gujarat and in the national government in the 1990s by stressing a return to ancient Hindu ideals.

These two models of religious adaptation – the ethnic/hierarchical and the national/ecumenical – are the most significant models that attract the allegiance of Hindus in the contemporary transnational context. Leaders of Swaminarayan Hinduism generally affirm the ecumenical aspirations of Hindu unity and pride even as they disavow any political aspirations or attachments. Leaders of the Hindutva movement blur ethnic distinctions at the same time as they try to attract the support of the hierarchies of neo-Hinduism to their political and cultural agendas. These are not antithetical strategies, but they are not the same. Future developments within Hinduism will be determined to a significant degree by dynamics and negotiations among these two models. These negotiations occur on a world stage and not only in India because of the transnational character of Hinduism and of Indian and Gujarati communities in many countries. The transnational movement and communication of leaders, information, finance, and people mean that events and processes of change in India have immediate effects around the world and the directions of adaptation in several countries abroad redound with remarkable swiftness upon Hinduism and Swaminarayan groups in India.

Swaminarayan Hinduism is on the move. In India it is developing new temples, structures, and institutions in its home state of Gujarat and expanding into urban areas where Gujarati residents provide a secure base from which it expands among other ethnic groups. In East Africa, especially in Uganda, it is enjoying some modest resurgence that accompanies greater political stability and unity and renewed emigration from India. Swaminarayan Hindus in Britain have gained through diligence and hard work a relatively secure economic base that provides support for new temples and initiatives. Indian immigrants to the United States following changes in the immigration law in 1965 are part of the brain drain, which enables the Swaminarayan Hindus very quickly to build temples and a strong infrastructure. They provide significant financial support for Swaminarayan activities in other countries as well. Thus far Swaminarayan Hinduism has attracted support exclusively from Gujaratis and a few other Indians. There has been no attempt to attract followers from other national or ethnic groups, which has shaped the nature of negotiations and relations with members of the settled societies where Swaminarayan Hindus live.

Once religious groups establish a firm foothold, they are generally long lived, so it is safe to predict that the current strength and success of Swaminarayan Hinduism will continue well into the new century. The major threats to continued growth are transnational economic developments and political changes that determine the shape and size of emigrations and population movements, relationships with religious and cultural groups among the settled societies in several countries that dictate freedom or restrictions on religious activities, technological advances that influence the character of transnational communication and movement, the power of cultural pressures on young people of the third and future generations of immigrant families that will influence how they accept the ethnic and hierarchical strategies of adaptation that were so effective for their parents and grandparents, and the quality of leadership Swaminarayan Hindus develop that can span the transnational scope of the group and still lead effectively in many different cultural settings. The challenges are great; the outcome uncertain. Most contemporary religious groups face similar challenges and opportunities. Swaminarayan Hinduism provides a fascinating study of the developments within contemporary religious groups that will shape religion in the twenty-first century.

Glossary

ACHARYA [ācārya] a spiritual preceptor or teacher; the head of a sampradāya; the two hereditary leaders of the Ahmedabad and Vadtal dioceses of the Swaminarayan religion.

ADIVASI [adivasi] a collective name for members of tribal groups of an area; a term of recent origin meaning "original inhabitant" which gives tribal identity; scheduled tribes recognized as a special category for the purposes of special privileges guaranteed in the constitution.

ADVAITA [advaita] the philosophical doctrine of non-dualism associated with Śankara; the doctrine that Brahman is the only reality.

AHIMSA [ahiṃsā] not to injure or harm any living being; specifically, not to kill or eat animals; non-violence; a central vow of Jains and Swaminarayan Hindus.

AKSHAR [akṣara] the abode of the supreme person; an eternal state; thought to have an impersonal form as a state of being and a personal form as an abode of god.

AKSHARDHAM [akṣardhām] the heavenly abode or state of the supreme person; equivalent to akṣara in the impersonal form.

AMSAVATARA [aṃśāvatāra] fourteen partial manifestations or descents of the deity that appear in Vaishnava literature and iconography.

ARTHA [artha] one of the four traditional goals of life; material gain.

ARTI [ārati] a waving of a lighted lamp before the deity; the ceremonies of daily worship in the temple or before the home shrines in which the lamps are waved before the images.

ASHRAMA DHARMA [āśramadharma] the traditional division of the human life into four stages: brahmācarin or student; gṛhastya or householder; vānaprastha or retired; sannyāsin or world renouncer.

AVATAR [avatāra] a descent or manifestation of a deity; specifically of a human or animal form assumed by Viṣṇu; the *Bhāgavata Purāṇa* names twenty-two, but adds that they are numberless.

BHAGAT [bhagat] the first stage of initiation into the ascetic life; ascetics who wear white clothing; ascetics from lower castes in the temples of Ahmedabad and Vadtal dioceses; same as pārṣādā or pālas.

BHAGAVATI DIKSHA [bhagavati dīkṣā] the ritual by which a person is initiated into an order; the initiation ritual for a sādhu.

BHAKTI [bhakti] religious devotion as a way to salvation; fervent devotion to god; participation in a devotional cult.

BRAHMACHARI [brahmacārin] (1) generally, a religious student for whom chastity was the most solemn obligation; one of the four āśramas or stages of life of a Hindu; (2) a specialized use in the old school of the Swaminarayan sect for initiates into the ascetic life from the Brahmin castes; Brahmin ascetics who wear saffron and white clothing and care for the images in the temples.

BRAHMAN [brahman (neuter)] the supreme creative principle; the substratum and substance of existence; frequently identified with any one of the chief gods and as Parabrahman and Puruṣottam; in some Swaminarayan literature distinguished from Parabrahman as the term for akṣara so that Parabrahman is Puruṣottam and brahman is akṣara.

DARSHAN [darśana] a looking at or viewing; the act of looking at the image of the deity in the shrine; sometimes of seeing a holy person.

DHARMA [dharma] obligations incumbent upon a Hindu according to his or her social status or stage of life; the basis of social order; duty and custom; codes of conduct for individuals and groups.

DHARMASHALAS [dharmaśālāh] rooms or apartments provided for pilgrims or guests in the temples or at sacred shrines.

DHARMASHASTRA [dharmaśāstra] texts which deal with personal domestic and caste duties; a class of religious texts containing codes of laws and duties.

DIKSHA [dīkṣā] the initiation of a disciple by his guru; initiation into a sampradāya; *see also* bhagavati dīkṣā.

DVAITA [dvaita] the philosophical doctrine of dualism associated with Mādhva; the doctrine that Brahman and the individual soul are separate and distinct.

EKADASHI [ekādaśī] the eleventh day of the bright and dark halves of the lunar months; a fast day for Swaminarayan ascetics.

GADI [gādī] a couch; a throne-like chair for the acāryā of the Vallabha and Swaminarayan Hindus; the seat of the acāryā in Ahmedabad and in Vadtal.

GOLOKA [goloka] the heavenly abode of Kṛṣṇa.

GOPIS [gopīs] the herdswomen with whom Kṛṣṇa danced; his relations with them symbolize the relation of the deity to his devotees; according to the *Bhāgavata Purāṇa*, he multiplied his form to dance with each.

GOTRA [gotra] exogamous group within castes among the three "twice-born" varnas, defined by its members as being descended from the same (remote, probably mythical) male ancestor through an uninterrupted patriline.

GURU [guru] a religious teacher or adviser; a preceptor; especially one who gives initiation.

GURUKUL [gurukul] traditional school, often in the residence of the guru.

GURUPARAMPARA [guruparamparā] the lineage of religious teachers back to the founder of a tradition [sampradāya]; the list of gurus chanted as part of some religious rituals.

HARI MANDIR [hari maṇdira] maṇdir is a temple; a hari maṇdir has pictures of the deities and not statues of stone or metal.

HAVELI [havelī] a stately house or palace; the residence of the ācāryas of the Vallabha sect where worship of images is performed; the residence for female ascetics in Swaminarayan temple compounds.

ISHVARA [īśvara] the lord; the gods or deities. Some Swaminarayan scholars translate it as "demigod" to distinguish it from parabrahman.

JANJAGRUTI [janjagruti] preaching tours to the villages; evangelistic visits to the villages.

JIVA [jīva] the self; a state of consciousness implying identity.

JNANA [jñāna] knowing; the path to salvation by knowledge of the ultimate reality.

KAMA [kāma] one of the four traditional goals of life; pleasure; sexual desire as distinguished from ascetic practices (tapas).

KANTI [kānti] a double-strand necklace of 108 wooden beads worn by satsangis; the necklace given to the person at the time of initiation into a sampradāya.

KIRTAN ARADHANA [kīrtan ārādhanā] performances of devotional songs accompanied by drums and instruments; a concert of sacred songs performed by the sadhus.

KOTHARI [kothārī] an adviser of a temple; usually an ascetic, but occasionally a layman; the ascetic who cares for the stores and guests of a temple; a manager not obligated to undertake preaching tours.

LINGA [linga] an image form of Śiva; symbol of generative power; a phallic symbol.

MAHANT [mahant] the ascetic appointed or elected as head of a temple and as leader of the ascetics resident there; a religious leader and preacher for the satsangis of the villages associated with the temple.

MANTRA [mantra] hymn or formula used in ritual worship and meditation; words or phrases which possess sacred power; a sacred phrase or chant given in the initiation ritual; for example, "I take refuge in Swaminarayan."

MAYA [māyā] illusion, the flux and change in which all existence apart from Puruṣottam and akṣara is bound.

MOKSHA [mokṣa] emancipation; salvation; release from the cycle of birth, death, and rebirth; specifically, the presence in akṣardhām with Swaminarayan.

MUDRA [mudrā] a symbolic hand gesture in iconography and dance; positions of the hands, fingers, and arms to express meanings; hand positions of the images of the deities in Swaminarayan shrines.

MUKTA [mukta] from mokṣa; one who has gained release; a released soul returning from akṣardhām.

MURTI [mūrti] material form of the deity; image of the deity installed in a temple; a picture, statue, or relief image of a deity.

NIVRTTI [nivṛtti] the life and discipline of the sādhu or world renouncer; to be distinguished from the discipline of the householder.

PADHRAMANI [padhrāmaṇī] a visit to the home or business of a devotee by a religious leader; ritual of blessing the homes and businesses of devotees.

PALAS [pālās] *see* bhagat.

PARABRAHMAN [parabrahman] the supreme brahman; equivalent to Puruṣottam.

PARAMHANSA [paramhansa] the fourth, the highest stage of ascetic renunciation.

PARAYANA [pārāyaṇa] a series of discourses on a religious text; meetings in which a religious text is chanted and interpreted.

PARSHAD [pārṣadā] *see* bhagat.

PARSHADI DIKSHA [pārṣādi dīkṣā] initiation into the first stage of ascetic life; *see* bhagavati dīkṣā.

PRADARSHAN [pradarśana] an exhibition.

PRAN PRATISTHA [praṇ pratiṣṭha] the ritual act of endowing an image of the deity with life; the rites to install the deity in the image of the temple; the final acts of the dedication of a new temple.

PRASADA [prasāda] a gift; grace; food distributed after having been offered to the deity in the temple or at the home shrine.

PRAVRTTI [pravṛtti] the life and discipline of a householder; to be distinguished from the discipline of the sādhu or sannyāsin.

PUJA [pūjā] an act of worship; daily worship in household, temple, or shrine; used especially of the morning and evening worship of satsangis.

PUJARI [pujārī] one who performs the act of worship (pūjā); the priest who cares for the deities in the temple and performs the daily rituals.

PURANA [purāṇa] a class of Hindu sacred writings containing ancient myths and legends; stories about Viṣṇu, Śiva, and Brahma; the *Bhāgavata Purāṇa* emphasizes devotion to Viṣṇu in his incarnation as Kṛṣṇa.

PURNAVATARA [purṇāvatāra] the ten main manifestations of Viṣṇu, which include Kṛṣṇa and Rāma.

PURNIMA [pūrṇimā] the day of the full moon; hence an auspicious day for religious celebrations.

PURUSHOTTAM [puruṣottama] Supreme [para], Reality [sat], Self [ātmā]; the supreme person, the highest divine reality; equivalent to Parabrahman.

SADGURU [sadguru] an ascetic appointed to be leader of other ascetics.

SADHAK [sādaka] a period of preparation before initiation to the first stage of ascetic life.

SADHU [sādhu] a Hindu ascetic; one who has renounced the world; one who has received initiation (parvati dīkṣā) and taken the vows of the Swaminarayan ascetics.

SAMADHI [samādhi] a trance-like state of oneness with the supreme person resulting from intense mental concentration or devotion.

SAMKHYA YOGINI [saṃkhya yoginī] female ascetic; a woman who takes vows of chastity and poverty; woman ascetic who lives in the Swaminarayan temples or institutions.

SAMPRADAYA [samprādaya] a tradition handed down from a founder through successive religious teachers which shapes the followers into a distinct fellowship with institutional forms; a religious fellowship; a sectarian group.

SAMSARA [saṃsāra] the continuing cycle of life, death, and rebirth in which status and condition in rebirth are governed by a person's actions.

SATI [satī] or suttee; the practice of a widow committing suicide by burning herself on her husband's funeral pyre; a woman who immolates herself.

SATSANGI [satsangi] a companion of the truth; follower of a religious path; member of a religious fellowship or satsang.

SEVA [sevā] service to a deity or to a guru.

SHALAGRAMA [śālagrāma] a black riverstone of a type found at Dwarka, believed by many devotees to be pervaded by Viṣṇu's presence; a small unformed stone worshiped as an image of the deity.

SHRUTI [śruti] heard; the sacred *Vedas* heard by the ancients and transmitted through the generations; the most sacred religious texts; to be distinguished from smṛti.

SIKHARA MANDIR [śikhara maṇḍira] maṇḍir is a temple; the śikhara designates a temple with tall towers which indicate that metal or stone images are inside.

SISHYA [sishya] student, pupil, disciple.

SMRITI [smṛti] remembered; post-Vedic classical Sanskrit literature; to be distinguished from the more authoritative śruti.

THAKORJI [thākurjī] a small image of the deity taken by the sādhus on their tours and kept in the temples; one image that is always with Pramukh Swami.

TILAK [tilaka] a sectarian mark on the forehead; generally affixed as a part of morning worship; the Swaminarayan mark of a U made of sandalwood paste (yellow) with a circle of kumkum (red) in the middle.

TULSI [tulsi] a type of wood used for religious articles.

VAIKUNTHA [vaikuṇṭha] an eternal abode or state of Viṣṇu; here associated with his form as Rāma.

VARNA DHARMA [varnadharma] the traditional division of people into four classes: brahmins or priests; kṣatriya or rulers; vaiśya or merchants; śudra or laborers.

VISHISTADVAITA [viśistādvaita] the philosophical doctrine of qualified non-duality associated with Rāmānuja; the doctrine that the human soul is a distinct reality but subordinate to Brahman.

YAJNA [yajña] sacrifice; worship; a gathering for a sacrificial ritual.

References

Babb, Lawrence A. 1975. *The Divine Hierarchy: Popular Hinduism in Central India*. New York: Columbia University Press.

Badhwar, Inderjit. 1980. Indians in America at the crossroads. In *India Tribune*, 15 August.

Barot, Rohit. 1973. A Swaminarayan sect as a community. In *New Community: A Journal of the Community Relations Commission*, 2 (1): 34–7.

Basch, Linda, Schiller, Nina Glick, and Blanc-Szanton, Christina. 1994. *Nations Unbound: Transnational Projects, Postcolonial Predicaments, and Deterritorialized Nation-states*. Langhorne, Penn.: Gordon and Breach.

Baumann, Martin. 1998. Sustaining "Little Indias": Hindu diasporas in Europe. In *Strangers and Sojourners: Religious Communities in the Diaspora*, ed. Gerrie Ter Haar, pp. 95–132. Leuven: Peeters.

Berger, Peter and Luckmann, Thomas. 1967. *The Social Construction of Reality: A Treatise in the Sociology of Knowledge*. Garden City, N.J.: Anchor Books.

Bharati, Agehananda (Austrian name: Leopold Fischer). 1967. Ideology and the content of caste among Indians in East Africa. In *Caste in Overseas Indian Communities*, ed. Barton M. Schwartz, pp. 282–320. San Francisco: Chandler Publishing Company.

1972. *The Asians in East Africa: Jaihind and Uhuru*. Chicago: Nelson & Hall Company.

1979. Indian parents and their American children. In *Illustrated Weekly of India*. Bombay, 11 November, 27–31.

Bhatt, Govindlal Hargovind. 1953. The school of Vallabha. In *The Cultural Heritage of India*, ed. H. Bhattacharyya, vol. III, pp. 347–59. Calcutta: Ramakrishna Mission.

Bhatt, Purnima Mehta. 1976. A history of Asians in Kenya, 1900–1970. An abstract submitted to the faculty of the Graduate School of Howard University. Ann Arbor, Mich.: University Microfilms.

Brent, Peter. 1972. *Godmen of India*. London: Penguin.

Burgess, James. 1872. Narayan Swami. In *The Indian Antiquary: A Journal of Oriental Research*, 1: 331–6.

Carman, John B. 1974. *The Theology of Ramanuja*. New Haven, Conn.: Yale University Press.

1981. *Vachanamritama*: a note. In *New Dimensions in Vedanta Philosophy*, ed. R. S.

Srivastava, Part i, pp. 204–20. Ahmedabad: Shri Akshar Purushottam Sanstha.

Chakaravarti, V. R. Srisaila. 1974. *The Philosophy of Sri Ramanuja*. Madras: V. R. S. Chakaravarti.

Clarke, Colin, Peach, Ceri, and Vertovec, Steven, eds. 1990. *South Asians Overseas: Migration and Ethnicity*. Cambridge: Cambridge University Press.

Daniels, Roger. 1989. *History of Indian Immigration to the United States: An Interpretive Essay*. New York: The Asia Society.

1990. *Coming to America: A History of Immigration and Ethnicity in American Life*. New York: HarperCollins.

Dave, Harindra. 1981. *The Cup of Love: Fifty-Four Poems of Swaminarayan Saint-poets*. Bombay: Bharatiya Vidya Bhavan.

Dave, Harshadrai T. 1974. *Life and Philosophy of Shree Swaminarayan*. London: George Allen & Unwin.

1977. *Shree Swaminarayan's Vachanamritam*. Bombay: Bharatiya Vidya Bhavan.

Dave, Ramesh M. 1978. Ethics of the *Shikshaptri*. In *Swaminarayan Magazine*, pp. 9–10. Ahmedabad: Akshar Purushottam Sanstha.

Desai, Neera. 1978. *Social Change in Gujarat: A Study of Nineteenth Century Gujarati Society*. Bombay: Vora Company.

Dimmitt, Cornelia and van Buitenen, J. A. B., eds. and trans. 1978. *Classical Hindu Mythology: A Reader in the Sanskrit Puranas*. Philadelphia: Temple.

Divyavigrahdas Swami. n.d. *Shree Swaminarayan Gadi*. Ahmedabad: Maninagar Shree Swaminarayan Gadi.

Dodwell, H. H., ed. 1963. *Cambridge History of India*, vol. v. New Delhi: S. Chand & Co.

Dumont, Louis. 1970. *Religion/Politics and History in India*. Paris: Mouton.

Embree, A., Saran, P., and Varma, Baidyanath. 1980. Hinduism in a new society. In *The New Ethnics: Asian Indians in the United States*, ed. P. Saran and E. Eames, pp. 216–32. New York: Praeger.

Farquhar, J. N. 1967 [written in 1914]. *Modern Religious Movements in India*. Delhi: Munshiram Manoharlal.

Fisher, Maxine P. 1980. *The Indians of New York City: A Study of Immigrants from India*. Columbia, Mo.: South Asia Books.

Freed, R. S. and S. A., 1964. Calendars, ceremonies, and festivals in a North India village: necessary calendric information for fieldwork. In *Southwestern Journal of Anthropology*, 20: 67–90.

French, H. W. and Sharma, Arvind. 1981. *Religious Ferment in Modern India*. New York: St. Martin's Press.

Fuchs, Stephen. 1965. *Rebellious Prophets: A Study of Messianic Movements in Indian Religions*. Bombay: Asia Publishing House.

Geertz, Clifford. 1973. Thick description: toward an interpretative theory of cultures. In *The Interpretation of Cultures: Selected Essays*, pp. 3–30. New York: Basic Books.

Ghai, D. P. and Y. P. 1970. *Portrait of a Minority: Asians in East Africa*. Nairobi: Oxford University Press.

Ghurye, G. S. 1964. *Indian Sadhus*, 2nd ed. Bombay: Popular Prakashan.

Gillion, Kenneth. 1969. *Ahmedabad: A Study in Indian Urban History*. Canberra: Australian National University Press.

Goody, Jack. 1968. *Literacy in Traditional Societies*. Cambridge: Cambridge University Press.

Gupta, Shakti. 1974. *Vishnu and his Incarnations*. Bombay: Somaiya Publications.

Heber, Amelia. 1830. *The Life of Reginald Heber*, 2 vols. London: John Murray.

Heber, Reginald. 1846. *Narrative of a Journey through the Upper Provinces of India from Calcutta to Bombay 1824–25*, 2 vols. London: John Murray.

Heimsath, Charles H. 1964. *Indian Nationalism and Hindu Social Reform*. Princeton, N.J.: Princeton University Press.

Hess, G. R. 1976. The forgotten Asian Americans: the East Indian community in the United States. In *The Asian American: The Historical Experience*, ed. Norris Hundley, pp. 157–78. Santa Barbara, Calif.: Clio Press.

Jaini, Padmanabh S. 1979. *The Jaina Path of Purification*. Berkeley, Calif.: University of California Press.

Kaye, John W. 1856. *The Life and Correspondence of Major-General Sir John Malcolm*, 2 vols. London: Smith, Elder & Company.

Leach, Edmund. 1968. Ritual. In *International Encyclopedia of Social Sciences*, ed. David L. Sills, vol. XII, pp. 520–6. New York: The Macmillan Company.

    1976. *Culture and Communication: The Logic by which Symbols are Connected: Introduction to the Use of Structural Analysis in Social Anthropology*. Cambridge: Cambridge University Press.

Lévi-Strauss, Claude. 1963. *Structural Anthropology*. New York: Penguin Books.

Lyon, Michael H. 1973. Ethnicity and Gujarati Indians in Britain. In *New Community: A Journal of the Community Relations Commission*, 2 (1): 1–11.

Mahadevan, T. M. P. 1960. *Outlines of Hinduism*, 2nd ed. Bombay: Chetana.

Majumdar, M. R. 1964. *Cultural History of Gujarat: From Early Times to pre-British Period*. Bombay: Popular Prakashan.

Majumdar, R. C. 1977. *The Maratha Supremacy*. Bombay: Bharatiya Vidya Bhavan.

Malcolm, John. n.d. "Minute on visiting Cutch." In "Copies of minutes of Major-Gen. Sir John Malcolm, Gov. of Bombay 1823–1830, 23 April 1829–15 October 1830 [Lithographed]," British Library, Add. Ms. 22082, pp. 154–200.

    1824. *Political History of India 1784–1823*, 2 vols. London: John Murray.

    1833. *The Government of India*. London: John Murray.

Mallison, Françoise. 1973. L'epouse ideale: la "Sati-Gita" de Muktananda traduite du "Gujarati." In *Publications de l'Institut de Civilisation Indienne*, fascicule 35. Paris: Institut de Civilisation Indienne.

    1974. La secte krishnaite des *svami-narayani* au Gujarat. In *Journal Asiatique*, 262 (3–4): 437–71.

Marfatia, M. I. 1967. *The Philosophy of Vallabhacarya*. Delhi: Munshiram Manoharlal.

Mehta, Dhawal. 1979. Perspective/Indians in America: the temple builders. In *India Times*, 5 February, p. 7.

Mehta, Kalpana. 1964. The temple in the politics of village Bariapur. In *Politics of a Periurban Village*, ed. A. H. Somjee, pp. 24–33. Bombay: Asia Publishing House.

Miller, Barbara D. 1980. Female neglect and the cost of marriage in rural India. In *Contributions to Indian Sociology*, New Series, 14 (1): 95–129.

Miller, David and Wertz, Dorothy. 1976. *Hindu Monastic Life*. Montreal: McGill-Queen's University Press.

Monier-Williams, Monier. 1877. *Hinduism*. Calcutta: Susil Gupta reprint of 1951.

——— 1882a. Sanskrit text of the *Siksha-Patri* of the Swami-Narayana sect and translation of the foregoing *Siksha-Patri*. In *Journal of the Royal Asiatic Society of Great Britain and Ireland*, New Series, 14: 733–72.

——— 1882b. The Vaishnava religion, with special reference to the *Siksha-Patri* of the modern sect called Swami Narayan. In *Journal of the Royal Asiatic Society of Great Britain and Ireland*, New Series, 14: 289–316.

Morgan, Kenneth, ed. 1953. *The Religion of the Hindus*. New York: The Roland Press.

Mukundcharandas Sadhu. 1999. *Handbook to the Vachanāmrutam*. Amdavad: Swaminarayan Aksharpith.

Munshi, Kanaiyalal M. 1935. *Gujarata and its Literature: A Survey from the Earliest Times*. Calcutta: Longmans, Green & Co.

Nagar, R. 1997. The making of Hindu communal organizations, places and identities in postcolonial Dar es Salaam. In *Environment and Planning D: Society and Space*, 15:707–30.

Naseem, Abdul Waheed. 1975. Nature and extent of the Indian enterprise along the East African coast and subsequent role in the development of Kenya, 1840–1905. Ph.D. Thesis, St. John's University. Ann Arbor, Mich.: University Microfilms SEG 106.

Pandya, R. B. 1974. *Pramukh Swami Maharaj*. Nairobi: General Printers.

Panigrahi, Lalita. 1976. *British Social Policy and Female Infanticide in India*. Delhi: Munshiram Manoharlal.

Parekh, Manilal C. 1943. *Shri Vallabhacharya: Life, Teaching and Movement, a Religion of Grace*. Rajkot: M. C. Parekh.

——— 1980. *Shri Swaminarayan*, 3rd ed. [1st ed. 1935]. Bombay: Bharatiya Vidya Bhavan.

Parrinder, Geoffrey E. 1970. *Avatar and Incarnation*. New York: Barnes and Noble.

Pocock, David F. 1973. *Mind, Body and Wealth: A Study of Belief and Practice in an Indian Village*. Totowa, N.J.: Bowman & Littlefield.

——— 1976. Preservation of the religious life: Hindu immigrants in England. In *Contributions to Indian Sociology*, New Series, 20: 341–65.

Ramanuja Swami. 1969. *Gitabhashya*, trans. M. R. Sampatkumaran. Madras: Rangacharya Memorial Trust.

Raval, R. L. 1987. *Socio-religious Reform Movements in Gujarat during the Nineteenth Century*. New Delhi: Ess Ess Publications.

Reynolds, David J. 1978. The Gujarati Indians of England and Wales. An unpublished paper prepared for Bible House, London.

Richardson, E. Allen. 1988. *Strangers in this Land: Pluralism and the Response to Diversity in the United States*. New York: The Pilgrim Press.

Sahajanand Swami. n.d. *The Lekh: Document for the Apportionment of Territory*, trans. G. P. Taylor. Ahmedabad: Shri Swaminarayan Temple.

Saran, Parmatma. 1980. New ethnics: the case of the East Indians in New York City. In *Sourcebook on the New Immigration*, ed. R. S. Bryce-Laporte, pp. 303–11. New Brunswick, N.J.: Transaction Books.

Schiller, Nina Glick, Basch, Linda, and Blanc-Szanton, Christina, eds. 1992. *Towards a Transnational Perspective on Migration: Race, Class, Ethnicity, and Nationalism Reconsidered*. Annals of the New York Academy of Sciences, 645. The New York Academy of Sciences.

Schubring, Walther. 1962. Sahajananda und die Svami-Narayaniyas: eine reformierte brahmanische Gemeinde. In *Nachrichten der Akademie der Wissenschaften in Göttingen, Philologisch-Historische Klasse*, pp. 95–133. Göttingen: Vandenhoeck & Ruprecht.

Segal, Aaron. 1993. *An Atlas of International Migration*. London: Hans Zell Publishers.

Sharma, Arvind. 1981. Relevance of Swaminarayan and contemporary Indian thought. In *New Dimensions in Vedanta Philosophy*, ed. A. Sharma, pp. 18–25. Ahmedabad: Akshar Purushottam Sanstha.

Singer, Milton. 1972. *When a Great Tradition Modernizes: An Anthropological Approach to Indian Civilization*. New York: Praeger.

Singer, Milton, ed. 1966. *Krishna: Myths, Rites, and Attitudes*. Honolulu: East-West Center Press.

Singer, Philip. 1970. *Sadhus and Charisma*. Bombay: Asia Publishing House.

Sollors, Werner. 1986. *Beyond Ethnicity: Consent and Descent in American Culture*. New York: Oxford University Press.

Srinivas, M. N. 1953. Prospects of sociological research in Gujarat. In *Journal of the Maharaja Sayajirao University of Baroda*, 2 (1): 21–35.

　1962a. A note on sanskritization and westernization. In *Caste in Modern India and Other Essays*, pp. 42–62. Bombay: Asia Publishing House.

　1962b. Hinduism. In *Caste in Modern India and Other Essays*, pp. 148–60. Bombay: Asia Publishing House.

　1966. *Social Change in Modern India*. Berkeley, Calif.: University of California Press.

Staal, J. F. 1963. Sanskrit and sanskritization. In *Journal of Asian Studies*, 13 (3):261–75.

Steel, David. 1969. *No Entry*. London: C. H. Hurst & Co.

Stern, Stephen and Cicala, John Allan, eds. 1991. *Creative Ethnicity: Symbols and Strategies of Contemporary Ethnic Life*. Logan: Utah State University Press.

Thakur, Murli. n.d. *Gandhivani*. Ahmedabad: Sastu Sahitya Vardhaka Karyalaya.

Thapar, Karan. 1979. Britain and the Indian immigrant. In *The Overseas Hindustan Times*, 19 July.

Tinker, Hugh. 1977. *The Banyan Tree: Overseas Emigrants from India, Pakistan, and Bangladesh*. Oxford: Oxford University Press.

Toothi, N. A. 1935. *The Vaishnavas of Gujarat.* Calcutta: Longmans, Green & Co.

Turner, Victor. 1980. Social dramas and stories about them. In *Critical Inquiry*, 7 (1): 141–68.

Underhill, Muriel M. 1921. *The Hindu Religious Year.* Calcutta: Association Press.

van Buitenen, J. A. B. 1959. Aksara. In *Journal of the American Oriental Society*, 79: 176–87.

Warren, Robert. 1980. Volume and composition of U.S. immigration and emigration. In *Sourcebook on the New Immigration*, ed. R. S. Bryce-Laporte, pp. 1–14. New Brunswick, N.J.: Transaction Books.

Williams, Raymond B. 1981. Presentation of the *Shikshapatri* to Sir John Malcolm. In *New Dimensions in Vedanta Philosophy*, ed. R. S. Srivastava, Part 1, pp. 114–22. Ahmedabad: Shri Akshar Purushottam Sanstha.

1982. Holy man as religious specialist: the acharya tradition in Vaishnavism. In *Encounter*, 43 (1): 61–97.

1984. *A New Face of Hinduism: The Swaminarayan Religion.* Cambridge: Cambridge University Press.

1985. Holy man as abode of God in the Swaminarayan religion. In *God of Flesh / God of Stone: The Embodiment of Divinity in India*, ed. Joanne Waghorne and Norman Cutler, pp. 143–57. Chambersburg, Penn.: Anima Press.

1986. The guru as pastoral counselor. In *Journal of Pastoral Care*, 40: 133–40.

1987a. Negotiating the tradition: religious organizations and Gujarati identity in the United States. In *Migration and Modernization: The Indian Diaspora in Comparative Perspective*, Studies in Third World Societies, ed. Richard H. Brown and George V. Coelho, pp. 25–38. Williamsburg, Va: Washington & Lee.

1987b. Hinduism in America. In *The Christian Century*, March, 247–9.

1988. *Religions of Immigrants from India and Pakistan: New Threads in the American Tapestry.* Cambridge: Cambridge University Press.

1990a. Asian Indians. In *Dictionary of American Immigration History*, ed. Francesco Cordasco, pp. 45–50. Metuchen, N.J.: Garland Publishing.

1990b. Asian-Indian Muslims in the United States. In *Indian Muslims in North America*, ed. Omar Khalidi, pp. 17–26. Watertown, Mass.: South Asia Press, 2nd ed., 1994.

1992a. *A Sacred Thread: Modern Transmission of Hindu Traditions in India and Abroad*, ed. Raymond B. Williams. Chambersburg, Penn.: Anima Press and New York: Columbia University Press edition, 1996.

1992b. Sacred threads of several textures. In *A Sacred Thread: Modern Transmission of Hindu Traditions in India and Abroad*, ed. Raymond B. Williams, pp. 228–57. Chambersburg, Penn.: Anima Press and New York: Columbia University Press edition, 1996.

1994. The Swaminarayan temple in Glen Ellyn. In *American Congregations*, eds. James Lewis and James Wind, pp. 612–62. Chicago: University of Chicago Press.

1995. America, Hinduism in. In *Harper's Dictionary of Religions*, ed. J. Z. Smith and W. S. Green, pp. 42–4. New York: HarperCollins.

1996. *Christian Pluralism in the United States: The Indian Immigrant Experience.* Cambridge: Cambridge University Press.

1997a. Religions of South Asian immigrants to the United States. In *A New Handbook of Living Religions*, 2nd ed., ed. John Hinnells, Oxford: Blackwell. London: Penguin (paperback), pp. 796–818, 1998.

1997b. South Asian Christians. In *American Immigrant Cultures: Builders of a Nation*, vol. II, ed. David Levinson and Melvin Ember, pp. 829–35. New York: Macmillan.

1998a. Training religious specialists for a transnational Hinduism: a Swaminarayan sadhu training center. In *Journal of the American Academy of Religion*, 66 (4): 841–62.

1998b. Asian-Indian and Pakistani religions in the United States. In *The Annals of the American Academy of Political and Social Science*, 558: 178–95.

1998c. Immigrants from India in North America and Hindu-Christian study and dialogue. In *Hindu-Christian Studies Bulletin*, 11, 20–4.

2000. *The South Asian Religious Diaspora in Britain, Canada, and the United States*, ed. Harold Coward, John Hinnells, and R. B. Williams. Albany: State University of New York Press.

Yajnik, J. A. 1972. *The Philosophy of Sri Swaminarayana.* Ahmedabad: L. D. Institute of Indology.

Zaehner, R. C. 1962. *Hinduism.* London: Oxford University Press.

n.a. 1823. Indian sect: memorandum respecting a sect lately introduced by a person calling himself Swamee Naraen. In the *Asiatic Journal and Monthly Register for British India and its Dependencies*, 15: (January/June) 348–9.

n.a., n.d. *A Short Introduction to Shri Swaminarayan Gurukul, Rajkot, Junagadh and Ahmedabad.* Rajkot: Shri Swaminarayan Gurukul.

GOVERNMENT DOCUMENTS AND NEWSPAPERS (BY DATE)

1872 *Gujarat State Gazetteer.* Ahmedabad: Directorate of Government Printing, Stationery and Publications, Gujarat State. The revised edition of the original *Gazetteer* of the Bombay Presidency.

1905 Civil Suit No. 22 of 1902 in the Court of the District Judge at Ahmedabad. The decision was given on 23 June 1905.

1943 Appeal No. 165 of 1940 in the Court of the District Judge, Kaira, at Nadiad from Decree in Reg. Civil Suit No. 519 of 1936 of the Court of the Sub-judge Mr. P. B. Patel of Borsad.

1965 Public Law 89–236. Eighty-ninth Congress, H.R. 2580. 3 October 1969. *Naturalization Laws.* Washington: U.S. Government Printing Office. 1981: 404–15.

1973 Exhibit 908 Civil Suit No. 136 of 1963 in the Court of City Civil Judge, Fourth Court at Ahmedabad. The decision was given on 4 April 1973.

1975 *The 1975 Annual Report.* Washington: Immigration and Naturalization Service.

1977 *The New York Times*, 2 August, p. 47.

1978 *Chronicle of Higher Education*, 17 (10): 14.

1979 *Annual Report of the Immigration and Naturalization Service.* Washington: U.S. Government Printing Office.

1980 Race of the population by states: 1980. In *The 1980 Census of Population, Supplementary Reports.* Washington: U.S. Government Printing Office.

1982 *Annual Report of the Immigration and Naturalization Service.* Washington: U.S. Government Printing Office.

Index